Vision & Change
Elements of Intuition and the I Ching as inner teachers

Vision & Change

Elements of Intuition and the I Ching as inner teachers

ALLEN DAVID YOUNG, Ph.D.

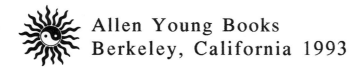
Allen Young Books
Berkeley, California 1993

Vision & Change
Elements of Intuition and the I Ching as inner teachers
By Allen David Young, Ph.D.

Published by:

Allen Young Books
2625 Alcatraz Avenue, P.O. Box 232
Berkeley, California 94705

© 1993 Allen David Young, Ph.D.
All rights reserved.
ISBN 0-9633319-1-4

No part of this book may be reproduced or used in any form, or by any means, without written prior permission of the author.

The graphics and illustrations are from various copyright-free books. Cover design and diagrams by Allen David Young.

Library of Congress Catalog Card Number: 92-91049

Manufactured in the United States of America

Acknowledgements

Writing this book was a one-person task, but there were many teachers who helped me get to this point and several talented people who helped me produce it.

I would first like to thank my primary teachers over the last twenty years: Howard Thruman (mysticism), Lewis S. Bostwick (psychic development) and Strephon Kaplan-Williams (Jungian psychology). For what I have learned from their books and teachings I would like to thank: Richard Wilhelm, R. L. Wing, John Blofeld and Yi Wu (the I Ching); Carl Gustav Jung (depth psychology); Ernest Holmes, Margaret Stortz and Victor Postolaki (Religious Science and mysticism); Robert Hand, Steven Arroyo and Isabel Briggs-Myers (element or personality types). And to my best teachers, all my clients and students over the past twelve years, I offer this book in gratitude.

Special thanks goes to Janet Livingstone for her painstaking attention to detail in proofreading and editing this book, and to my wife Ursula for creating the book's title and making invaluable suggestions. I am also grateful to Gordon Burgett, Malcolm Barker, Dan Poynter and John Kremer for sharing their wisdom about the business of self-publishing.

I am dedicating this book to my wife Ursula, my mother Willie Ora Franklin and to the memory of my father Fred Odell Franklin.

Contents

  Acknowledgments   5
1 *Introduction*   9
   Part One: Voluntary Self Discovery
2 *Self-Study*   13
  Discovering My Self   16
  Self-help Journal Work   20
  Expressing the Self Within   21
  The Right Attitude   24
3 *Personality Types and Relationships*   27
  The Four Elements   29
   Fire   Air   30
   Water   Earth   33
  Perceiving and Judging   36
  Extroversion, Introversion and Centroversion   36
  Elements and The Creative Process   39
  Wholeness and the Element Types   41
  Element Type Model (diagram)   43
  List of Element Types   44
  Finding Your Element   46
  Scoring the Element Type Survey   47
  Element Type Survey   48
  Elements and Occupations   50
  Unconscious Elements   52
  Unconscious Elements Defined   54
  Element Pairs   55
   Fire and Air   55
   Fire and Water   56
   Air and Water   57
   Fire and Earth   57
   Air and Earth   58
   Water and Earth   59
  The Healthy Personality   60
  The Healthy Relationship   62
 Part Two: Intuition and Decision Making
4 *Imagery and Intuition*   65
  Imagery and Structure   67
  Reading the Aura and Colors   68
   Common Colors Defined   69
   Aura Layers Defined   71
  Reading the major Energy Centers   73
  The Seven Chakras Defined   73
  House Reading   76
   Rudiments of House-as-Self Defined   77

Open-ended Visualization 80
Assets and Liabilities 83
Seeing the Future 84
Numbers 86

5 *Elements of the I Ching*   91
The I Ching As Defined by Itself 95
Divining and Sampling 96
Talking to the Unconscious 97
Hexagram Elements 98
The Eight Trigrams 99
The Lower Trigram 101
The Upper Trigram 101
The Six Hexagram Lines 102
Finding the Most Important Changing Line 106
Hexagram Stability 106
Grading Hexagrams 107
Methods of Interpretation 108

6 *Counseling or Psychotherapy*   111
Psychic or Intuitive Counseling 114
Being of Help 116
Levels of Knowledge and Attachment 118
A Personal Comment 120

7 *Applications*   123
Getting Acquainted 124
The Case of Sarah 128
The Case of Ralph 140
Advertising and Education 143

Part Three: Consulting the I Ching

8 *Consulting The I Ching*   149
The One-coin Method 152
The Three-coin Method 153
The Shorthand Yarrow-stalk Method 154
Creating Elements and Trigrams 156
The Sixty-four Hexagram Titles and Grades 158
Table of Trigrams and Hexagrams 160
The Sixty-four Hexagrams 161

Appendix A   225
Rules for Changing Lines • Line Meanings • Trigram Attributes

Appendix B   227
Trigram Titles and Symbols

Appendix C   229
Books and Tapes You Can Order

Notes   233

Recommended reading   235

Index   239

1

Introduction

Vision & Change is written to help all truth-seekers discover what is right for them. As a self-help spiritual guide it offers a way for serious readers to discover, clarify and resolve the hidden problems that are common-place in everyday living.

Vision & Change deals with speaking to the deeper mind and listening to its message. Practically and specifically this book shows you how to converse with the inner universe in its language of imagery and symbols. It is a book that hopefully will show you "how" to nurture your authentic Self. This book shows the gate to every spiritual path. It shows what the gate is and how to pass through it. And more, it is a comment about spiritual truth.

Vision & Change makes it as easy as possible for you to learn how to use your intuition to work toward the fulfillment of your potential. Its goal is to help you to understand and improve your present situation. In the pages that follow you will learn to use two intuitive tools or "inner teachers" of extreme age: clairvoyance and the I Ching. The book presents new ways to train your intuition, new ways to use the I Ching, and new ways to work with personality types. If you are not already familiar with these techniques you will find them remarkably precise, practical, and within your reach.

In presenting the techniques of clairvoyance, the I Ching, and personality types I have changed the language of interpretations so that they speak to you and me, in terms we can understand, in ways that consider the realities of our present everyday situation and place in history. By reading the real life examples in this book you will learn to focus your intuitive gifts to foretell events, assess the present or past, and resolve problems.

This book shows you how to understand the unconscious and use its infinite resources to promote self-directed growth. If there is one single overriding theme in this book it is to help you to acknowledge, understand, and express your spiritual nature. It teaches you how to ask the right questions and how to read answers from the deeper mind.

Throughout this book you will find people like yourself or people whom you know. You will find examples and cases of people who want to understand and resolve their career, relationship and personal problems. You will see people finding insights about themselves and others, making the "right" decisions, planning the future, and working to develop their full spiritual powers. Through these examples you will be able to apply the principles and techniques in this book to your own life.

A word about my background may be in order. Before changing my career to that of psychic counselor and management consultant more than ten years ago, I worked as a university professor for more than ten years. This means that during a period of two decades I have been helping a broad sampling of adults in our population. These individuals have come in for consultations with a wide diversity of personal problems. For five years I taught several undergraduate courses as a full time faculty member at California State University, Hayward. For two of these years I also served as associate dean of its School of Business and Economics. I then took a leave of absence for two years to work as a statistician and project leader for the Federal Reserve Bank of San Francisco. Since 1982 I have taught psychology and management, part-time at Lincoln University, because I love to teach.

I mention my educator's background so that readers can get a sense of the nature and tradition of my primary background. My training consisted of more than five years of study at the Graduate Theological Union, the Berkeley Psychic Institute, the Jungian-Senoi Institute, and in Religious Science. But I have had no "board certified" training as a psychotherapist or counselor. Despite this lack of conventional training, I have been very successful as a psychic counselor and management consultant with many long-term clients. I regard it as a deep privilege to have had the opportunity to teach and advise a large number of people how to listen to their own inner voice.

Before starting my own counseling practice, I had no facts to suggest I had something to offer on a personal and intimate level to a diverse multitude of people. But growing into this role has been as natural for me as walking. Out of this experience I have collected many stories from clients and insights about spiritual growth with increasing momentum over the last decade. I have presented this material to share my counseling and teaching experience in communicating with the deeper Self .

My experience has been that society tends to obscure approaches to higher consciousness based on the I Ching, clairvoyance, tarot, etc. Why? Muddy thinking on the part of society as a whole. These tools are unorthodox—identified with nonsense, occultism and heresy by some, and with mysticism by others. However, the truth is that we can find healing through almost any approach that we desire. [1] Even though many approaches declare that only God heals or is central to the healing process, others avoid religion altogether, while most fall somewhere in between. As a self-help spiritual guide this book falls in the middle. I am hopeful that it will achieve the goal of teaching readers how to listen to the inner teacher as a guide for what to do next and how to do it.

Part One

Voluntary Self-Discovery

To realize fully how much of our present daily life consist in symbols is to find the answer to the old, old question, What is Truth?

Thomas Troward,
Collected-Essays

2

Self Study

*The mystery is not what we want it to be,
but what it is.*

W. Brugh Joy, M.D.

In *Practical Mysticism*, Evelyn Underhill defines mysticism as the art of attaining union with Reality (the inner teacher and the unconscious in this book). She defines the mystic as a person who has attained that union in greater or less degree; or who aims at and believes in such attainment. [1] When people equate psychic abilities and methods for communicating with the unconscious with mysticism, they do so without full consciousness. Despite the variety of differences between psychic powers and mysticism these domains are two sides of the same coin. Throughout this book, psychic methods come together with the practice of mysticism. These domains are means to an end, union with God, and not the end itself.

Because of historical associations with miracles, occultism, witchcraft, unusual happenings, and numerous other reasons, various religious traditions and many non-religious people associate psychic powers with mysticism and nonsense. This association is often unconscious. It takes the form of believing that if a person displays any kind of ESP or psychic ability, he or she is more spiritual than ordinary people. The idea of having some special power or knowledge (psychic or otherwise) implies spiritual maturity is silly. For example, we can learn to use our intuitive abilities or tools without regard for mysticism, self-healing or helping other people. Likewise, the mystic is not wholly conscious, nor wholly alive to his human potential without the use of intuitive abilities.

I know many psychics who use clairvoyance and know about mysticism but few who truly integrate both domains. When rooted in mysticism, clairvoyance develops a technique all its own in locating and reporting to us its findings. With full consciousness of our unity with God we can make accurate interpretations of psychic impressions. As a result, we can be to the deep Self what we could never be without such awareness. In his book *The Inward Journey*, mystic Howard Thurman makes an excellent comment on this mature use of

Whatever is true of the Universe as a Whole must also be true of the individual as part of this Whole.

Ernest Holmes

clairvoyance:

> We are accustomed to thinking of the imagination as a useful tool in the hands of the artist as he reproduces in various forms that which he sees beyond the rim of fact that encircles him. . . . We recognize and applaud the bold and audacious leap of the mind of the scientist when it soars far out beyond that which is known and established, to fix a beachhead on distant, unexplored shores.
>
> But the place where the imagination shows its greatest powers as the *angelos* of God is in the miracle which it creates when one man, standing in his place, is able, while remaining there, to put himself in another man's place. To send his imagination forth to establish a beachhead in another man's spirit, and from that vantage point so to blend with the other's landscape that which he sees and fees is authentic—this is the great adventure in human relations. But this is not enough. The imagination must report its findings accurately without regard to all prejudgments and private or collective fears.

Psychic preoccupations may be and often are a major obstacle in the way of genuine spirituality.
Alduos Huxley

Since ancient times the great mystics have told us that various spiritual gifts, e.g., clairvoyance (creating mental pictures and directing the movies of your mind), become available with the attainment of certain states of consciousness. It is a major theme of this book that such spiritual gifts be integrated into the practice and teaching of mysticism. Speaking as an educator, psychic counselor and mystic, it is clear to me that the development of psychic abilities as a singular goal is not desirable. As a singular goal this development tends to divert us from genuine spiritual growth. This diversion is dangerous when we become attached to psychic powers in ways that don't further our spiritual growth or relationship to the Self within and may hinder it. Aldous Huxley discusses the differences between the psychic and the mystic in *The Perennial Philosophy:*

> The Sufis regard miracles as "veils" intervening between soul and God. The masters of Hindu spirituality urge their disciples to pay no attention to the *Siddhis*, or psychic powers, which may come to them unsought, as a by-product of one pointed contemplation. The cultivation of these powers, they warn, distracts the soul from Reality and sets up insurmountable obstacles in the way of enlightenment and deliverance.

Often the words "mystical," "mystic," and "mysticism" simply convey the idea of being religious, and they meet with approval by some religious people. However, people identified with the words "psychic," "clairvoyance," "occult," and "astrology" to name a few, are perceived as irrational, confused, unreliable, and even amoral. [2] To make matters worse, the moment the mystic or the psychic describes an experience labelled "other-worldly," (e.g., religious, spiritual or psychic) he or she alienates a whole group of people.

It is this problem of alienated opposites, of good and evil, of superior and inferior, etc., which tends to separate the mystic and the psychic from one another and from society. Blacks represent the "shadow" among many white Americans, just as clairvoyants, psychics and even mystics make up the shadow among mainstream religious professionals. Seen from the one-sided viewpoint of traditional religious values, the occult is an inferior component of our relationship to God, and is consequently repressed. However, unless these opposing domains become conscious, forward movement is hindered. Jung describes this superior versus inferior phenomena in the following way:

> Conscious and unconscious do not make a whole when one of them is suppressed and injured by the other. If they must contend, let it at least be a fair fight with equal rights on both sides. Both are aspects of life . . . and the chaotic life of the unconscious should be given the chance of having its way too—as much as we can stand. This means open conflict and open collaboration at once. That, evidently, is the way human life should be.

Again and again we are overwhelmed by the littleness of our lives.
Howard Thurman

Many people from all backgrounds use clairvoyance under various related names and in various degrees, e.g., visualization, mental imagery, applied intuition, hypnosis. Yet the sole possession of such an ability does not give a deep, inner sense of life or unity with the whole of life. Generally, clairvoyants are mystic when their visions put them in touch with the spiritual center.

Clairvoyance without mysticism is unconcerned with the atmosphere of God: it seeks the fulfillment of personal desires rather than transpersonal need. It fails to distinguish personal desire from guidance from the Self within. Such individuals tend to magnify their own ills, distort their own problems, and enlarge their misery. As a rule, what we do not permit ourselves to do in the work of understanding others, turns in upon ourselves with disaster and sometimes terror.

The basic proposition of mysticism that all life is one is difficult to comprehend because we tend to experience and interpret our lives in terms of events. When the mystic says he experiences unity with God (regardless of the path taken) he is talking about that familiar part of the human experience called meaning. The interpretation of the meaning is always a reflection of the path we have taken to arrive at the meaning. In the end, every road that leads to the center is the road that leads to the center.

This applies to quieting the mind, self-sacrificing, or following the inner teacher through visualization or the I Ching or tarot cards.

There is one mind common to all individual men. Every man is an inlet to the same and to all of the same.
Ralph Waldo Emerson

(The I Ching and tarot are excellent divination vehicles to expand our intuition and awareness. These simple tools take us beyond the outer mind's ideas of time and space.) In arriving at this unaware state of consciousness what we experience is what we already know. The higher state of consciousness that we seek already exists within us. It is how we experience this state that makes one person seem religious and the other not.

Discovering My Self

Before age thirty my highest goals were academics, material security, and political power. I never thought I would earn three graduate degrees, practice mysticism, or develop my psychic ability, but that is what happened. I knew nothing about mysticism or the psychic realm, nor did I have a reason to know. From an early age I had always assumed that academic achievement and business ownership led to real security. Although these goals and assumptions were valid in the material sense, I simply outgrew them.

By age thirty I had climbed to the top of the mountain. I felt like "superman." I attained my goals. I earned my Ph.D. I was an entrepreneur. At age twenty-seven I was associate dean of the business school at California State University. Two years later I left to run for the Oakland City Council, and won the primary election. My influence seemed great until I lost the runoff election (by five percent). These gains were rapid and short-lived. Afterwards I felt as if I had stepped off the stage to blend with the audience. About this time, my second marriage of three years ended in divorce. My greeting card and word processing business went bankrupt—my money, my family's money, all lost. During the next year I felt hurt, defeated, and rejected. I could not integrate my deflated ego, lower social status and new identity as a former "superman." Although I was determined to turn my setbacks around and avoid the same mistakes, it didn't occur to me to seek professional help.

Some teachers are hallways and some are staircases; to have breadth and depth in your expanding awareness, find both kinds.
W. Brugh Joy

My best friend who was taking a psychic healing course suggested that I get a clairvoyant reading from one of his teachers. As I just mentioned, I was thirty years old at the time and had managed to ignore the subject up to then. While interested in psychology, I knew little about the inner psychic world. This tape-recorded reading turned out to be a life-altering experience. I replayed this tape several times during the next month or so and then concluded that there was something of great value about this psychic stuff. I was in awe of this stranger who seemed to know more about me than I knew about myself.

It was this experience that inspired me to take steps to become clairvoyant. This stranger had what I wanted and said I could learn it for a price. I was an eager customer and soon became his student. His modest 1975 price of $1,200 was well-worth it. Within the the next several months I discovered that I too could give good clairvoyant readings. While I didn't think much about my ability, almost all the people I read gave me loads of validation. This validation was central to my belief that the movies in one's mind have meaning. The process of learning by doing readings convinced me that my psychic abilities were priceless. I found I was getting high on learning about myself and helping others.

The more I got paid for reading other people, and teaching others to read, the higher I got. I became increasingly elated about the possibilities inherent in clairvoyance, but something was missing—the religious factor. How did psychic powers relate to my Baptist background? What was so weird about being psychic? Why did the people around me (mainly the university community, friends and fellow bankers) scoff at my psychic interests?

In my first three years as a student of clairvoyance and self-discovery I was a newcomer to everything. This included my inner world, my job as a statistician for the Federal Reserve Bank, the Berkeley Psychic Institute (BPI) with Lewis Bostwick, Pacific School of Religion with Howard Thurman, the Graduate Theological Union (GTU), and the Jungian-Senio Institute with Strephon Williams.

As a student of the inner world and a statistician in the outer world I came across some striking parallels. The process of giving meaning of the inner pictures seen by clairvoyants was analogous to the process used by statisticians to give estimates based on sampling. In both cases we draw particular inferences about an unknown universe based on sampling its contents. Collect sample pictures from the inner psychic domain or sample data from the outer physical domain, and the unknown reveals itself. Select I Ching hexagrams at random (divining), create mental pictures (visualization), or collect data at random from a predefined whole (sampling), and the conscious mind sleeps while the unconscious mind goes to work. It is in this interval of time that the unconscious speaks to the conscious. After this we can call back our conscious mind to give a rational meaning to the message from the unconscious. Because we have to live with the veil between the aware and the unaware states of consciousness, we should understand how to remove it to experience the awareness we need. To do this we find ourselves sampling or divining (estimating or predicting or foretelling) the unknown in some way. Even though this process is largely nonscientific it works. These statistical laws can assist us in understanding how the process works.

After a few months of psychic training I found myself questioning many of my religious assumptions about life. Perhaps there was more to religion and being a good Christian than going to church, reading the Bible, and praying to God than I had learned as a child. My exposure to clairvoyance was the first major step in opening my awareness to wider possibilities of viewing life than my rational, systems approach and scientific background allowed.

Usually when someone belives in a particular religion, his attitude becomes more and more a sharp angle point away from himself.
Shunryu Suzuki

This firsthand psychic training led me to the world of my inner Self, my emotional life, and my hidden attitudes toward women and relationships. It paved the way to my interest in dreams and subsequently to mysticism. My training progressed and I wondered, "How do I integrate this experience with religion?" I pondered this question and wondered how I could become one with God. As my passion to find out about God intensified I had two great dreams:

Lucid dream on June 26, 1977
   A large white light entered my bedroom as I stood on a platform above my bedroom. The white light became a figure like Jesus. I saw an umbilical cord flow down from my navel as an observer to the navel of my body. The cord became silver and grew thicker. I felt myself become more attached to this cord. I then saw all of my attachments: my home, property, job, clairvoyant training program, three girlfriends, academic degrees, etc. I looked down and Jesus said, "Now that you see yourself and the mess you have made of your life, are you ready to follow me, your true guide within?" I quickly answered, "yes." He then asked, "Are you ready to give up all of your possessions." I hesitated a moment and then said yes. He then said, "Cut the silver cord and follow me?" I said "no" to myself out of fear. From what I had read and heard about from psychic sources, one detaches from the silver cord at death. Jesus just waited behind me. It was a stand off. I thought to my self, "I may never get another chance like this again." I then created a razor blade and cut the cord.

This dream was a life-altering experience. Since that moment I have not been the same. It was as if God became another being, moved into my inner space, took up half of my consciousness. Later that evening I had a short second dream:

   A woman dressed in white led me to a special series of rooms in a large hotel. She asked me to take a shower, to leave my old friends behind, and to prepare myself for living in my new home with God.

This dream validated the first dream and formally launched my journey to God. Within days I ended my psychic studies. My interest in psychic development became secondary to my interest in God. Within weeks I started a two-year period of celibacy and began my formal study of religion and mysticism.
   As I galloped through the teachings being offered at the various GTU seminaries I began to understand my inner world in relation to religion. I entered God's world on a chariot pulled by a team of white horses, on the ground and then upward. The more course work I took, the more I felt as if I was running a cross-country race at top

speed. I gave my full attention to God. I fell deeply in love with God. My power increased. I had finally arrived in my personal journey to God.

In my final months at the GTU I studied with Howard Thurman. In perhaps his last class before he died, titled "Mysticism and Social Change," we met for nearly three hours, four days a week for about a month. To this day he remains the most influential mystic that I have met. From him I discovered that nothing in life is more important than the search for God. He taught me that despite any good works it is necessary to find my own soul to save myself. He taught me that finding God was the most important goal in life. To this day his influence on me remains the greatest of any mystic I have ever met. I credit him with putting mysticism into my lap and raising profound questions for me. For instance, in describing the mystics' experience of the meaning of God, he asked, "What is meant by meaning? Does it mean you understand it or it understands you?" His melodic voice continued, "Does God move out more and more in creative exploration? If so, does this mean that before there can be a new earth there must be a new heaven?"

In talking about his own death Thurman asked, "When you see the end of your days marked by death, do you sense or know that the night into which you are entering will be followed by day?" He was a master at using silence when he had something important to say. On one occasion he put it this way: "There are two important questions you must ask (silence). Where am I going (silence), and Who is going with me (silence)? You're in trouble if you don't answer in the right order." I felt alienated from most religious groups before this meeting. I was unable to share with them my psychic experiences. My relationship to religion shifted for the better when Thurman assured me that spiritual experience is always personal and private. He added that this experience is available to everyone, but that religious professionals have the hardest time accepting and experiencing it. With this he confirmed what I had already begin to sense.

Unlike my first clairvoyant reading, I don't recall my first I Ching consultation, but I remember getting acquainted with it in 1978. I first discovered the *I Ching or Book of Changes* by Wilhelm/Baynes from a course taught by a Jesuit priest at the GTU. But initially, I used *The I Ching Workbook* by R.L. Wing. It is difficult to describe my personal experience or use of the oracle without sounding absurd, but I will try to outline what happened for me. In the first two years of my association with the I Ching I felt very limited, weighted down, and even oppressed by its guidance.

To make matters worse, the people around me, those who knew me but not the I Ching, wondered why I was following its guidance instead of making up my own mind. They didn't understand that my mind and the I Ching were one and the same thing. Those who knew me from the sixties and seventies felt that I was running from life's

If you must choose between how I feel and how I think which way do you choose?
Howard Thurman

responsibilities, and losing my ability to make decisions. In retrospect, what they observed about me was somewhat true. I withdrew from the world and became a mere shadow of my former self.

As the years went by the I Ching became a greater and greater ally. I viewed it as the path to my higher Self. Instead of feeling imprisoned by its advice, I felt comforted by it. I knew of no one who consulted the oracle as much as I did. And those I knew who followed its advice relied on it less than I did. I became isolated from my former life by simply taking its advice. Except for clients and students, my world became totally introverted. My whole way of dealing with the outer and inner world depended upon the I Ching and clairvoyance to an equal degree. I reasoned that since it did such a good job so far, why not use it more? For me there was no such thing as talking to God too much.

To know God is to be God.
Emma Curtis Hopkins

Within six years I became an expert in the eyes of those around me. Instead of being held back as mentioned earlier, I learned to move forward by staying put. I learned to gain peace of mind, to see and tell the truth, to free myself from bondage and entanglements, and to rise above problems. Along with my desire for union with God, the I Ching and clairvoyance became my torch to light up the darkness, my sword to slay confusion, my interpreter for talking to God.

Self-help Journal Work

The greatest aid in my own psychic work has been the process of keeping a journal. This is the place I record my insights from the unconscious, and summarize my psychological episodes. When I have done this with the sparks of new thoughts and impulses that flash through my mind they become like seeds I have planted in the ground. Being written down and later evaluated has enabled them to grow and develop in a mature fashion. This is also the place I write down and investigate a sampling of those rare negative thoughts and temptations I have from time to time such as wanting to see so-and-so hurt, or venting anger by breaking new dishes, or seeking revenge and the not-so-rare thoughts of "other" women. I have found that examining these thoughts serves to reverse inappropriate ones, and to energize appropriate ones.

In our everyday life our thinking is ninety-nine percent self-centered.
Shunryu Suzuki

After years of observation I have accepted that the greater part of what emerges into my consciousness comes from the unconscious. Since 1979 my use of "thinking" has continued to decrease rather, my thoughts have increasingly come to me from my inner teacher. I have a sense that this was true earlier but I was unaware of it. These impulses, affects, emotions, imaginary events, and conversations that we call "fantasies" stream through us from the unconscious. When taken seriously, they are greatly beneficial. Many people before age thirty, including myself, pay too little attention to the source of consciousness. Consequently, they miss the presence of the unconscious and travelling the subjective spiritual path. For me, keeping a journal has reversed this state of neglect. It takes into account the unseen dimensions of my psychic life.

Keeping a journal helps us to be psychologically honest. Perhaps the greatest obstacle to our own wholeness is psychological dishonesty. This happens because there is much about ourselves that we prefer not to see. This comes up for me when I choose bold actions without first consulting the I Ching or looking for inner pictures to get a sense of where things are going. To some degree we all prefer to rationalize, to blame others for our unhappiness or some outer circumstance for our behavior, rather than look within. The habit of carefully writing down the thoughts (from significant events) that go through our screen of consciousness will help us overcome the psychological dishonesty inherited from our early years.

The journal of my dialogue with the unconscious has been a great aid in my creativity. As already mentioned, if we have a creative thought and write it down it is like planting a seed in the ground. Later, we will find that some of our creative thoughts or inspirations have a chance to grow and develop. Now enlarged, the original idea comes back to us in an expanded form. In this way our growing creative thoughts come from the unconscious and not from our ego. Keeping a journal will enlist the help of the higher Self in our creative efforts, and in the creative efforts of others. Keeping a journal is simple in principle. Everyone should do it. It is perhaps the most basic form of self-healing and self-expression.

Everything in the unconscious seeks outward manifestation.
C.G. Jung

Expressing the Self Within

Every experience we have is a building block for what we are today. Conscious or unconscious, we filter every experience we have through our self-view. We screen out evidence that contradicts our self-opinion. We selectively take in evidence that supports it. Over the long run our thoughts, choices, and beliefs form a relationship with the people, activities, places and things around us. Solidly and consistently, our experiences from within ourselves and from with-out shape us. This process continues until we consciously decide to reinterpret these experiences. Writing about this phenomenon in his book *Diagrams for Living*, Dr. Emmet Fox says:

> You have built your present. If you want to know what sort of job you have made of it, just look in a mirror. That is what you have built. If you have poor lungs, they have been broken down by your thoughts and your emotions. Your home and occupation have been built by your thought. Indeed, all the conditions of your life have been built by the thoughts and feelings you consistently entertain.

Collectively as a race we have built the present conditions of the earth. The conditions and circumstances on this globe we live on are the outpicturing of the thoughts of mankind. Beautiful scenery is the outpicturing of man's understanding of beauty, while the squalor and meanness in other places is the outpicturing of man's belief in lack and limitation. Fire, flood, and famine are the outpicturing of the race consciousness. Tornados, cyclones, and earthquakes are the expressions of man's hatreds and fears, resentments and apprehensions.

We build as individuals and we build as a race, and the things we build manifest as our conditions, our bodies, and our world. Because we build our lives all day long by the thoughts we think, the beliefs we accept, and the feelings we entertain, we should build with conscious choices. By conscious choice I am referring to choices based on insights from the Self or voice within. When viewed as a path to God, such choices are *means* to this end rather than the end itself.

Before we can express the Self within we must find out what it is really saying, and have the courage to answer its call obediently, even if hesitatingly. In addition to making conscious choices, conscious self expression requires being responsible for our actions. Inherent in this dual awareness-of-Self and responsibility requirement is the fact that the expression of this truth makes a person what he is. The conscious pursuit of inner wisdom and subsequent actions to alter one's life, are the first signs that an individual has begun the process of self-realization.

Wholeness exists to the extent we are conscious and receptive to our inner images and motivations. All of us can learn about our inner Self and move responsibly toward the wholeness it provides, no matter how small and insignificant the steps we take in the beginning. We do not have to be or have all that we want to choose to act on behalf of the inner Self. Taking small, gradual steps leads the way to trusting ourselves and to taking larger steps later on.

Healing impressions and images appear when the quiet Self within hears our conscious intention. The inner world of the Self is largely unconscious and mysterious, but it is not incomprehensible. Whether we first turn to spiritual teachers, therapists, counselors, books or solitary intuitive tools such as visualization and the I Ching to strengthen our bond to the inner world, these are only instruments. These are only vehicles that offer an opportunity to accelerate the expansion of awareness. To be effective it is important to accept and act upon this subjective information. Despite the risks, despite the complications such knowledge may add to our life, healing can only take place when we surrender to this transcendent wisdom, to the joy of being nurtured by the deeper Self.

Done for a regular and lengthy period, the solitary discipline of consulting the I Ching and interpreting the subjective world of visualization creates inner strength. One of the most pragmatic uses of

The strength of the personal life is often found in the depth and intensity of its isolation.
Howard Thurman

these disciplines is to connect us quickly with our center. These tools are highly personal. They lift us out, up and away from our socialized, established personality as understood (by us, our family, friends and associates) since infancy. We can all learn these paths of personality- or self-transcendence regardless of our age, but this learning is not instant. And we must never think that our path to the inner Self compels it to be present. Speaking from personal experience, there is no guarantee that if we do our part the inner Self will do its part. Who knows what it will do?

Communicating with the unconscious is learnable because we can learn to improve the way we solve problems, and we learn to solve problems by having problems to solve. If we want to improve our relationship to our inner Self, we will have to put ourselves in a sort of Catch-22 position. We need to have real life problems upon which to communicate with the unconscious, home of the Self within. Because success leads to success, the more we see ourselves as able to act in accord with our subjective impressions the more trust we will have in them. This includes our ability to solve our most relevant concerns, and to get what we need for ourselves.

By setting aside a part of each day for travelling the subjective spiritual road, through these solitary disciplines, we can gain the benefits of both. These practices, and a host of others that I have not discussed, lead to successful development and wholeness because they serve as a channel of communication for the unconscious Self. Because we reach the unconscious by indirect means such as dreams, intuitive insights or feelings, images and symbols, transcending the conscious mind in some way, these disciplines are effective. According to psychiatrist William Glasser, in his book *Positive Addition*, a discipline must meet six requirements if it is to help people grow:

- It should be non-competitive and be done, for the most part, alone.
- It should be a practice which is not dependent on others for execution.
- It should be easy to do, should not require much mental effort (e.g., straining to make the mind blank turns people away from meditation despite their sound intentions).
- It should be a practice which is done regularly, about one hour per day (or twice a day in equal amounts of time).
- It should be something that the doer *believes* will improve his mental/physical state. He must see his own improvements, without needing an "expert" or guru to tell him he's getting better—in other words, in every respect it should build self-sufficiency rather than dependence upon another.
- It should be something which can be done without inordinate self-criticism or comparison to someone else's progress.

When we pursue life's challenges with commitment, we come to see all problems as opportunities for growth. The often-needed intuitive response to problems may be hard to come by for two reasons: first, the types of problems that are helpful in training us to use our intuitive abilities are exactly what risk-averse people avoid second, most people fail to believe in themselves—they forget that they have access to all the skill, intelligence and wit required to meet their every need.

By choosing to act according to the transcendent inner Self we grow in insight and understanding. We also learn about our strengths and weaknesses. With each conscious choice to live out what is most helpful to us, we become more fully human. Every choice, however insignificant it might seem, in line with what we feel is highest and representative of our inner voice, supports our true life goals. In this manner we tend to create a more positive cycle of thinking, habits and outcomes. All choices, all day-to-day decisions have the energy to transform our lives if we are open to the messages and cues from the inner teacher.

I will prepare and someday my chance will come.
Abraham Lincoln

Nobody can keep us from our own center if we choose to go there. No self-help book, seminar or guru can choose the directions we take for us. Neither is there a pill to swallow or "quick fix" that will cause the uplifting effects that healthy choices can have on our lives. Self-honesty, awareness and an ongoing inward listening can open us to our inner predispositions and talents. As we cultivate an "ear" for the subjective inner voice, we help with our growth and development.

The Right Attitude

To commit oneself to the instruments or techniques or paths of getting at the true Self rather than the goal of attaining wholeness is to miss the mark. There is no guarantee that if we do our part to become one with God (the deep Self) we will get what we want. The method we use is merely the road we take. What we believe and the way we act offer the most accurate statements of who and where we are. In gaining access to the vast wisdom of the unconscious, there is no way to guarantee the success we desire (even through the most authentic spiritual methods). That is to say, just because I seek and receive insight from the inner Self does not mean that I will understand it, or that this insight will satisfy my personal needs.

When one separates the method from his or her self, the method becomes an agent of self-deception and of evading one's truth. This is easy to do for beginners because it appears that the method or tool is not part of who we are. An ancient Chinese mystic said it this way: "If the wrong person uses the right means, the right means work in the wrong way." [3] This statement conveys an invaluable truth from mysticism and should serve as a guideline for using clairvoyance, the I Ching or any technique for getting information out of

Self-Study

the unconscious. This saying dispels the common belief that using the "right" tool leads to the right result irrespective of the person who applies it. This saying tells us that one's search for the true Self depends on the person and has little to nothing to do with the method. Even though we tend to look for personal success and outer physical security, the deep Self always seeks the attainment of wholeness. It seeks to integrate all aspects of personality. According to this reality all roads to the true Self lead to transpersonal rather than personal ends.

We must not allow any consideration whatever, any instituition, or organization, or any book, or any man or woman, to come between us and our direct seeking for God.
Emmet Fox

3

Personality Types and Relationships

That which shrinks must first expand.
That which fails must first be strong.
That which is cast down must first be raised.
Before receiving there must be giving.

Lao Tzu
6th Century B.C.

We pride ourselves on knowing today that matter contains over a hundred elements, each with peculiar affinities. Chemistry has discovered something very similar to fire, air, water, and earth as physical states of matter. In addition, many cultures throughout the world refer to the four elements as philosophical, mythological, or religious symbols. To understand what we are really working with in any practice using the four elements one has to understand them. To do that, we need to look at not only the physical and psychological significance of the elements, but also to view elements from the vantage point of spiritual awareness.

The elements serve as a vehicle that connects each person with him-or-herself. As in structured visualization, the elements give us a view of ourselves and the world around us. Depending upon how we organize and interpret our elements they provide us with a view of our personality, current life stage, relationships, problem areas, life goals, and creative potentials. As finite and highly structured inner pictures the elements give us a fairly objective model for understanding the unknown. By knowing your elements you can know the form through which your inner teacher expresses and how to gain access to the riches within.

In relation to the infinite number and ever-changing mental pictures, the elements move slowly. Although few, and limited in information the elements have much to tell us. They allow us to "freeze" our reality and study it in greater detail. As a model of human consciousness the elements reside on the surface of awareness. Through rational, left-brain thinking we can access them.

There is nothing supernatural about the study of life.

Ernest Holmes

While inner pictures fall beneath the surface of awareness and must be accessed through intuitive, right-brain thinking, the elements gives us an objective view of the relationships between conscious and unconscious, personal and transcendent, and the aware and unaware aspects of life.

The elements appear in the holy scriptures of India (such as the Bhagavad Gita), and form the philosophical basis of Indian Ayurvedic Medicine. Like Tibetan and Indian expressions of their outer physical and inner psychic nature, the Chinese describe the elements on many levels. Ancient Greek philosophy has its roots in the doctrine of the elements, which relate to man's four faculties: moral (fire), intellectual (air), aesthetic and soul (water), and physical (earth).

Medieval and Renaissance Europe correlated the elements with the four "humors" which in turn lead to four specific human temperaments. These show up in all the early medical writings of Europe as well as in the works of Shakespeare and other literary artists. These examples reveal how the elements were not only a vital reality faced by ancient peoples, but indeed the foundation of reality itself.

Ralph Metzner provides another example by suggesting a correlation among the four personality types discovered by Jung and the four elements of the astrology signs. [1] In this correlation the pioneering spirit, enthusiasm, and perception of the three fire signs (Aries, Leo, Sagittarius) fit with the intuitive function. The air signs (Libra, Aquarius, Gemini) which deal with concepts, information, intellectual communication and evaluation match the thinking function. The water signs (Cancer, Scorpio, Pisces) relate to the feeling function and the earth signs (Capricorn, Taurus, Virgo) fit with the sensation function.

The division of life into four parts or elements is obviously a model, a conceptual system to help us to understand and deal with life. In real life, we function in all four elements at the same time, though one of them is always the primary focus. The concept of the four levels of life (physical, emotional, mental, spiritual), the four element model, and by extension the eight trigrams of is just one "way" to describe life. Yet this "way" has been extremely useful to ancient and modern man alike. While models are not final and total truth, they are somewhat useful ways to simplify a more complicated reality, and to help us to deal with it more effectively. Models of elements, like all models of life, are not the same as life, or a substitute for life, but they help us to get a handle on life.

The elements give us a definitive vision of the dualism in nature. They embrace the yin and yang, active and passive, optimistic and pessimistic, extroverted and introverted, beautiful and ugly, etc., and these opposing sides neutralize themselves into a stalemate. Generally, an individual's character and psyche takes the form of the unique interaction of these contrasting forces. In relationship matters, the four elements from ancient times describe reference points within the whole personality. The elements represent our most basic level of conscious and unconscious activities and patterns of behavior. They provide a careful measurement of our unique attitude, motivation and temperament.

Character is nature in the highest form.
Ralph Waldo Emerson

As a rule, elements are extremely stable for long periods of time and usually describe unchanging patterns of behavior. As already pointed out, the symbolic language of elements has worldwide recognition and appears in every culture.

The Four Elements

Just as everyone has freedom of choice, conformity to one's element pattern is a matter of choice. This amounts to the same thing as saying that it rests with each individual to form his or her own personality. However this form carries with it the inevitable result that we will manifest the conditions corresponding to the sorting of elements we accept as our pattern. What we shall eventually express is not what we merely wish, but our type or pattern. The reason is that we cannot transcend our elements. We can, however, move beyond the expression of our elements as a law of averages or norm. We can move into the recognition of our spiritual nature, and hence expression of our artistic self.

As already mentioned all material things, including our own bodies, are composed of combinations of the four elements. Jung believed that God and all of creation labored through time to bring conscious awareness into the universe, and that it is the role of human beings to carry that evolution forward. He showed that the unconscious and its language of symbols is the creative source of all that evolves into the conscious mind and into the total personality of each. It is out of the raw material of the unconscious that our conscious minds develop, mature, and expand to include all the qualities that we carry potentially within us. The unconscious is the primal matrix out of which our species has evolved a conscious mind and then developed it over the millennia to the extent and the refinement that it has today. Every element, every capacity, every feature of our functioning consciousness, was first contained in the unconscious and may find its way from there up to the conscious level.

Jung emphasized the uniqueness of each person's psychological structure. It is his conviction that the more we face the unconscious and combine its contents with what is in the conscious mind, the more we derive a sense of our unique individuality. He shows how universal traits and possibilities manifest in each person in ways that are unlike those of anyone else. He used the term Individuation to refer to the lifelong process of becoming the complete human being we were born to be. Individuation means waking up to our total selves, allowing our conscious personalities to develop until they include the basic four elements inherent in each of us at the unconscious level.

Fire

The native language of fire is expressed through subjective perceptions—the metaphor, the imagination, the symbol, visions from the Self within. The fields that personify fire are those that include creativity and inspiration. Fire abhors routine because it leaves nothing for inspiration to accomplish. Those influenced by fire tend to get caught up in the excitement of their projected vision or dream. They are often impatient with the demands of present reality and find it difficult to see things through to completion. Fire is by far the most self-expressive or yang of the elements. It is always getting it out, pouring forth its energy and life substance by direct action.

The mental picture of a family sitting around a dinner table as a baby crawls away describes the way of fire. This picture suggests that fire is a baby in relation to other elements. It implies independence, immaturity and playfulness because the child crawls away from the older family group. Those influenced by fire are childlike; its presence always points to a struggle in growing up, being consistent, and assuming responsibility. It suggests freedom from social rigidity and an escape from well structured social activities. Fire may constructively influence other elements when its conduct is firm, correct and in alignment with the established order. Otherwise it finds it difficult to deal with close relationships such as marriage, family, or well-defined social situations. Influenced by fire, people tend to have little regard for the "proper rules," living the "right" way and following regulations.

Where fire dominates, people tend to push their way through life. They find it difficult to wait for times when external energies can provide them with the needed impetus. Fire manifests the qualities of progress, change, and evolution. The fire element tends to be impatient with more sensitive or gentler elements, especially water and earth. It feels that water will extinguish it, that earth will smother it, and it therefore resents the emotionalism and heaviness of these elements. Fire is an emotional element, like water, but it tends toward the more active and dynamic emotions—anger, joy, and enthusiasm.

The fire element appears in initiators, inventors, promoters and those having no taste for life as it is. Those influenced by fire are often in danger of being fickle, changeable, and lacking in persistence. They tend to be imaginative at the expense of observation, restless, and to desire opportunities and possibilities. In fire the will to be and to express oneself freely is rather childlike in its simplicity. It has a quality which at times appears endearing to other people but at other times seems an offense to those who are more cautious and sensitive.

Fire represents faith or confidence in one's own resources. It is eager, dynamic, dramatic, refusing to do anything outside its own desire and will. It marks the zest and excitement of life, a recuperative power that can bounce back from anything. Fire is a universal radiant energy. It is the essence of creativity, doing something new or more than has gone before. This element inspires people to follow where their interest leads them and to become totally absorbed in whatever excites them. They will work constantly and rapidly as long as their interest level remains high. They dislike waiting and when they want something, they want it now. Barriers and delays that seem minor to others can often halt fire's effort altogether.

The fire element can be the most difficult element because we tend to label those who live fully in the moment as irresponsible or shallow. While it is not appropriate to designate fire as problematic alone, it is fair to say that it tends to magnify problems if problems do exist. Those strongly influenced by this element cannot tolerate boredom, and when it is present people rarely relax and do nothing. What it lacks in patience and endurance, it compensates for through diversity. Here people are most successful when they start several projects and follow through with the most promising option. Fire lives fully in the now. Current relationships, social prejudice and peer rejections affect it more deeply than other elements.

Air

The combination of abstractness and practicality is an essential quality of the air element. Air is at its best with the impersonal, and when it is present people find it easy to deal with things impersonally. It evaluates according to truth or falsity and works best as a logical process aimed at an impersonal finding. The objective judge and the scientist, for example, tend to rule out all personal input. The air element is easy to see in fields such as biology, science, technical writing, investigating, and research.

Don't get caught up in airy philosophical debate. Keep your eye on reality.
David K. Reynolds

Air actions include reading a book, talking to someone, thinking or trying to "figure something out." Air alternates between ideas and words, and the testing of ideas or theories in the physical world. Another way to get a feeling for air is to think of backing away after an experience and putting air (space) between oneself and the experience. With distance we can see the broad perspective and not get hung up in the details. Air symbolizes the capacity to "take things lightly." It inspires people to assign meaning to their experiences and to make up models to help them explain reality.

Air is the world of ideas behind the veil of the physical world and cosmic energy actualized into specific patterns of thought. Although air produces impractical dreamers, it plays a part in the actualization of creation on the broadest social level. Its ideas can eventually touch the lives of millions of people.

The air element produces an interest in organizing conceptual structures or models to fill the needs of human nature. The picture of someone attempting to nail down the loose ends of a large tent in the midst of a windstorm helps to explain how this element operates. The windstorm is symbolic of concepts and information that threaten to uproot new ideas and knowledge. The tent represents tentative and new knowledge that is not yet a part of earth's reality. This picture may serve as a warning that any individual and cultural society should be wary of the dangers inherent in venturing far away from the socially structured way of life. Here we see that uncontrolled thoughts (air) may damage whatever people build to venture away from solidly individualized and conscious realities. In meeting the hardships inherent in air's close existence to earth, strength, efficiency and intelligence must be present to work with the tenuous link between air and earth.

Air or wind has been a metaphor for the soul or spirit because it animates living matter in the same way, causing other objects to move while it itself is invisible. In fact, the word "animate" relates to words meaning air. Air operates extensively, rather than intensively, trying to cover as much ground as possible to gain a comprehension of the whole. Like fire, air can become so involved in abstractions that it looses touch with physical reality and practical considerations. Unlike fire, air hovers just above the earth's surface, so that though it is fond of abstractions, its abstractions are closer to physical reality than those of fire. Air and earth deal with a reality external to the self, while fire and water deal with personal, inward truths. More than other elements, air represents a strong social quality and is more likely than fire to make accommodations to the social group, but needs a great deal more freedom than earth. Although air is a social element it does not handle real intimacy as well as water.

Air has a detached and objective quality. The air element allows people to deal with more data faster and more efficiently than any other elemental type. It can combine the best of the other elements and signify truly effective and innovative thought. All fields of study involving the development of new techniques, methods, and practices are air. Air's detachment enables people to work effectively with many problems without becoming heavily involved with emotions.

With air, our thoughts are such a dominating force that we feel threatened if our opinions go unnoticed. Water and earth are the most likely to devalue air's ideas, for those ideas don't usually meet the test of emotional depth or practicality that water and earth insist upon. When air is present people don't want the limitations of earth, nor do they wish to have their freedom curtailed by the feelings and reservations of water. Although air admires the strength and confidence represented by fire, it tends to think things over before committing itself, a habit that can be annoying to fire.

Water

The water element governs values and relationships, through subjective judgments of situations, personal objects, and psychological states. In teaching and counseling, in acting and the other arts, in oratory and all branches of persuasion, in the relations of clergy to their congregation, in family life, in social contacts and public relations, and in any rather personal service, water provides the bridge between one human being and another. The water element is people-oriented and the people who prefer it also prefer to help others. When this element is present, people evaluate situations according to their subjective likes and dislikes.

Nothing in the world is as soft and yielding as water. Yet for dissolving the hard and inflexible, nothing can surpass it.

Tao Te Ching

The element of water, like the nature of water itself, has no solidity or shape of its own. Its fluidity adopts the form of other elements, particularly the earth element, which has the solidity that water can trust and rely upon. With water people tend to dislike those who are boisterous or who have strong personalities, such as fire personalities. Water feels most comfortable with others who are rather secretive and self-contained, which give it a greater feeling of protection and security.

The symbolic picture of someone running from a crowd of people describes another aspect of the water element. Here we see that water inclines people toward privacy, and influences them to turn their back on peers and social groups. It is through this act that water learns to individualize its consciousness. This suggests that water allows the individual to step out of the bondage of collective patterns and ideals. Through this image we see that water represents protection from outside influences to assure itself of the inner calm necessary for privacy and reflection.

The realization of the true nature of our emotions and yearnings is a slow and often painful process. But as long as we face our real motives, our inner contentment will increase as the years pass. The water element corresponds with the process of gaining consciousness through the slow but sure realization of our essential nature.

Of the four elements, water is the most difficult to understand. Early cultures understood the water element and gave it an honored place in daily life, but in the modern psyche water refers to a very primitive internal level. Even those who comprehend this element from first-hand experience cannot readily communicate what they comprehend. It is not that those influenced by water are poor at communication or unwilling to communicate. It is just that what they have to communicate is extremely difficult to put into words. Communication is difficult because water represents non-linear, non-rational, non-discriminative modes of thought, the very opposite of air. Often the best way for water to communicate is by means of art, especially poetry and music.

Whereas fire rises, air moves horizontally, and earth stands still, water tends to sink and to penetrate. In moves down until it surrounds the root of all things. More than any other element water deals with the unconscious, the eternal, unknown, and unchanging background that exists forever, against which the drama of the individual life plays out. Water requires some earth to actualize its potential. But true creativity, as represented by this element, also requires the ability to see a possible existence where there was no existence before. Thus, those influenced by water have an opportunity to bring new insights into human nature. It gives us the ability to understand ourselves better. If water retreats into private fantasy, it is only creativity without earth to actualize it, or insight without the air to communicate it.

Earth

The earth element represents situations that are sound, factual and realistic. Earth is effective at actualization and turning dreams into reality. It points to the objective perception of immediately present data, facts, and events. It is the most effective adapter and the most skillful in dealing with the material aspects of the environment of the four elements.

The mental picture of an individual riding an ascending elevator helps to explain another aspect of the earth element. This image mainly refers to the drive for advancement along structured or traditional paths of growth. This scene suggests that earth is responsible for assisting those who seek upward mobility within modern man-made structures. It tells us that earth deals with making progress and supporting others. Here we see that earth inspires people to share in the simple skills needed to advance social existence, the ascending elevator.

Earth represents our capacity to enjoy the world of the physical senses. It also represents our capacity to work successfully, i.e., being competent, thorough, well-organized, focused on details, completing what we start, being conscientious and responsible. Those influenced by earth tend to exhibit remarkable strength and efficiency. The world of work tends to dominate their activities and their entire sense of self-worth tends to get threatened in the presence of an unforeseen change in such activities. Earth is a symbol of the physical universe and practical, commonsense matters. No matter how bound to our fantasies, ideals, beliefs, or abstractions, we must always deal with earth and its concerns. It is the ultimate arena in which the acts we perform become manifest. Because this elements imposes internal and external constraints, as well as structures, we cannot do whatever we wish or go wherever we want.

Unlike fire, earth is stable, the most stable of all the elements. Earth tends to resist change, and it can signify structures that break down under pressure because they lack the flexibility that allows adaptation. It often represents stubborn conservatism, in which an excessive concern for what is "real" at any moment blocks the ability for any new reality to come forth. Earth is passive: another element must act upon it. For earth to be really productive, there must be a positive assertive energy provided by fire, air or water.

If you lose the spirit of repetition, your practice will become quite difficult.
Shunryu Suzuki

Where fire wishes to change things, earth will usually try to make the best of the status quo. Earth signifies dealing with what is available. Earth people are adept at dealing with the details of in everyday reality to make it work effectively. Fire may provide the motivation, but earth provides the substance.

When earth dominates, people tend to be very aware of the outer world of the senses, but they are not so aware of emotional considerations. It attunes people to the world of "forms" that the senses and practical mind regard as reality. And their innate understanding of the material world gives them more patience and self-discipline than other elements. More than anything else, those influenced by earth should open themselves to the reality of the unseen world and to commit themselves to specific ideals as guidelines for their activity. Although the earth element is the most passive or "receptive" element it, like water, has the strength of endurance and persistence that enables it to look out for itself. Here people are suspicious or dubious about more lively, agile-minded people, and they react to fire and air with some degree of reserve. They feel that air is up in the clouds, playing with impractical schemes. And, that fire will parch it, storming through life much too quickly and forcefully to be trusted. Water on the other hand, shares earth's qualities of retentiveness, and self-protectiveness.

Perceiving and Judging

As mentioned in discussing the elements there are basic differences in the way we prefer to use our minds. Myers-Briggs gives an excellent description of how we differ in the way we perceive and the way we make judgements. [2] By definition, perceiving refers to how we become aware or understand people, things, happenings, and ideas through the senses. This includes the familiar five senses from earth as well as our intuitive sense from fire. By definition, judging refers to arriving at conclusions, through thinking or feeling, about what has been perceived. This includes rational and impersonal judgements from air as well as non-rational and personal judgements from water.

Extroversion, Introversion, and Centroversion

Traditionally, the four elements fall into two groups. The first group contains the extroverted, active and self-expressive fire and water elements. The second group contains the introverted, passive and self-repressive water and earth elements. These terms refer more to the mode of expressing the elements and to the method of self-actualization than to specific generalizations that are true for all people in a certain category.

The term centroversion refers to the act or habit of fixing attention at, in, or near the middle position between the extremes of extroversion and introversion. Neither extroverted or introverted centroverts, moderate by nature, fall between the extremes of fire and earth or air and water. As we shall see, each elements has the potential of being extroverted, centroverted, or introverted.

The elements of water and earth are more self-repressive than the air and fire elements in the sense that they live more within themselves. These elements don't allow themselves to project their essential energy outward without a good deal of caution and forethought. The air and fire elements are self-expressive in that they are always pouring forth their energy and life substance unreservedly. The elements of air and fire tend to spread out and rise, extending toward a perimeter in space. The elements of earth and water tend to fall under the influence of gravity and therefore concentrate and collect at the lowest level.

In working with the extroverted and introverted expression of the elements I have found it useful to expand upon the Metzner correlations between Jung's four personality types and the astrology signs, as mentioned earlier, in the following way. Aries and the first fifteen degrees of Leo correspond to extroverted fire while Sagittarius and the last fifteen degrees of Leo fit with introverted fire. Among the air signs, Libra and the first half of Aquarius fit with extroverted air whereas Gemini and the second half of Aquarius relate to introverted air. Cancer and the first half of Scorpio relate to extroverted water while Pisces and the second half of Scorpio relate to introverted water. Finally, Capricorn and the first fifteen degrees of Taurus fit with extroverted earth whereas Virgo and the last fifteen degrees of Taurus fit with introverted earth.

Although the first and second half of Leo, Aquarius, Scorpio and Taurus fit with extroversion and introversion they may be put into the category of centroversion in the following way. These signs relate to centroverted fire for Leo, centroverted air for Aquarius, centroverted water for Scorpio, and centroverted earth for Taurus.

The attitudes of extroversion and introversion are always present in everyone, and the dominance of one causes a polarization into one of the two major preferences. The inferior or shadow or nondominant attitude is always operative, but it remains in the unconscious. Thus each mode of expression has little or no awareness of its opposite until it reveals itself in primitive and distorted ways.

In the case of true centroversion we have an interesting situation. Its shadow is extroversion and introversion. The centrovert is seen as a generalist, a jack-of-all-trades, who meets its challenge in extroverted or introverted specializations. Centroverts have an outgoing and sociable orientation to life that operates within well-defined or familiar limits. They prefer being alone and with other people in moderation.

The extrovert's unconscious, and therefore underdeveloped introversion, makes him vulnerable to irrational and regressive internal processes. The introvert's unconscious, and therefore primitive, extroversion causes him to come across as childish and awkward in socially oriented situations. Since the preference for extroversion or introversion is completely independent of the four elements, these preferences may exist in any element. In all cases, things usually move faster for extroverts and in a more considered fashion for the introverts.

Extroversion is active and yang-like in nature. Extroverts often get inspired to lead, teach and encourage others. The tendency to seek

By nature men are alike. Through practice they have become far apart.
Confucius

gratification from what is outside the self points to being the center of attention or on stage. Extroverts don't function well in subordinate roles. The major asset with this element expression is friendly persuasion. It implies confidence, forward movement, impatience and youthfulness. Extroverts function like fire and air in the sense that these elements tend to spread out and rise, extending toward a perimeter in space.

With extroversion, people should exercise restraint over their opinions and belief systems to be more successful in their endeavors. Extroversion suggests great influence over one's environment when one learns to wait for the signs of sure success. Generally, extroversion signifies the ability to cultivate friendships openly and without inhibitions. To carry out its purpose, extroversion needs a strong inner determination, a gentleness and adaptability in external relations.

Introversion is reactive and yin-like in nature. Introversion implies restraint, caution, hesitation, uncertainty and wisdom. The tendency toward being concerned with one's own mental life lead to withdrawing from personal relationships. Introverts tend to question their actions, and to operate in the dark by experimentation and trial-and-error.

Introverts don't handle interpersonal situations very well and often feel that the world of people and objects are somehow impinging on them in a disagreeable fashion. Introverts often appear asocial, held back, and inhibited. It functions as water and earth in the sense that these elements tend to be under the influence of gravity and therefore concentrate and collect at the lowest level.

When introversion is present people gain freedom when they understand, accept and take action within the limits of their situation. They can reach the highest significance through discrimination and the setting of realistic restraints. This type of element expression suggests a good sense of timing and the ability to adapt to obstacles by bending around them. Here we find people who are introspective and experience decisive tree-like growth as a result of setting voluntary restraints. Introversion points to forward movement with maturity and the effort of will power.

When extroverted people come together with introverts or centroverts, the relationship calls for caution, because the extrovert tends to move quickly and avoid restraints. Generally, the introvert and centrovert feel superior to the extrovert and think of the extrovert as immature, frivolous or evasive. When centroverts and introverts unite both parties tend to relate like two introverts.

Extroversion's tendency toward active sociability runs counter to introversion's wish for privacy, especially if the extrovert's work is socially demanding. In spite of the problems, this combination can work if the differences between them transcend the issues of inferiority. At best, the relationship between extroverts and introverts offers an interesting variation in human nature, one that enriches the life of each partner.

Elements and The Creative Process

It is a major tenet of this book, and of the I Ching, that the creative process depends upon the interaction of polar opposites. This interaction is the basis of all evolution. The basis of our further evolution, our goal, is alignment with our inner teacher—the one spirit. What is the creative process? The interaction and union of spirit with the element forms—fire, air, water and earth. If these forms did not exist things would be perpetually flowing into each other so that no identity could be maintained.

The elements are the necessary channel for the self within to express itself in the variety of forms and things we have come to know as reality. While the elements and all forms oppose spirit, together they constitute one harmonious whole. Without this relation between opposites no external motion would be possible because there would be nowhere to move from and nowhere to move to.

The creative process in self-discovery can be diagrammed by a circle with spirit, the animating principle of life, above and the four elements, the forms used by spirit to contemplate and express its own nature, shown here.

All Things are born of being.
Being is born of non-being.
Tao Te Ching

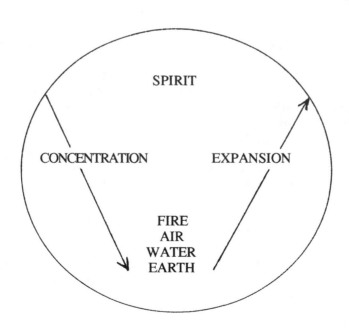

I have placed two arrows in the circle to symbolize the paths of concentration and expansion in the creative process. This diagram tells us how we get from our place of origin to the place we want to go. It tells us that the general direction we all want to go is that of putting more consciousness into the elements and getting more out of life than we have ever got before. The downward and upward arrows are intended to show that our further evolution is into a state of more activity, more experience, more aliveness, more awareness, and more wisdom than we have had before.

In this model we see that the path of concentration deals with attention, focus, and self-observation. This direction precedes the path of expansion, which deals with spreading out, growing, and self-recognition. The path of concentration describes the process of molding the realm of spirit into the form of our thoughts to produce experiences in the world. It is here that we apply the conscious mind to external facts or mental images. Since we can never stop creating element forms of some sort by our mental activity it rests with us to determine of what sort they will be.

The concentration arrow flows downward from spirit to earth. This is the path which spirit takes in seeking to manifest itself in structures that as yet exist only in thought. In the element of fire we find intuition, ideals and insights. Fire rules the ability to know without rational thought or inference. Following fire the creative process moves on to air. Air governs the ability to formulate ideas, create mental images, make plans, and design concepts of what things ought to be. At this level our intuitions and ideals take on definite forms that correspond to the outer physical world. Water follows the lead of air in that it responds to what air imagines and formulates to be true. Water governs inspiration, emotion and action. It gives the needed life, initiative, and excitement to bring air into expression. The final stage of concentration takes the form of earth. Through this element we experience the things, conditions, circumstances and other people that reflect our original intentions, intuitions and ideals.

To expand our knowledge and gain wisdom we must first concentrate our thinking by paying attention to something. The path of expansion refers to the process of spirit contemplating its own nature. No other life than the life we lead in our own conscious experience is possible—that is to say, life itself can only be realized by the conscious experience of living it ourselves. While this process may be almost imperceptible from one day to another, it will be perceptible at longer intervals.

Refining energy into spirit means keeping the clear and removing the pollouted.
The Secret of the Golden Flower

The direction of expansion, opposing the way of concentration, proceeds from earth back to spirit. In the process we come to see the truth and the reason for it—we come to know the truth firsthand for ourselves rather than from someone else. Because the truth becomes our own we can begin to learn how to use it. Through the foundation of earth we begin to extend our awareness back into the realm of our feelings and thoughts. This in turn leads us to the acquisition of wisdom, and the ability to use our knowledge and skills effectively. The next stage along the expansion path, just above the earth element is water.

Through water we learn to respond to physical experiences in the world in a variety of internal ways. Through it we become aware of our feelings and what nurtures us. At the level air we extract knowledge and form our beliefs based upon what we learned from water. In air we find that the quality of our experiences has much to do with our attitudes toward life and our own self-discovery. The last stage in the path of expansion takes us back to fire and the gaining of wisdom. At this point we begin to take back to spirit a deep understanding of our experiences—we discover their true cause, and understand what is universally true and eternal.

Wholeness and the Element Types

Much of our consciousness (how we perceive, judge and react to the world) comes out of our preference for extroversion or introversion. These represent opposing ways of looking at the world that are well known and well accepted by society as a whole. They represent two different orientations of consciousness, two personality types with which we are all familiar.

Normally in a person's life one of these attitudes assumes dominance and comes to rule behavior and consciousness. This does not negate the other attitude altogether. It exists but not as part of consciousness. It becomes part of the unconscious, where it is still capable of influencing behavior.

The model of elements presented in this chapter has much in common with Jung's model of psychological types and his theory of wholeness called "individuation." [3] Through them we see the relationships among the four elements and the I Ching. In many of our basic orientations to the world, only one element tends to be dominant in consciousness and the other three become part of the unconscious. Likewise, only one preference, i.e., extroversion or introversion, tends to be dominant. Only element from the fire and earth polarity, or the air and water polarity tends to be dominant in a person. This comes about because of the polarity itself. Generally, a person cannot react consistently to the world using both polarities at the same time. However there are many cases in which incompatible elements have a way of sharing the limelight.

The following element type model diagrams the elements, the polarities of extroversion and introversion, and the combinations of element relationships into one model. It shows the relationships between the elements and the attitudes of extroversion, centroversion, and introversion.

By identifying your position in the type model and the corresponding positions of the people with whom you relate, you may gain valuable insights about your relationships. Generally, easy relationships occur between identical elements (fire and fire, air and air, water and water, earth and earth) and compatible elements (air

No experience contains all.
Howard Thurman

and fire, water and earth). Opposing elements (air and water, fire and earth) and incompatible elements (air and earth, fire and water) result in difficult relationships. The following summary presents a simple rating of potential element combinations on a scale of "easy" to "difficult." This rating may be applied to the combinations that come about within and between individuals.

Combination	*Rating*
Introvert & Introvert	Easy
Centrovert & Centrovert	Easy
Introvert & Centrovert	Easy
Extrovert & Extrovert	Easy & Difficult
Extrovert & Centrovert	Easy & Difficult
Extrovert & Introvert	Difficult
Fire & Fire	Easy & Difficult
Air & Air	Easy
Water & Water	Easy
Earth & Earth	Easy
Fire & Air	Easy
Fire & Water	Difficult
Fire & Earth	Difficult
Air & Water	Difficult
Air & Earth	Difficult
Water & Earth	Easy

The typology and indeed this chapter will help us to identify our primary elements and element combinations, and therefore our relationship to all areas of life. Difficulties in communication that are otherwise extremely frustrating can, with enlightened awareness of the innate differences, be resolved into productive and creative synergistic companionship.

Since opposites exist between air and water, earth and fire, and introversion and extroversion, we usually choose one way of dealing with the world to a greater degree than its opposite. If this choice is not made we will combine the opposite elements rather than specialize in one end of the polarity.

Unconscious elements are the most powerful and potentially harmful. They have the deepest roots because they contain the primitive animal instincts from our pre-human ancestry. These are particularly troublesome elements because they encompass the best as well as the worst aspect of our nature, and we must express both of them.

Element Type Model (diagram)

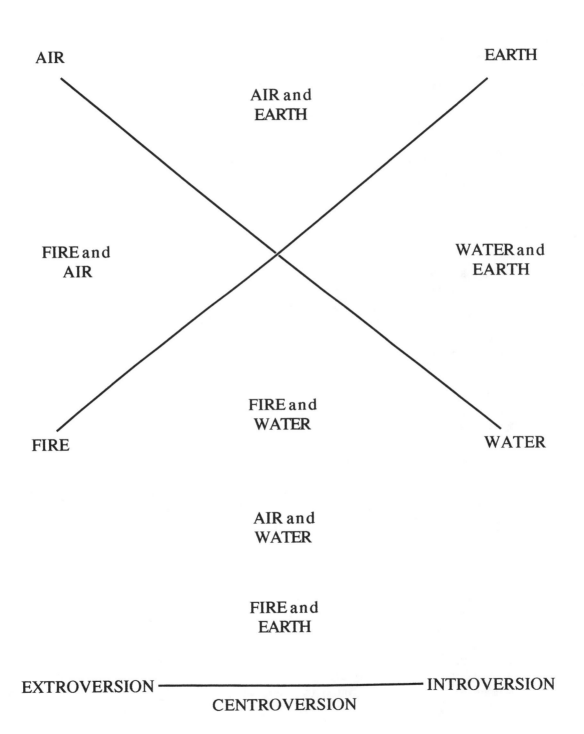

List of Element Types

Specialist

Fire	supported by Air or Water
Air	supported by Fire or Earth
Water	supported by Fire or Earth
Earth	supported by Air or Water
Fire	supported by Air and Water combined
Air	supported by Fire and Earth combined
Water	supported by Fire and Earth combined
Earth	supported by Fire and Earth combined

Generalist

Fire and Air combined	supported by Water or Earth
Fire and Water combined	supported by Air or Earth
Fire and Earth combined	supported by Air or Water
Air and Water combined	supported by Fire or Earth
Air and Earth combined	supported by Water or Fire
Water and Earth combined	supported by Air or Fire
Fire and Air combined	supported by Water and Earth combined
Fire and Water combined	supported by Air and Earth combined
Fire and Earth combined	supported by Air or Water combined
Air and Water combined	supported by Fire or Earth combined
Air and Earth combined	supported by Water and Fire combined
Water and Earth combined	supported by Air and Fire combined
Fire and Air combined,	Water and Earth combined
Fire and Water combined,	Air and Earth combined
Fire and Earth combined,	Air and Water combined

Each of these preferred element combinations may be expressed through extroversion, centroversion, or introversion. As a result, there are sixty-nine potential element types, twenty-four "specialists" and forty-five "generalists." Specialist have distinguishing features and tend to devote themselves to a particular function or area of study. Generalist are not well-adapted to specific functions or areas of study and tend to have broad general interests in several areas.

Your element type may be found by using the Element Type Survey in following section. Each element type represents a complex of characteristics that distinguish the totality of behavioral and emotional traits, attitudes, or habits from other types.

On the negative side, our most suppressed element (our unconscious elements) contains our dark side or shadow and we must bring it into consciousness if we are to get along harmoniously with others. If we don't suppress the impulses of this element to a large degree we are likely to run up against the mores and laws of our society. Yet if we totally suppress them we may reduce or destroy the desirable qualities the element possesses. The unconscious elements are not only the source of animal instincts, they are also the wellspring of spontaneity, creativity, insight, deep emotion, and all characteristics necessary for full humanness. When unconscious or non-dominant elements remain fully suppressed, the personality becomes dull and lifeless, and cut off from the instinctive wisdom of the past.

It is not desirable, then to suppress non-dominant elements totally, only enough to civilize some particular behavior or situation and allow for the expression of its positive side. We cannot develop a one-sided personality and hope to be whole. To attain a healthy personality, there must be a harmonious blend or balance between opposites. When we are able to regulate the forces of the unconscious, allowing equal expression of both aspects, the person is lively, vigorous, and zestful. To attain wholeness means the person's emotional and conscious awareness becomes alert and responsive in the spheres of all elements. The expression of some unconscious elements, i.e., essentially animal instinct, through a balanced interplay between the conscious and unconscious explains why highly creative people seem so full of life, bursting with animal vitality.

The idea of attaining wholeness through the elements integrates central aspects of Jung's theory of wholeness called individuation, and the Book of Changes or I Ching. The I Ching and individuation are processes at the core of the unconscious; processes that integrate our conscious and unconscious elements. Although those who pursue wholeness will face many doubts, the result is a healthy life. This means a healthy personality and healthy relationships.

Those that pursue wholeness in earnest over the long-run have weathered the severe crises that result from the changing nature of their personality during that time. When they continue in contemplation of their inner Self, their ambitions, hopes and goals, they allow the unconscious to express itself and be manifested. In doing this, they gain an awareness of the previously suppressed side of their nature. These people will achieve a high level of self-knowledge; they will know themselves at both conscious and unconscious levels. They understand and accept the dark side of their nature, their animalistic, primitive impulses such as destructiveness and selfishness. This does not mean that they get pushed around by them or give in to them, but simply that they accept their existence.

Individuation does not shut one out from the world, but gathers the world to oneself.

C.G. Jung

Moving toward wholeness is central to the I Ching in that all elements and element combinations, including extroversion and introversion, express themselves without regard to our historical preference for certain ones. In the I Ching as in individuation, there is no dominance of any one facet of personality (or element). In every case of consulting the I Ching and following its guidance, the range of all elements come into harmonious balance. That is to say, we make a conscious choice to adopt all element combinations. With individuation, paradoxically, individual differences disappear because the person no longer fits any one category. Through working with element and element combinations in the I Ching we approach wholeness as the search for and discovery of meaning. Not a meaning we consciously devise, but the meaning embedded in life itself.

Individuation is a work, a task that calls upon us not to avoid life's difficulties and dangers, but to perceive the meaning in the pattern of events that form our lives. As a process, it integrates our conscious and unconscious elements. Although those who pursue this path to the inner Self face many doubts, the result is a healthy personality as discussed earlier.

Becoming whole does not mean being perfect, but being complete. It does not necessarily bring happiness or pain, but growth. In the strictest sense, it is not getting out of life what we think we want, but is the development and purification of our consciousness. To put it more precisely, individuation brings the authentic person out of the unconscious.

Finding Your Element

The Element Type Survey that follows aims to reveal our most conscious and unconscious elements. It comes out of my work with Jungian types, the four elements of astrology, and the eight trigrams of the I Ching. The survey attempts to tap the attitudes, feelings and behaviors of the different elements, and therefore element types. Jung identified four basic preferences (intuition, thinking, feeling and sensing) and suggested that they were functions of the personality. They are seen as elements in this book and viewed as part of the very processes of life. While the Element Survey only estimates our preferred way of being it is an aid to understanding our lives in relation to our mental pictures and I Ching results on a concrete rather than abstract basis.

The measurements taken by this survey have much in common with surveys based on Jung's theory of psychological types. [4] Of these tools the Myers-Briggs Type Indicator is by far the most widely used personality measure for non-psychiatric populations. Such surveys, including this one, go beyond quantitative measures and can only be expressed in qualitative human terms.

As already mentioned, the Element Type Survey provides a rough estimate of who we are in the language of elements. This survey measures three sets of twelve item polarities based on our preferences between extroversion (ONE) versus introversion (TWO), between fire (THREE) versus earth (FOUR), and between air (FIVE) versus water (SIX). High scores on any list of items indicate a high preference for that disposition or element. Even though most people who take this survey will have at least one high and low preference, a few survey takers will have equal scores on the three sets of polarities.

Scoring the Element Type Survey

I have divided the six item lists in the survey into three parts. The first list deals with extroversion and the second with introversion. The third and fourth lists deal with fire and earth, and the fifth and sixth lists deal with air and water respectively.

High scores (totals) on extroversion or introversion should be combined with the highest remaining score between fire and earth, and air and water. For instance, my total on introversion is nearly twice as high as my total on extroversion. My total on fire is nearly twice as high as my total on earth; and my totals on air and water are nearly identical. These scores identify my first preference or speciality as introverted fire, my second preference as extroverted air and water (combined). They identify my shadow element as earth in general, and extroverted fire and earth in particular. Generally, the second element or preference expresses itself in the second or inferior mode. That is, the introverts second choice is extroversion and the extroverts second choice is introversion. Equal or approximately equal totals (those totals within one point) on any of the three sets of polarities point to equal preferences or combined elements.

A young man in one of my workshops produced the following scores:

```
14  extroversion              11  introversion
11  fire                      10  earth
10  air                       11  water
21  perceiving (fire+earth)   21  judging (air+water)
```

While these scores indicate a slight preference for extroversion, the remaining two polarities are identical. With these results he wondered if the survey had any thing to say about him. He couldn't find his shadow or preferred element. In his case I concluded that he

Element Type Survey
by
Allen David Young

Directions

This is a survey of YOUR ELEMENT preferences. Responses should reflect your historical pattern instead of what you want or need to be like from time to time. There are no right or wrong answers. Please go through each list and leave the items that don't apply blank ( ), mark those that apply to you somewhat with a (1), and those that apply strongly with a (2). Then total each list.

ONE
(___) I am outgoing and sociable
(___) I enjoy working with others
(___) I enjoy many relationships
(___) I find self-expression easy
(___) I seek out new experiences
(___) I enjoy meeting new people
(___) I express my feelings to others
(___) I speak first, then think
(___) I enjoy being popular
(___) I am ruled by outer conditions
(___) I value popular opinions
(___) I am pleasure-loving
_____

THREE
(___) I am fiery and hot-tempered
(___) I am inventive and creative
(___) I am youthful and impatient
(___) I enjoy motivating people
(___) I enjoy new challenges
(___) I am optimistic and confident
(___) I am spontaneous
(___) I enjoy leading people
(___) I enjoy being first
(___) I enjoy freedom and variety
(___) I value independence
(___) I get around rules, laws
_____

FIVE
(___) I am rational, objective
(___) I am a clear thinker
(___) I enjoy analyzing
(___) I enjoy research
(___) I am fair and reasonable
(___) I appreciate systems
(___) I communicate very well
(___) I am sociable and detached
(___) I am impersonal
(___) I enjoy new ideas
(___) I am often insensitive
(___) I am truthful, then tactful
_____ Totals

TWO
(___) I am private and unsociable
(___) I enjoy working alone
(___) I prefer limited relationships
(___) I find self-expression difficult
(___) I tend to avoid new experiences
(___) I enjoy being quiet and alone
(___) I keep feelings to myself
(___) I think first, then speak
(___) I am cautious and uncertain
(___) I am ruled by inner feelings
(___) I value my own ideas
(___) I am hesitant and selective
_____

FOUR
(___) I am even-tempered
(___) I am conventional, traditional
(___) I am mature and patient
(___) I tend to accept life as it is
(___) I dislike new problems
(___) I am pessimistic and reserved
(___) I am conservative, reserved
(___) I prefer to follow leaders
(___) I enjoy following orders
(___) I am consistent and stable
(___) I value fact and tradition
(___) I accept rules, limits
_____

SIX
(___) I am irrational, subjective
(___) I find it hard to express ideas
(___) I enjoy serving people
(___) I am aware of feelings
(___) I am concerned for others
(___) I appreciate feelings
(___) I am people-oriented
(___) I am humane and sensitive
(___) I am personal
(___) I value imagination, dreams
(___) I am sympathetic to pain
(___) I am tactful, then truthful
_____ Totals

_____ Totals (THREE+FOUR)   _____ Totals (FIVE+SIX)

Your Elements and Relationships 49

was generally extroverted in the elements of fire and earth combined or the elements of air and water combined. Because he preferred the four elements to an equal degree I suggested that he was a generalist rather than a specialist. Upon hearing this he remarked, "So I'm a jack-of-all-trades and master of none." "In a manner of speaking" I replied. While he had no first or second element preference his shadow was introversion and "specialization," sticking with one element.

One woman of 28, an administrative aid to a local state senator wanted to change jobs and work toward a more fulfilling career. Before working for the senator she had obtained her BA degree in history and worked in the Peace Corps. She felt she was good with children and teaching foreign languages, but didn't want to teach or work in a nursing school environment. Since her job was fairly secure and she had no ideas about where to go from here, I suggested that we look at long-term plans. I gave her the Element Type Survey to put us in the right playing field for planning her next occupation. The idea here was to find occupations and potential careers within her element. Her results:

Everyone has vocational decisions to make and vocational problems to resolve.
John I. Holland

1 2	extroversion	0 9	introversion
1 3	fire	0 8	earth
0 7	air	1 4	water
2 1	perceiving (fire+earth)	2 1	judging (air+water)

Her scores suggest specializations in extroverted water and introverted fire (her first and second choices). Careers in her inferior elements, extroverted earth and introverted air would be just that, unfulfilling. With these totals I suggested that she consider extroverted careers that combine the elements of water and fire.

After deciding that additional schooling was her next best move we looked at typical water-fire occupations in the diagram of Elements and Occupations. This partial listing prompted her to express an interest in taking a deeper look at pursuing an MA/MS program in School Counseling and an MPA program in Public Administration. Upon discussing these two options described in the local college catalogues I had, she decided against the MPA route. That left School Counseling. At my suggestion we consulted the I Ching to get at what her inner Self had to say about pursuing this course. She got Hexagram 50 (The Cauldron) changing to Hexagram 55 (Abundance). I explained what these hexagrams meant and told her that this was an excellent course to pursue, but not the only course. I made this point to encourage research and possibilities beyond our session. This additional exploration tends to increase one's certainty about the direction being considered or pursued.

Since this survey, and indeed all surveys of psychological preferences will only estimate one's personality we should ask, "Do the survey results fit the survey taker?" For example, if someone scores high on introversion or extroversion, air or water, fire or earth, does it mean they agree with the score? Not necessarily. Some people deplore the idea of being typed. However, those who score high on a preference are more likely to agree that this element describes him or her better than the opposing element. If this is not the case those taking the survey should reexamine their responses to relevant survey lists and make the necessary adjustments. An additional survey technique is to read the descriptions of extroversion, introversion and the elements, and then select the right elements.

Elements and Occupations

In our culture, most persons can be categorized as one of six types: realistic, investigative, artistic, social, enterprising or conventional.
John I. Holland

The map of Elements and Occupations that follows includes a small sampling of typical occupations for the six element combinations. This diagram applies the Element Type Model presented earlier. The occupations in this map come out of John Holland's *Making Vocational Choices: A Theory of Careers*. In this book he explains vocational behavior, and the relationship between career choice and personality type. His work expands the popular Strong-Campbell Interest Inventory and provides practical self-help aids (mainly surveys) on the subject matter. Although these works deal with the same occupational themes, and their relationship to personality types, they ignore the role of elements. As a practical matter these two domains (elements and occupational themes) relate as shown here.

Fire	Artistic Occupations
Air	Investigative Occupations
Water	Social Occupations
Earth	Realistic(and Conventional) Occupations
Fire & Earth	Enterprising Occupations
Air & Water	None

By listing a sampling of occupations for each quadrant (Air and Earth, Fire and Air, Fire and Water, Water and Earth) and the opposing element combinations (Air and Water, Fire and Earth) I have identified the relationships between occupations and element combinations.

Your Elements and Relationships 51

Diagram of Elements and Occupations

Air

BUSINESS RELATIONS/CLERICAL/PROCESSING WORK
Farmer   Fire Fighter   Physical   Police Officer
Carpenter   Secretary   Janitor   Draftsman
Mechanical Engineer   Logger   Foreman
Truck Driver   Accountant   Banker
Telephone Operator   Rancher
Mail Carrier   Locksmith
Air Traffic Controller
Gardner

Earth

THE SCIENCES
College Professors
Librarian   Astronomer
Systems or Research Analyst
Electrical Engineer   Inventors
Scientist   Computer Programmer
Manager   Advertising Specialist
Architect   Reporter   Astrologer
Mathematician   Economist
Laboratory Technicians
Radio Announcer
Airplane Pilot

PUBLIC SERVICE/
SALES
Home Economist   Baker
Cook   Training Directors
Animal Keeper   Bartender
Educational Administrators
Personnel Director   Caterer
Social Worker   Hair Stylist
Food Service Manager
Health Professionals
Gudiance Counselors
Parole Officer
Salesperson

SERVICE/
THE FINE ARTS
Entertainers   Buyer
Politician   Writer   Artist
Philosopher   Minister   Priest
Musical Director   Lobbyist   Teachers
Religious Science Practioner   Promoter
Public Relations Specialists   Interior Decorator
Tour Director Managers   Officials   Dancer   Designers

Fire   **Water**

Fire & Earth   Entrepreneur, Real Estate Salesperson, Insurance Sales Person, Attorney, Business Owner-Manager, Sales Manager, Automobile Dealer

Air & Water   Humanities Teacher, Poet, Psychic, Interior Decorator, Playwrite, Artist, Journalist, Writer-Editor (human interest), Spiritual Teachers and Counselors

Unconscious Elements

The unconscious is a much larger realm than most of us realize, one that has a complete life of its own running parallel to the ordinary life we live day to day. Unconscious elements are the secret source of much of our thought, feeling, and behavior. They influence us in ways that are all the more powerful because of being hidden and unexpected.

Much of ourselves and most determinants of our character live within the unconscious. Yet, we modern people are so out of touch with it that we encounter it mostly through luck, psychological distress, accidents, and physical illness. To get a true sense of who we are, and to become complete and integrated we must go to the unconscious, home of our inner teacher, and set up communication with it.

The idea of unconscious elements derives from the simple observation in daily human life: there is material contained in our minds that we are not aware of most of the time. We sometimes become aware of a memory, pleasant associations, ideals, and beliefs that well up unannounced from the unconscious. Sometimes these hidden elements can be embarrassing or violent, and they often humiliate us when they show up. At other times we experience strength and fine qualities within ourselves that we never knew were there. We draw upon hidden resources and do things we normally could not have done, express wisdom we did not know we had, or understandings of which we never knew we were capable.

Our isolation from our hidden elements is synonymous with isolation from God—from the teacher within. It results in the loss of self and often our religious life, for it is through the unconscious that we find our individual conception of God. The purpose of taking the subjective spiritual through the I Ching, and therefore the four elements, by way of the I Ching, is not just to resolve our conflicts. We should find in them a deep source of renewal, growth, strength, and wisdom. Through them we learn to connect with the source of our evolving character; we cooperate with the intelligence that brings the total self together.

In terms of the Element Type Survey, the hidden or unconscious elements show up as the lowest scores on the three sets of polarities. For example, consider the survey scores:

```
15  extroversion           14  introversion
 9  fire                   16  earth
12  air                     7  water
25  perceiving (fire+earth) 19  judging (air+water)
```

In this case both fire and water reside in the unconscious. These elements take a back seat to earth and air; they receive little attention in the person's everyday life. As such they are both the unconscious elements and the most creative modes of self expression. This comes about because the unconscious always expresses itself in creative ways. Its expression is free from the limitations or controls imposed upon it by the conscious mind. On a practical level "unconscious elements" are important because they point the way to getting in touch with our full potential and to expressing our creative nature. By making a conscious effort to operate within and express these elements we give life to the deeper Self. Since the preference for extroversion and introversion are nearly identical, in this case, the "unconscious preference" would consist of sustained introverted or extroverted activity.

Unconscious elements are weak because they are not expressed in a conscious way. These elements are avoided by choice and as such they oppose our preferred elements. As seen in the Element Type Model, air opposes water and fire opposes earth. This means that a greater preference for air or water weakens the opposite element; a preference for either fire or earth makes a weak element out of its opposite. The unconscious elements should not be judged as necessarily negative features in a person's approach to life, but as areas of future growth. These elements tell us about the nature of our limitations and how we can gain access to the deeper mind—that is to say, to how we can integrate such elements in ourselves. In his book, *Astrology, Psychology, and The Four Elements,* Stephen Arroyo gives an excellent description of under represented elements. [5] In addition to drawing from my own experience, I have borrowed some insights from Arroyo's work.

The Unconscious exists and functions whether we are consciously aware of its existence or not.
W. Brugh Joy

Unconscious Elements Defined

Fire: Negativity in attitude. Rigid. Tendency toward pessimism and apathy. Lacking in enthusiasm and spontaneinty. Risk averse. Difficulty in seeing the value of new ideas, theories and possibilities. Dislike of the unfamiliar or complex.

Air: Over emphasis on feeling and personal point of view. Too sensitive. Difficulty in accepting to new ideas, criticism or disagreeable facts. Tendency to avoid the truth and jump to conclusions rather than think things over. Inability to be brief or businesslike in talking with others.

Water: Too little regard for other people. Cool and aloof. Lacking in worldly experience. Trouble in dealing with feelings. Tendency to misjudge others and to mistrust intuitive knowledge. Must learn to listen to other people's points of view.

Earth: Dislike of routine, detail and limitations. Tendency toward being unstable undependable, fickle and easily discouraged. Inability to shape inspirations into effective action. Too idealistic. Too much imagination. Tendency to feel totally out of place in the world.

The Element Type Survey provides another way of identifying unconscious features within the elements. These hidden features, representing doorways to the unconscious, may be identified by writing down the "blank" items on each list. For example, if an introvert left blank the item *I enjoy being popular* on list ONE this item would represent a specific doorway to the unconscious in general and to extroversion in particular. In this case the introvert could, for say one day of the month, make it a point to be popular or do something widely liked or appreciated. Just as items marked "2" or "1" represent one's preferred way of being, items left "blank" indicate an unconscious feature within that element. As such these unmarked items point to specific opportunities for growth and creative expression.

Element Pairs

Element pairs exist because the four elements come together in several ways, e.g., fire with fire, air, water or earth. The presence of introverted, extroverted, and centroverted expressions of each element account for numerous pairs. Since there are two basic ways to express each element (introversion and extroversion) we have eight primary element dispositions, the number of trigrams. The descriptions that follow give the basic combinations of elements ranging from those that are most like fire to those that are most like earth: fire and air, fire and water, air and water, fire and earth, air and earth, water and earth. These descriptions serve to explain key relationships within the element typology model, and insights into the eight trigrams that make up the I Ching's sixty-four hexagrams. In addition to the presence of the element pairs within every individual they exist in relationships as well. The fact that definite relationships exist between elements makes it valid for individuals, couples, groups, organizations, and other interactions between people.

Fire and Air

The presence of fire and air points to people who tend to be independent, analytical, and impersonal in their relations with others. Here people are more apt to consider how others may react to their endeavors than how they may affect others. This combination of elements brings together the qualities of enthusiasm, leadership, logic, and scientific thinking. Fire and air prefer to look at the world through "the big picture." Their main interest is exploring possibilities beyond the present, obvious or unknown. Fire appears to heighten air's intellectual interest, curiosity about new ideas, tolerance for theory and taste for complex problems.

The fire and air elements signify an interest in the broad picture rather than detailed procedures or facts. Here people surround themselves with those who are quick on the uptake, with minds that work in the same fashion as their own. At best these elements represent an idealistic, aspiring, positive-thinking person or situation whose intentions and motives are above reproach.

Fire and air's approach to life are not particularly realistic, however, and they often find that they must learn about the darker side of life through hard experience and disillusionment. Those influenced by this combination often neglect the very needs and feelings that can give them more stability and inner strength.

The fire and air hexagrams, i.e., 13, 14, 17, 25, 34, 38, 49, and 54, represent an exceptionally creative combination, working to harmonize ideas, inspirations, and plans with the ability and drive to execute them. These combinations suggest the ability to put our personal ideas into action and the capacity to gain a perspective on the meaning and implication of these actions. The danger with this emphasis is that it points to people living in their head and aspirations, and thereby neglecting emotional problems and dealing with physical necessities. The problem with really getting things done comes from the fact that these elements lack grounding. They would rather rise above the more mundane necessities of dealing with responsibilities, emotional needs, and persistent work.

Fire and Water

Water and fire are yin and yang, yin and yang are essence and life, essence and life are body and mind, body and mind are spirit and energy.
The Secret of the Golden Flower

Fire and water refer to the expression of everything emotionally, excitedly, and rather impulsively. This is a combination of intensity, emotional extremes, and surprising sensitivity to what others think of them. Here people function in a high-pressure state and, as a result, they do best when challenged by outer circumstances. There can be a conflict between freedom and attachment, between future aspirations and security needs, between ego and selflessness. However, this combination enables people to moderate their enthusiasm with sensitivity and to express directly their feelings for others.

As seen in the fire and water hexagrams, i.e., 5, 6, 9, 28, 44, 47, 60, and 61, these elements manifest as "the pressure cooker," where the water holds back the fire until it builds up enough pressure to explode. These elements suggest a lack of self-restraint or control or discipline that leads to severe swings of mood. Both elements emotional, so the combination is intensely emotional. The natural conflict here is greater than with any other two elements. At worse, these elements are explosive, unpredictable, and given alternately to inspirations and deep frustrations. In all cases, fire wants to express outwardly and water wants to hold back.

Individuality as measured by fire and water appears hidden because people care enough about harmony to try to win, rather than demand, acceptance of their purposes. When the fire and water combination finds itself surrounded by people and their problems, it does not have as much opportunity to dwell on the unforeseen as the air and fire combination does. Here, a masterpiece of insight into human relations may not look unusual at all. These elements suggest a concern for human welfare, and a contribution made independent of a mass movement. Occasionally, the individual contribution represented by this combination of elements starts a mass movement or a religion or a crusade.

Air and Water

The air and water combination refers to a situation in which people feel pulled between intellectual and emotional perspectives on life. At best air and water points to people who are in touch with both realms of experience. This results in people giving emotional depth to their ideas, and in gaining detachment and perspective on their feelings. Neither the abstract-intellectual nor the feeling-intuitive is alien when these elements are present.

This is the most sensitive of all combinations (physically as well as psychologically). Although this sensitivity suggests dreaming, escapism or highly idealistic endeavors, the sensitivity need not dominate all of one's life. These elements point to imagination, exceptional creative abilities in the arts or sciences, and specialized skills for dealing with people in the counseling and healing arts. With this combination we have maturity in handling human relationships, and a talent for organizing facts and ideas about the depths within human nature.

The air and water combination refers to the conscious and unconscious aspects of mind. It is a good combination for psychotherapists and psychics, and indicates the ability to become conscious of the unconscious Self. The combination marks the widest expansion of awareness, the capacity to understand people and life, and the capacity to communicate this understanding. The desire to tune in on the subtler perceptions of the unconscious and being able to verbalize it concisely shows up in all hexagrams that combine air and water, i.e., 3, 32, 37, 40, 42, 50, 63, and 64. With the air and water elements, our personal decisions depend upon some think-ing and some feeling. As a result, people don't reach the same result from a given set of facts. This combination tends to make people aware of what is pleasing or displeasing, supporting or threatening, and logical or inconsistent at the same time.

The river flows a winding course to the sea. We must be equally flexible if we hope to reach our goals.
Nelson Boswell

Fire and Earth

The fire and earth elements are dominant, very different, and have almost nothing in common. With these elements people tend to be energetic, adventurous, self-confident and dominant, and still going when the rest of the world has fallen by the wayside. This combination signifies strength and exceptional endurance.

The fire and earth combination represents the urge to keep on going until something solid gets done. In this combination, earth slows fire, making it more careful and persistent. When the fire and earth elements come together, things happen and the world is different. But, when they work against one another, people tend to be insensitive and difficult to be around. People influenced by these elements should do well in executive positions, political campaign management and promotional work. These elements suggest opportunities for consistent and repetitive in work with creative ideas.

Earth gives sustaining power to the drive for self-expression represented by fire. The earth element gives more patience and discipline to fire, while fire provides the confidence and spontaneous faith that earth lacks. The initiative of fire and the practicality of earth with its urge to produce in tangible form makes this the most creative and productive of the element combinations. All the fire and earth hexagrams, i.e., 11, 12, 19, 26, 31, 33, 41, and 45, represent the impetus to conserve and direct rather formidable vitality and to channel enthusiasms toward specific ambitions. Those influenced by these elements are happiest when they go off on their own to meet the challenges of the outer world rather than relying on established social roles for success.

The primary problem of this combination is a certain grossness and insensitivity. Here people are neither reflective about themselves nor careful about whom they crush in their efforts to get where they are going. Therefore, they would do well to give more attention to the subtler aspects of life, such as their own inner life, ideals and values. In this way we see an active manifestation of steadiness, reliability and productivity.

Air and Earth

The air and earth combination signifies logic, analysis, and decisiveness. In this combination we see that people tend to give any amount of help if they can see the need for it. Their logic rebels against anything that doesn't make sense to them. This combination brings to light the alternating pull between abstract-conceptual and practical-efficiency orientations. Although these elements are not compatible, there is some harmony because both are objective and concerned with reality.

The air and earth combination suggests self-restraint and the setting of realistic limitations. The air part seeks to explain the limits, obstacles and structures, and the earth part seeks to take action within them. In this pairing, earth does its part by making new ideas and knowledge both solid and systematic. Thus air is more consistent, more realistic, and more deliberate than we in all other combinations. Earth is similar to air in that it moves forward by consistency, repetition and thoroughness. This is a fine combination for mental work that involves accuracy, details and clearly stated facts. As a group all the air and earth hexagrams, i.e., 16, 22, 24, 27, 35, 36, 56, and 62, tend toward dealings with variations in the known and familiar rather than with what is entirely new.

Your Elements and Relationships

The air and earth combination represents the practical grounding upon which ideas rest. It provides a particularly innovative perspective on getting things done in the material. This combination describes bureaucratic situations. They can process a wealth of concrete details without getting overwhelmed by the demands of their nervous system.

The air and earth elements describe the work of bookkeepers, accountants, tax lawyers, administrators, computer programmers, researchers. They also describe anyone who has to take things apart, uses logic and experience to calculate, to solve a problem, or to follow some procedure to get desired results. Modern science and the modern educational system depend upon the enterprising use of air and earth.

Water and Earth

Water alone can be either dependent (absorbed into something bigger) or nurturing (absorbing others into itself) in its concern for preservation. The strength and responsible conscience of earth provides the stable, dependable base which makes society possible. Water and earth refer to people and situations that are people-oriented. However, earth is less appreciated, less modest, and less easygoing than water. In this combination, water remains still, but everything seems to move forward with greater ease. These elements assist in the fields of sales, banking and business activities that deal with people. They signify a talent for adapting to a routine and following the leadership of those in the material world.

The water and earth elements as well as hexagrams, i.e., 4, 7, 8, 18, 20, 39, 46, and 53, lead to friendliness, tact, and ease in handling people, and in making sound and practical estimates of them. When these elements appear we see an emphasis on loyalty, consideration toward others, and the common welfare. The dominant characteristics of this combination are a profound depth, seriousness, and self-protectiveness in all activities. They suggest awareness of survival needs, security needs, and others' reliance on their solidity and resources. The compatibility between water and earth adds to their strength of endurance and ability to survive any trouble. This combination points to attachment to security (water) rather traditional values (earth) and may manifest through family, home, and community responsibilities.

On the problem side the water and earth combination may be understood from the viewpoint that people with such elements are motivated by feelings, fears, habits, past conditioning, and security needs. This creates the tendency to manipulate others to meet their own security needs. Although water and earth indicate material growth and expansion, they exhibit a lack of faith and optimism.

The Healthy Personality

The healthy personality is open to the unfamiliar and attempts to make use of all elements and element combinations. Conversely, the unhealthy personality shuts out unfamiliar elements and element combinations.

Whatever is true of the Universe as a Whole must also be true of the individual as part of this Whole.
Ernest Holmes

From the viewpoint that your body lives in you to a far greater degree than you live in it you have multiple personalities. At least ninety-nine percent of who you are is unknown and unseen. In this sense all human beings have multiple personalities at the level of the unconscious. Viewing the elements and element combinations as distinct personalities within the unconscious is an extremely helpful way of understanding the relationship between known and unknown personality elements. Although the vast majority of these personalities reside in the unconscious they represent the fullness of who and what we are—a fullness far beyond our current level of awareness. These personalities may be defined by elements or hexagram or trigram symbols, or by other symbols such as those seen in mental pictures.

Through the I Ching, the Self within tends to influence the conscious mind, and in time leads to genuine spiritual unfoldment. However, this unfoldment requires at least a primary understanding of this universe. From the perspective that the I Ching regulates all elements through the intelligence of the inner teacher, we can understand how the conscious mind learns what elements it needs for optimum health. This realization suggests calling forth appropriate hidden or unconscious personalities and behavior. The following research example from Brugh Joy's *Avalanche* shows how some personalities are associated with certain illnesses and conditions.

> When lecturing on the multiplicity of Beingness or related topics, I usually use some examples given by the Institute of Noetic Sciences, wherein they report cases in which allergies are detected when one personality is present and no allergies are detected when another personality is present. Doesn't that just boggle the mind? From the viewpoint of my scientific background, this information is simple a noncompute. We are supposedly allergic lifelong, not personality-long! Another example that upset the physician within me is that of cases which have been reported where diabetes mellitus is present and detectable in one personality and not in another. (Remember this is the same body with a different self in charge of the consciousness.) Even eye color was reported to change in one case of multiple personality.

This tells us that by producing psychological changes, we can change our state of mind, conditions, health, etc. This research is nearly identical to research at the National Institute of Mental Health on how different personalities in the same body may affect health and disease. [6] As mentioned earlier, this idea appears in Jung's theory of the healthy personality, Individuation, which aims to integrate all aspects of our diverse personality.

For the individual there are unconscious elements which reflect aspects of his or her private inner world that may or may not be acceptable to the outer world or outer sense of self. Depending on the person's circumstances the I Ching will reflect particular family, social, cultural or collective unconscious elements. The idea that personalities correspond to different levels of health and disease is common to all approaches to wholeness. Although we can't be certain about which thoughts and behaviors produce these personalities, there is little doubt that they are related. We do know with certainty that the unconscious brings to light the thoughts and behaviors that lead to wholeness and health. When we are receptive to the unconscious we can be about as happy and whole as we make up our minds to be.

The model of health which follows integrates central aspects of Jung's theory of wholeness, namely individuation, and the I Ching. The I Ching and individuation are processes at the core of the unconscious; processes that integrate conscious and unconscious elements as follows.

The outer circle contains the universe of elements and element combinations. This universe includes every potential element type and the I Ching's sixty-four element relationships. The inner circle represents our conscious, limited, personalities and relationships. The outer circle contains all personalities and relationships, known and unknow, conscious and unconscious.

I am of the opinion that the psyche is the most tremendous fact of human life.

C.G. Jung

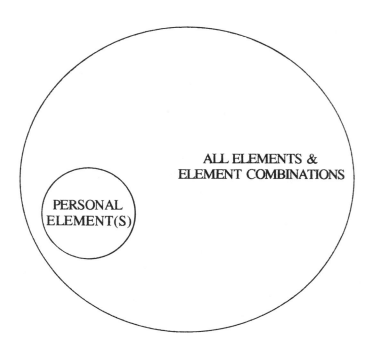

Because every personality and relationship lives within the whole and is one with the whole you can choose to receive and express any part of the whole at any time. And the degree to which you receive and express the whole is the degree to which you attain health in your personality and relationships.

Although those who pursue individuation and the I Ching will face many doubts, the result is a healthy life. This means a healthy personality and healthy relationships. Becoming whole does not mean being perfect, but being complete. It may not bring happiness, but will bring growth. It is not getting out of life what we want, but rather the development and purification of our consciousness.

The Healthy Relationship

Know the personal, yet keep to the impersonal: accept the world as it is.
    Tao Te Ching

From the viewpoint of elements the healthy relationship has much in common with the healthy personality. How? The various element combinations that come in to play when two individuals unite is nearly identical to the dominant element pairs at work within one person. Just as individuals tend to prefer certain elements over other elements, relationship have attitudes that assume dominance over other attitudes. When the partners prefer any one element or pattern in excess the relationship remains out of balance and out of full health.

The process of moving toward healthy relationships is patterned after the process for healthy relationships. The main difference is that relationships allow greater opportunities to be objective about opposing elements and attitudes. As such the healthy relationship remains open to and includes all patterns of behavior, conscious and unconscious, familiar and unfamiliar, etc.

Part Two

Intuition and Decision Making

There is much to be said for the intensity of life focus which structures and defines where the individual places the living emphasis of his days.

Howard Thurman,
The Inward Journey

4

Imagery and Intuition

At a practical level, visualization has an uncanny ability to improve the quality of our lives. It does this through its power to heal the body and spirit, to reconstruct the past, and to reveal our hidden truths.
Adelaide Bry

The word "clairvoyance," a form of mental imagery, comes from the French and means clear seeing. It refers to acute intuitive insight—to the visualization or reading of images through the mind's eye. Its an excellent avenue through which you can view the workings of the human psyche. Everyone is clairvoyant to some degree. Every person is intuitive. We all have intuition and the ability to see mental pictures such as colors, forms, entities, etc. It is for this reason, and this reason alone, that this ability merits our serious attention.

While clairvoyance allows us to see the objective aspect of the inner world it does not imply knowledge and understanding. Clairvoyance or mental imagery permits us to see, but clairvoyance itself is not the highest level of investigation. The highest level of is to perceive and understand intuitively without seeing forms or colors or anything else. For example, a great many people who see forms and colors are unable to interpret them correctly. Consequently, what good does it do them to be clairvoyant? Intuition, on the other hand, is a blending of intelligence and sensitivity. When combined with spiritual truths and knowledge of the subject matter under investigation the insight given by intuition is full and complete.

The creation or visualization of images, when interpreted, sets into motion both unconscious psychological processes and conscious attitudes. But the clarity of the insight received will depend on your level of development and on the work you have done. That is to say you can only attract and understand images that have an affinity with your own inner state. This is the law! When interpreted, mental images are an effective tool for reaching and transforming your conscious and unconscious mind, and in turn the actions you take in the outer world. This mature use of imagery provides the missing

I believe in the direct revelation of Truth through our intuitive and spiritual nature, and that anyone may become a revealer of Truth who lives in close contact with the Indwelling God.
Ernest Holmes

link between the conscious and unconscious elements of personality. It bridges the rational and non-rational mind.

Visualization is the basis of mental healing. Through this technique you can look at the past, present, and future in the same way. Its mastery is fundamental to all the ancient mystery schools and to Hermetic teaching. The visualization of mental images is currently practised in education and training, in clinical psychology, in sports and in physical healing. At a practical level the mental imagery is the central technique in Christian Science, Religious Science, Science of Mind and all other organizations that practice the power of mind over matter.

You are not inside your body; your body is inside you.

W. Brugh Joy

More and more people, nowadays, are interested in mental imagery (the conscious, self-controlled imaging of any thing or situation that we can experience in any way). When you recognize that the use of imagination is natural, you can understand what imagery contributes to your self-knowledge, and to your knowledge of others. Imagery is available to all of us to describe the characteristics and properties of everything. Through visualization you have an uncanny ability to improve the quality of your life. This comes about by gaining access to that power within the unconscious that heals the body and spirit, which reconstructs the past, and reveals your hidden truths. Through personal observations and examples this chapter lays the ground work for many practical uses of imagery.

An understanding of visualization can enrich and enliven your life in many ways. The terms visualization and clairvoyance refer to methods of getting information out of the mind to set goals. "A vivid imagination," said Aristotle, "compels the whole body to obey it."

Clairvoyance also refers to methods of solving problems, explaining the unknown, and answering "what if questions." Anyone who creates or sees mental pictures, and then understands them, make use of intuition and clairvoyance. There is nothing weird or magic about this inner experience. And nothing is more important than to have a clear vision of the universe.

You can absorb faster and remember longer by calling up visual images of the internal and external characteristics of persons, places or things. The more you experience mental images and stories about items of interest to us, the better your chances will be of remembering them. In my work with clients and students, participants learn specific things about themselves and others by learning to relax with their eyes closed and experience whatever images or impressions come to mind. Since there is no right or wrong answer, everything has some validity.

As in outer visual images taken by camera, the use of clairvoyance to see inner pictures is what you make of it. According to Adelaide Bry, these inner pictures or movies-of-the-mind have been explored and used since the beginning of time.[1] If you believe clairvoyance can be meaningful you will have and remember meaningful images; if you believe them to be helpful you will have and remember helpful images. Just as existentialists claim that the meaning of life is the meaning we give it, the meaning assigned to images is the meaning we give them.

Unlike the English language and its logical orientation, the language of imagery comes out of our intuitive-based right brain. The right brain governs imagery, intuition, dreams and wholistic perception; the left brain controls logic, verbal expression and analytical thinking. The major difference between the language of imagery and the spoken or written word is that an image has only one individual as its audience. However, the spoken or written word may reach thousands or even millions of people.

The fact that individuals alone create their images means that clairvoyance cannot be the direct object of study except by the individual. For images to be interpreted objectively it is necessary for the individual seeing them to tell us what he or she has seen. Any interpretation of pictures from the inner world is really an interpretation of the images communicated by the image-maker. It is fruitless to ask how much of the image narrative resembles the original image unless we fully transcribed the original image.

Imagery and Structure

As suggested earlier, we absorb information about personality and behavior faster and remember it longer when we look for items familiar to the image-maker. For example, you can choose to have known physical entities such as houses, colors, auras, numbers, chakras, animals, machines, and so forth, appear on your inner screen. You can then interpret these pictures as symbols.

Structured imagery works well because the image-maker sees something familiar. Since these forms are commonplace in the outer physical world, the conscious mind finds it easy to relax and give up its tendency to control. Many pictures will come to you by visualizing precise forms, while others emerge spontaneously on the open, or blank, unstructured screen of the mind's eye. Structure forces the mind's eye to create and visualize the endless stream of lifelike images from the unconscious in some familiar format.

The process of structuring inner pictures is most effective when you know the characteristics and functions of the structure. For instance, there are many feelings about colors and their psychological properties. In his self-help book, *The Lüscher Color Test*, Max Lüscher provides a thorough discussion of eight basic colors. [2] As a result, it is fairly easy to assign meanings to colors as stand-alone qualities or to the color of any familiar object. A gray

house, for instance, would have a meaning other than a white or brown house. These rather traditional colors convey qualities which are very different from red, black or green.

Because animals exhibit habit patterns and lessons that relay symbolic messages to anyone astute enough to observe them, they make an excellent choice for structured imagery. As in other forms, animal symbols provide valuable insights about individuals as well as life situations. The use of animals to describe psychological or spiritual qualities may be as old as humankind. In their divination book, *Medicine Cards*, Sams and Carson provide symbolic meanings of the healing powers of some forty-four animals. [3] The uses of animal symbols appear in the fields of mythology, religion, American Indian traditions, and in the zodiacs of China and western culture, to name a few. The uses of structured and open-ended imagery apply to questions such as, "What animal comes to mind to describe my personality or the personality of this group, or my assets and liabilities?"

Of all the forms for structuring or programming mental pictures, numbers may be the most natural. As in astrology and numerology, numbers in the psyche convey qualities rather than quantities. That numbers measure quantity is an ingrained self-evident reality. In their original form numbers also indicate the quality or the pattern of a structure. In his book, *Synchronicity: An Acausal Connecting Principle*, C. J. Jung regards numerical symbols in the psyche as structured constants of consciousness. [4] He believed that numbers are the most primitive element of order in the human mind and that their spiritual aura remains intact. In the development of number-theory in the West this aura has slowly fallen behind. However, numbers developed from the opposite or symbolic end in China, and serve to describe quality rather than quantity. In her book *Your Days Are Numbered*, Florence Campbell offers an excellent discussion of the number symbols. For instance, number symbols reveal information about the qualitative structure of self, and mirror the qualities of situations as well as things. [5]

Reading Auras and Colors

Conceived and created out of a higher order of intelligence, individuals create out of their own intelligence as well. Whenever you visualize another person's aura, you create a subtle form of the imagined person. While the shape and clarity of this imagined form varies from image-maker to image-maker the form tends to be similar when we agree beforehand that it looks a certain way.

Whether colors or the aura have some physical existence, or whether they are the creation of minds who claim to observe them makes little difference. For practical purposes, enough individuals have seen approximately the same phenomena regarding auras and colors to make them real. [6] Consequently, it is safe to assume that

Imagery and Intuition

the aura exists independent of the observer's awareness—even though no two perceptions will be identical.

The healthy aura surrounds the body and extends about one foot from head to toe depending upon the individual. But in some cases the aura may cover only the upper body, from the knees, waist or even shoulders to head, or extend to many feet out from the body. These differences indicate levels of energy and points of concentration.

As already mentioned, everyone is clairvoyant and sees mental pictures to some degree. Because of this everyone can learn to see auras. Clairvoyance, seeing and directing mental images, is one of your basic powers—one of the natural powers available to all individuals. Although the proper and controlled use of clairvoyance can be of great help in your daily life this power alone will not give you the wisdom to solve your problems. The obstacle to the easy use of clairvoyance is not becoming clairvoyant or getting new visual information out of the mind through clairvoyance. The obstacle is seeing the inner pictures as a true statement from the Self within and interpreting their presence with our full mental powers.

When attempting to see and read auras two things shoud be kept in mind: colors and aura layers. To see and read colors simply imagine that you see them as part of any picture that comes to mind or as colors by themselves. For instance, tell yourself to see the color(s) that define your personality or another person's character. Yet some definitions are necessary. The meanings that follow are simple guides; as the reader grows in experience they should expand. The following list contains the twelve most common colors. The meanings of these colors come out of my experience and the book by Yogi Ramacharaka, *Yogi Philosophy and Oriental Occultism.* [7]

Each individual receives the degree of clairvoyance that matches his level of evolution; those who are still mired in the lower regions of the astral plane are bound to suffer because they will only encounter the entities of that plane.
Omraam Mikhaël Aïvanhov

Common Colors Defined

Red: Intensity, high energy or vitality. Force. Impatience. Passion, desire and sensuality. Assertiveness. Maybe anger violence when dark or combined with black.

Black: Unknown. Uncertain. Unconscious. A Question mark. Some thing mysterious, secret or hidden from view. Confusion Strength. Letting go. Maybe evil.

Blue: *Light Blue*—Tranquil. Peaceful. Feelings. Feminine nature. Sensitivity. For additional meaning see green.
Dark Blue—Wisdom. Ethics. Laws, orders or limits. Religious concepts. For additional meaning see purple.

Brown: Tradition. Stability. Prudent and business-like. Greed. Application. Management. Practical. Material security. *Light Brown* takes on additional meaning from yellow while *Dark Brown* takes additional meaning from red.

There is nothing good or bad but thinking makes it so.
Shakespeare

Green:
: New growth. Youthfulness. Open-mindedness. Creativeness. Fertility. Renewal. Abundance. A change for the better, but not yet mature. *Light Green* comes closer in meaning to yellow and *Dark Green* comes closer in meaning to blue.

Gold:
: The attainment of mastery and self-knowledge. Union with God or mystical consciousness.

Grey:
: Sadness or depression. The death or loss of a loved one. Overly serious, detached or isolated. Coolness. Apathy.

Orange:
: Healing in general and mental/spiritual healing in particular. Warmth. Energy. Positive thinking. Leadership. Vitality. Inspiration.

Pink:
: Divine love. Acceptance of others. Compassion. A loving or friendly nature. Benevolence. Gentleheartedness.

Purple:
: Inner-directed passion and intensity in general. Royalty in general and spirituality in particular. Leadership. Like Purple, *Violet* combines the qualities of red and blue.

Silver:
: Great wisdom and experience. Great occult knowledge. Highly developed psychic or intuitive ability.

White:
: Purity of heart and intention. Innocent. Blameless and good. Pursuing the truth, self-discovery and personal growth. Perfection and integration.

Yellow:
: Mental power. Analysis or objective thinking. Clarity of mind. Intellectual attainment, light, spirituality. *Light Yellow* takes on additional meaning from orange and *Dark Yellow* takes on additional meaning from green.

These basic colors form endless combinations and blendings and may show up in varying degrees of brightness and size. Colors reveal the predominant tendencies of your inner and outer personality. When swept along by some strong passion, feeling, or emotion, the entire aura seems colored by the particular hue or hues representing it. For instance, the color bright red splashed upon a black background or red spotted with black dots would almost certainly symbolize anger or violence. However the principal colors in an aura change more slowly, over a period of weeks, months, and even years.

Colors in the aura provide useful statements about personality, health or basic life conditions. Seeing objects or scenery or activities may give useful insights as well. In some cases people don't see auras at all. Instead they intuitively sense how an aura would look and what colors might appear if they could see them. While some traditions use as many as seven or more auric layers, and offer guidelines for reading colors and shapes in relation to the chakras, I use three layers. [8] I have found it useful to work with three layers as follows:

Aura Layers Defined

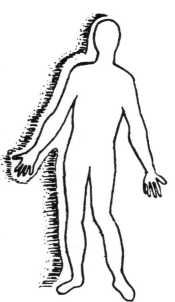

First Layer: Describes your private world or inner personality. Information confined to your personal attitudes, thoughts, and behaviors. (This layer is next to the body.)

Second Layer: Describes the your status in relationship. This middle layer shows your style or way of relating to others. (This layer follows the first or inner layer.)

Third Layer: Describes the mask you present to others and behaviors about yourself that tend to be obvious to others. The first impression you make upon others. (This layer follows the second layer.)

To see the aura simply imagine three layers of energy surrounding or emanating from the body. Further, imagine each layer is a few inches thick and has its own color or mixture of colors, and perhaps images. When I do this I typically look for colors around the person's shoulders. For instance, you might imagine the colors red, white and blue as separate colors in the outer, middle and inner layers or see all three in a single layer. In the first case each layer would correspond to a single color as defined above. In the second, a single layer would draw its meaning from three colors.

Anything and everything may come up when you attempt to see auras. You may get very clear or dim colors, and images of reality. The pictures and colors you see may either be identical to familiar objects, places, activities, and people, or very different. In some cases, you may feel uncomfortable, or see something unappealing, or see nothing but darkness. At the other extreme you may feel great joy, excitement, or a sense of something profound and sacred. Simply accept whatever comes up, as it is, as part of the person or thing being observed. Just report what you see. You don't know what the unconscious is trying to say until you report it.

In working with one couple I saw a sunflower in the woman's outer layer and a policeman directing traffic in her middle layer. For the man I saw a yardstick and then the colors orange and yellow. Despite the attraction between them they acknowledged that their relationship was well described by the opposites suggested in these images. The woman was upbeat and positive on the surface yet controlling in the relationship. The man came across a cautious and measured yet his approach to the relationship was always positive.

One woman, Janet, who was in charge of a small environmental lobbying coalition group, came in for a psychic reading. Janet told me about her interest in getting a more traditional job to create financial stability, and about her problem with the insensitive man who would replace her when she left her present position. She had heard about aura readings and wanted to get one as the first part of her session.

With this request I relaxed, collected my insights, turned on my tape recorder and told her what I saw. In the first layer of Janet's aura I saw a large half open eye floating around in a room without lights, complete darkness. We saw this image as a message about her attempts to discover what is unknown about her situation in life. Despite her doubts about what she was doing and where she was going, she interpreted this picture as looking for enlightenment on a part-time basis.

In Janet's second layer I saw light green in the background and many hands greeting one another in the foreground. No people were present. The presence of hands rather than whole people suggested an inner personality characterized by an open-minded, friendly, and detached attitude toward others. Her contacts were superficial when it came to meeting many people and expressing warmth.

Her third layer needed little interpretation. In its background I saw red with a tinge of pink around the edges, and a steamroller in the center. Generally, this combination suggests an intense, forceful nature that is gentlehearted on the surface, and hard to refuse. She remarked that some people had described her as having an iron fist in a velvet glove.

Initially, Janet seemed ashamed about the colors in her third and fourth layers, but she acknowledged their accuracy. The color gray, suggesting apathy and depression, was predominant in Janet's fourth layer.

As the reading proceeded to her relationships, assets and liabilities, and life goals it was obvious that she wanted to keep many feelings secret because she feared others might not approve. She constantly blamed herself for not meeting her own self-imposed standards of perfection that she thought she must achieve to be worthwhile. After a short period Janet seemed to understand why she had trouble accepting the man scheduled to replace her, projecting many of her undesirable traits upon him. She also gained more clarity into the nature of her depression and indifference, and her feelings of hopelessness about finding another job.

Reading the major Energy Centers

Like the aura, chakras are centers of spiritual energy based on yoga psychology. Elaborate knowledge about them appears in the psychology of tantra and kundalini yoga. Central to this system is the belief that our central nervous system is an organized top-down structure, and that energy and consciousness are inseparable. In addition to the aura, most books on the subject include some discussion of the seven major chakras or energy centers. Because of this the following summary definitions (adapted from Jeffrey Mishlove's *Roots of Consciousness* and Dr. Brugh Joy's *Joy's Way*) are given:

The Seven Chakras Defined

The Seventh Chakra—An area 2 to 3 inches in diameter around the center or top of the head. The highest subtle center of consciousness, the crown chakra, the thousand-petaled lotus, that which joins humankind with the infinite. Describes one's relationship to God and to divine wisdom and understanding. Its element is spirit. Its ideal color is violet.

The Sixth Chakra—An area 1-1/2 to 2 inches in diameter situated just above the line of the eyebrows. This center is some times called the mind's eye or third eye. The organ of psychic visualization or clairvoyance. Describes one's relationship to visualization or seeing mental pictures, intuition and perception beyond duality. Its element is spirit. Its ideal color is dark blue.

The Fifth Chakra—An area 1-1/2 to 3 inches in diameter situated at the throat. This chakra mediates vocal expression and conveys the self image or personality we project to others. Describes how we communicate and express ourselves to others. Its element is spirit. Its ideal color is light blue.

The Fourth Chakra—An area 1-1/2 to 4 inches in diameter centered just to the right of the heart. This chakra mediates the emotion of divine/unconditional love and devotion. It describes our openness, love, acceptance, compassion and affinity to and for other people in general. Its element is air. Its ideal colors are green and pink.

The Third Chakra—An area 1-1/2 to 4 inches in diameter located about a hand's width above the navel. The solar plexus or power chakra describes one's ability to lead and control situations, and the nature of one's personal power. It element is fire. Its ideal color is yellow.

The Second Chakra—An area 2 to 4 inches in diameter centered in the lower abdomen about a hand's width below the navel. This chakra is associated with sexual energy, passion and, giving and receiving. It Describes the quality of one's feelings and emotions and one's relations to family and loved ones. Its element is water. Its ideal color is orange.

The First Chakra—An area 1 to 3 inches in diameter centered at the base of the spinal column between the anus and the genitals. This chakra is often called the root center. It describes the individuals relationship to survival, being stable, and material world success. It element is earth. Its ideal colors are red and black.

I can only know that much of myself which I have had the courage to confide in you.
John Powell

We can all project ourselves into the consciousness of another person, regardless of how near or far they are, or the nature of the relationship. In my own clairvoyant work with clients, about eighty percent of my readings take place over the telephone. More than the aura, the chakras provide us with a structure for describing and healing the whole person. The chakras are very useful for problem solving because we can ask them questions and get answers.

While there are seven major chakras, the chakra consist of an energy field with multiple levels ranging from the inner psychic body to the outer physical body and beyond. The visualization of chakras lets you examine yourself, other people, and your relationships. Visualization allows you to see people in a way that may be very different from what you believe about them. As a structure, the chakras provide an excellent vehicle for seeing the deepest parts of ourselves. It allows us to see the vital links between ourselves and others, and between ourselves and any established relationship such as our job or career or life goals.

In his work with the seven chakras, Dr. Brugh Joy reported the following observations in his book, *Joy's Way*.

- People who have weak energy fields in the lower parts of their bodies, especially in the knees and feet, tend to be flighty or "spacey." Relatively ungrounded, they are disconnected to varying degrees from their outer reality system. Most of their energy is located in the upper portions of the body.
- People who have strong energy radiating from the neck area tend to be not only very sensitive to energy transfer but also gifted psychically and artistically.
- Persons with strong energy radiating from the solar plexus tend to be emotional and power-driven.
- People with strong forehead energies tend to be mental types.
- Strong energy flow from the lower abdomen seems to indicate a sexually active individual.

While his observations correlate more with the physical measures of chakra intensity than with psychic measures of life quality, i.e., those based on inner pictures and colors, the result is similar. The chakras can be observed on multiple levels. In addition to the seven major chakras, eight or more other chakras can be found in the literature. These are minor energy centers and I do not consider them to be useful.

One woman came in for a psychic reading after having her marriage date cancelled for the third time. She had been dating her man for eight years and had planned to get married in about four months. Although he told her it was really over this time they continued to call one another. She wanted my insights on what went on between them and why, what she could do to heal the relationship, and where things were going.

She started telling me about the status of her current psychotherapy work on the subject and all the reasons her boy friend gave her for changing his mind about marriage. I interrupted after a few minutes, thanked her, and asked her to hold on. I asked her to tell me after I took a look at what was going on. I explained that some information was good but too much could interfere with my ability to be objective. "Why?" she asked. "It's something like this" I replied. "If I ask you not to think about or see something a certain way, you can't stop yourself from doing just that. And I might have that problem if I hear to much." Because she seemed nervous and had so many questions I suggested that we get started by taking a little time to look at her chakras. I told her how this would work and she agreed.

I then relaxed and allowed the pictures in her chakras to show up on my mental screen over the next minute or two. Starting with the fourth chakra I saw a large red heart about one foot across pinned upon her chest.

She stood next to the line dividing the left and right side of the screen facing him. The heart on her chest had a thin line running through it from top to bottom, a fracture. On his side of the screen, he stood on a block of ice. Although he faced her, he stood well back from the line. The heart pinned on his chest seemed to be 3 or 4 inches high. As I turned my attention to the other chakras, the various dimensions of this relationship began to unfold.

In the sixth chakra I saw her gazing into the evening stars and then shooting an arrow toward them. At the same time I saw his eyes fixed on the ground a few yards in front of him in broad daylight. In her fifth chakra she appeared to be looking up to him at a public gathering. At the same time, in the privacy of his room, he spoke to her by telephone. In the second chakra the two of them were making love on a submarine. Situated in her power chakra was a picture of the two of them facing one another with contented expressions. Emerging into view from her first chakra was yet another scene. He stood on a cloud next to her as she pumped oil out of the ground.

After presenting my observations from each chakra, just as I saw, them I added my interpretations. The pictures in chakras two and three identified the strong points in this relationship. They suggested deep emotional contentment and satisfaction, as well as balance and equality regarding matters of personal power. The potential problems in this relationship appeared in the other chakras. Each of the pictures here raises questions about differences and potential difficulties. After discussing the pictures and their meanings, she concluded that those in her fourth and sixth centers helped to pinpoint the major conflicts in this relationship. What was the heart chakra issue? She said that he was often cool toward her and she felt that she loved him more than he loved her. The scene from her brow chakra prompted her recall that he had never shared her hopes of the future with him. He had no interested in being pulled toward the future by her.

Upon clarifying their differences and her frustrations, I suggested that I ask her chakras what steps she could take to resolve things. Because her attachment to this man was clear to me, I asked her if she would accept this relationship without the prospect of marriage. She acknowledged that even though she wanted children and marriage, having a relationship with him was more important. As we continued, the pictures that came up suggested that she could help matters by doing more for herself. Further, she could accept him as he was, adjust her expectations of the relationship, and allow herself to both acknowledge and act upon her interest (in time) in other men. What she valued most in this relationship is their emotional ties and the feeling of being an equal.

House Reading

Can you create or imagine a house? If you can imagine what a house looks like you can do a house reading. Every time you imagine a house to describe another person, you create a mental picture of the imagined house. This comes about because the mind always reproduces itself in familiar thought forms and matter. Whether you are aware of it or not, your state of consciousness reflects a mirror image of both the outer physical and inner psychic house you have created as your place of residence.

As a structure know to all, houses give us an opportunity to create inner pictures in a form familiar to all. The process of visu-houses is easy because this particular form is easy to imagine. Viewing the house as a symbol of self provides us with insights of not only the personality and self-image, but of current life changes, problem areas, and creative potentials. Our house, surrounding environment, and interior designs, reflect how we view ourselves. This view describes us both as an individual psyche, and in relation to society and the outside world, and how we are presenting ourself to family and friends.

The following brief descriptions of typical house components will serve as a beginning. They summarize my experience of how the house-as-self linkage may manifest in individual and societal behavior and attitudes. However, the reader can add many more instances from his or her personal experience.

Rudiments of House-as-Self Defined

House: Gives information on how the person sees himself. One's self-image both as an individual and as a person in a certain socio-economic status or position in society. While the ideal house is free-standing, detached or single-family with yard "different" forms such as apartments or mobile homes reflect various stereotypes.

Neighborhood: One's relationship to other people in general. For example, just as homes without close neighbors point to privacy and the need to keep one's distance from outsiders, homes in densely populated areas tend to suggest the opposite.

Weather Conditions: Describes one's emotional status or state of mind. The presence of thick gray clouds might well suggest pessimism or depression, while sunny weather may imply a time of harvest or abundance.

Timing: A symbol of one's cycle in life. Typical examples include a time or perception of a sun-rise, sun-set, midday, mid-night, and the four seasons.

Front Yard: Gives information about the person's outer appearance and availability to the outer world. For instance, a fence or wall suggests inaccessibility and amouring. An open, well kept yard decorated by flowers or lawn suggest openness, warmth of feelings, and harmonious human contact. Trees suggest natural growth.

Living Room: This room describes the communal territory of several personalities. The appearance of this room—coloring, furnishings, windows—tells the individual's way of relating to others socially. Generally, the presence or absence of certain objects are good if not perfect clues to status and attitudes. Since the living room is the area where "performances" for guests are most often given, its "setting" must be appropriate to the performance.

Kitchen: Provides information on how one nurtures oneself as well as others. This can be deduced from the atmosphere, size, furnishings, how well the cupboards are stocked, the kind of food, etc. For example, cupboards full of baby food might suggest the nurturing of immature behavior as well as a new project or child. Generally, food stored on high shelfs symbolize spiritual nutrition, while food kept on low shelfs—below the waist would represent material or physical nourishment.

Bathroom: Gives clues on how much a person can eliminate and the kind of thoughts that go into creating their self-image. The colors, size, and style of this room represent various nuances of private behaviors. For instance, broken mirrors or toilets point to low self-esteem and difficulty in letting go of outlived habits. While full length, wall-to-wall mirrors suggest high self-esteem.

Bedroom: This room is often the only private space in one's residence. It is highly personal and symbolic of how the person relates to intimate others. The appearance and furnishings in this room give insight into one's sexual and emotional nature. While large, well decorated spaces suggest healthy relating habits, small, sparsely decorated, or locked bedrooms suggest feelings of inadequacy or even aloneness.

Backyard: This space describes the extent to which we allow ourselves to enjoy life and have fun. For instance, whether the backyard is well-defined or without boundaries, well kept or weed strewn, large or non-existent, etc., gives information about our private outer life—information that is known to the person but unknown to others.

In the widest sense every thing is a symbol of that which constitutes its inner being.
Thomas Troward

The house as a symbol-of-self is deeply ingrained in the human psyche. As such, it offers an excellent structure for describing many facets of human consciousness. Houses reflect how people see themselves as viewed from within and revealed only to those intimates who come inside. They also describe how people view themselves from the public exterior standpoint (the persona in Jungian terms) or the self that we choose to display to others. The items in your house, the way you arrange them, the outer designs and surrounding landscape all express how you see yourself, and what message you want to convey back to yourself and others. The varieties of exterior house designs tell us a great deal about our personal and social image.

As in auras and chakras the inner psychic house is a universal and ancient vehicle that connects an individual with him or her self. Generally, an ostentatious design describes the extroverted person or self-made individualist. The quieter, inward-looking design describes people in the helping professions, whose goals revolve around personal satisfaction rather than financial success. On the other hand, the average home owner looks down upon those who live in apartment buildings and mobile homes because they tend to violate the true image of home and neighborhood. Viewed as symbols, people who live in these houses are as unstable and transitory as the structure itself.

Generally, house interiors often symbolize the inhabitant's feelings about her or himself. The phenomenon of people, particularly women, rearranging the furniture in their house at times of psychic turmoil or changes-in-self, further evokes the house-self connection. Every room or space, e.g., living room, kitchen, bathroom, hallway, closets, basement and attic, provides additional meaning about the personal self.

In my workshops and classes I ask participants to sit in pairs. I have them close their eyes, relax, and then imagine the house and surrounding environment that describes their partner's consciousness. In addition to being fun, this exercise tends to work well because the house image is basic to human awareness; it gives us a fixed point of reference to structure the world about us. While some participants imagine houses that are quite similar to their partner's actual residence, this is not the point. The inner psychic house and the neighborhood around it represent interesting and nearly infinite nuances of our individual uniqueness. It is amazing how much ground we can cover.

One student saw his partners house as a tall narrow building made of stones. This house stood alone on a cliff overlooking an ocean. No neighbors were in sight. The partner saw the first student's house as a fancy mansion in a well-populated, expensive upper class neighborhood. These images reflect two very different personalities. The first one suggests an introverted and very guarded individual who tends to observe rather than participate in life's mysteries. The second image describes an individual who identifies with wealth and extroversion. These summary interpretations tell us something about the person and what other people tend to think of them. This approach to clairvoyance is easy and works well as long as we have a good grasp of what the item means as a symbol.

Just as the house imagery represents individual selves, house imagery describes the self-attributes of organizations and groups as well. In my work with organization clients and in teaching university students, commonplace items, the four elements, and the house model in particular, prove to be useful assessment tools. Although interpretations may vary for organization and individual houses, the process is identical.

I saw the following bedroom image for one my organization clients, a community mental health center:

"A million people crowded into one small bedroom—so many people that other items in the room can't be seen. In addition, dark rain clouds hover near the bedroom ceiling."

In function and therefore as a symbol, bedrooms are the only private spaces in houses and tend to describe intimate ways of relating and sexual activity. In this image the over-crowded bedroom served as a perfect clue about how health center counselors as a group related to their clients. Although the counselors should have followed ethical standards in serving their clients, this appeared to be a problem. For instance, some of the counselors had friendships with clients, and one had an ongoing sexual relationship with his recent client. While dark rain clouds often represent an emerging source of nourishment or withheld emotions, they point to sadness and depression as well. The evidence of these dark clouds may have shown up over the next few months. During this time, two counselors left for ethical violations.

Open ended Visualization

In *open-ended* visualization, the image-maker creates a question or theme, and then waits for pictures to emerge spontaneously on the open or blank inner screen. In this approach you attemt to understood images without structures. The unstructured or open-ended approach is extremely useful, direct and far more flexible than the structured approach which makes use of pre-selected forms from the material world.

He who has imagination without learning has wings but no feet.
Anonymous

The open-ended approach goes beyond specific forms; it is "tailor-made" to the image maker's understanding. Unlike structured approaches to imagery, the open-ended approach depends upon an accepting, receptive mind, one in which the image maker allows him or herself to work with whatever pictures the unconscious serves up. As such it brings us in close touch with the soul and with the deeper layers of our own personalities, our relationships, and the situations around us.

You can use open-ended visualization for all types of knowing and remembering. You can recall long-forgotten events from your childhood, birth, or past lives, and discover answers to your most pressing current problems. You can look into the future and determine how to act in the present and when to act based on what is coming up. You can use it to set the direction for the whole personality and to accelerate the acquisition of knowledge and skills. This kind of clairvoyance gives you access to a very deep and reliable wisdom.

I often ask clients and students to create mental pictures to answer their questions without the aid of structures. This works best when they have experienced seeing mental pictures and progressed beyond the stage of asking, "Does this make sense?" or "Why does this make sense? Is it only my fantasy?" These "experienced" individuals see the scenes, people and objects in images as being real—just as real as corresponding items in the outer physical world.

In using mental imagery to describe her personality, one young woman saw a town from a western cowboy movie in the foreground of a Hawaiian beach resort. Upon seeing this image she had no idea of what it meant. But as soon as I asked her to talk about the two scenes as separate insights, and the idea of foreground and background, it all made sense. The western scene described her "tough-guy" outer personality or persona (one with rough edges) while the beach scene explained her easygoing private or inner personality.

While this mental picture said a great deal about her personality, it described her attire and presentation as well. She was attractive, and added to her good looks with model-quality makeup. Yet she often wore tattered blue jeans over her stocky physique and sat behind her motorcycle helmet.

Another woman, a concert violinist described her current situation by the image of a dormant volcano. Despite the simplicity of this symbol, it is very economical in that it conveys a great deal in a short space. In her opinion the volcano explained how her stillness and outer reserve overshadowed her intense competitive nature and passion for making music. Despite describing her calm, introverted persona, it also depicts great inner strength. In explaining how this image applied she responded, "I am warm and enthusiastic, but my culture (Japanese) has taught me to only show it to the people I know well."

Open-ended visualization offers an entirely different way of getting at what is true for you by giving you a window through which you can create the unseen and unprecedented. Instead of figuring things out with our heads, i.e., calculating, reviewing, memorizing, trying or striving, the inward focus allows us to receive the wisdom we seek from the deeper mind. It is important to ask the right questions, and to allow the pictures to show up on your screen, and then accept that they are part of you. Whatever comes up, be with it. Observe it. Write it down. Accept it as being as real as what you see in front of you.

In my work with clients and students I have found the following sample questions to be helpful for most people. These questions have a way of coming up often and should be asked as often as needed.

- If you're unhappy ask, "What do I need to be happy?"
- If you're faced with circumstances beyond your control ask, "What is it that keeping me from having what I want?" or, "What do I need to change in my life to get what I want?"
- If you facing indecision ask, "What's true for my highest good?"
- If you're facing a difficult task or situation ask, "What is the nature of this problem?" and, "What can I do to solve this problem?"
- If your health could be improved ask, "What can I do to improve my health?"
- If you're ill ask, "What can I do to get well?" And perhaps when you're feeling better, "Why did I need my illness in the first place?"
- If you're searching for life direction ask for two images for each question, "Who Am I?" and, "What are my fears?" and, "What's my role?" and, "Where are my opportunities?"

You must not imagine that, just because some people have mediumistic capacities, this necessarily gives them access to every region of the invisible; on the contrary they will see only what corresponds to their own level of consciousness, their own thoughts and desires.
Omraam Mikhaël Aïvanhov

- Inasmuch as some people don't really want answers that come from within or feel they don't deserve them or can't accept them for any number of reasons, it would be wise for them to ask, "What am I resisting or why am I resisting it?" and, "What can I do to move through my resistance?"

Most people are about as happy as they make up their minds to be.
Abraham Lincoln

The aim of using clairvoyance as I have discussed is to help assess the quality and impact of one's way of being so that he or she can make appropriate adjustments if necessary. Clairvoyance provides a critical observing faculty that allows you to watch, editorialize, and know concretely what to do to achieve self-knowledge, wholeness, and maximum effectiveness in your daily life. By using the mind's eye to facilitate an ongoing dialogue with the unconscious, and therefore inner Self, we can alter the structure of our thinking and the things before us in a significant way. In time, the hidden elements come into the light of day. In accepting them they no longer function as liabilities that we tend to suppress.

By asking the right questions and following the lead of your inner movies, the true Self is free to emerge. The right questions include the following: "What can I expect if?" and "How do I or should I relate to this person or situation to get the best result?" Fortunately, as time goes by, the demands of the inner world are easier to hear.

Open-ended visualization works well when you set an agenda for the inner teacher to follow by asking questions about you concerns or decisions. In most case the more specific the question the better the answer will be. When clients do this before sessions our work tend to be efficient because we don't spend time clarifying or creating questions, or structures, that may be of interest to them. The following open-ended questions taken from one of my clients, over two sessions, gives an example.

"What was my relationship to my father (he died when I was seven years old)?"
"What is my relationship to other people?"
"Why didn't I develop the ability to listen to people?"
"Why do I sometimes become unclear when I speak?"
"Why is my fear of abandonment so strong?"
"Why do I frequently feel angry?"
"Where do my anxiety attacks come from?"
"Why am I insecure and uncomfortable with people?"
"Why don't I deal with people in a smooth, loving and caring way?"
"How can I become a successful person?"
"Why do I have sexual needs that are very intense?"
"What is important for me?"
"What are my goals?"

Imagery and Intuition

"What do I think about my self?"
"Why don't I smile and laugh more often?"
"Why don't I have a good and consistent sense of humor?"
"Why am I so serious?"
"Why am I here?"
"What affected and shaped me most in my childhood?"
"What is my relationship with my wife (we're separated)?"

The young man who wrote these questions, an engineer, is well-organized. (Most people don't actually write down their questions and when they do the list is short.) While he expected a different answer to each question, some questions were answered by the same image. This happens a lot with related question. And it's fairly common for the unconscious to answer unrelated questions with great clarity by the same mental pictures.

Assets and Liabilities

The assessment of personal assets and liabilities takes on an interesting dimension when viewed by the mind's eye. I often use this kind of assessment with new students and clients. After guiding participants to a quiet inner state, I have them take several seconds to relax and visualize answers to the questions, "What are my assets or what qualities do I have to attract the people and circumstances I need and want?" After viewing the asset picture on the inner screen, ask "What is my liability or what qualities do I need to change to attract the people and circumstances I need and want?" Raising such questions with the conscious mind allows the deeper mind through its universal language of imagery and symbols, to bring answers into the light of day.

While the meaning of these insights may vary greatly, report the mental pictures, images or colors just at they appear, no matter how ridiculous or faint, because they represent the deeper mind. While it is tempting to verbalize thoughts or feelings, doing so limits your ability to create pictures. For example, the statements, "my asset is intelligence," or "I feel great about myself" are not images and tell us very little about the quality of this asset. However, the mental picture of someone in a scientific lab or library, when viewed as a symbol, will tell us a great deal about the nature of one's intelligence. In the first case, we are dealing with the words "intelligence" and "great" and their literal meanings. In the second, there are several potential meanings for each picture of intelligence. When participants have trouble "seeing" I often give them permission by saying, "Fake it or pretend or make-believe, use your imagination." In this way they relax. There is less emphasis on doing it right, or seeing clearly.

The realization of truth consist in the ability to translate symbols.
Thomas Troward

If your seeing is not real, what is living, what is true?

The Secret of the Golden Flower

In one of my classes a young man shared his personal asset and liability images with other students. He saw his asset as a tortoise walking next to an oak tree and his liability as a motorcyclist attempting to pull a mobile home. According to him the asset picture served to validate his sense of stability, calmness, protection, and slow but sure movement toward desired goals. He saw his liability image as confirming his tendency toward arrogance and taking independent actions which border on stupidity. Although these images were easy to interpret some are not so obvious.

By reporting all pictures just as you see them, even the strange or confusing or dimly perceived ones, you honor the unconscious. You can always call back your rational mind to interpret the image, draw implications and formulate your response.

While knowledge of the dominant themes in our personal behavior, relationships or job situation is important, we also need to be aware that these are only principle qualities. These qualities vary in intensity depending on the individual or situation, as do other less obvious qualities. We each tend to be a type made up of certain qualities, but within each of us there lays every other type ready to come forth when the time is right.

Seeing the Future

In addition to identifying, setting, evaluating and revising personal, relationship and group goals, inner movies are very useful for seeing the future. Since individuals are by their nature goal seeking, goals give direction to their life and provide purpose. Whenever you act out of vision, you begin to manifest that vision.

You can see the future, a form of prediction, because it grows out of the deeper mind. Before anything in the future reaches the physical plane it lives as a thought form or picture in the unconscious.

While we create many of these thought forms or pictures with our full awareness, we create the vast majority of them (over 99 percent) without full awareness. As a result, much of what happens in our lives, happens without our full knowledge. This should not come as a surprise but it is just that for most of us. Because the future exists, we can see the future in the present. Although it lives in another dimension we can see it.

In my work with clients, a useful question to ask before making specific plans for the future is, "What can I expect by pursuing this course?" While it may not be obvious, implicit in this question is the question, "Based on my current situation or reality or plans or starting point or intention, what will happen?" For those prone to poor judgment, this kind of question ought to be answered before getting attached to or pursuing any significant goal. In asking life direction questions like, "What can I expect in the future?" you should specify a time such as the next month or year or decade. In addition, you should identify specific areas of concern business, job or relationship.

Specific questions are closed-end and give you direct control over your actions. Insights or "answers" to specific questions are relatively easy to interpret. General questions are open-ended and allow you to see futures that may surprise you. However, answers to these questions may not be easy to understand. In both cases the use of clairvoyance can help you determine what attitudes and actions will improve your situation or adjust it before it shows up in the outer world. If something unexpected or undesirable presents itself, you can change your thinking or plan and then act accordingly. Nothing of importance should be left to chance or fate.

Most people are especially enthusiastic about the future and work to control as much of it as they can. Given this human tendency to do forward planning, they turn to helpers such as psychotherapists, counselors, psychics, or to self-help techniques, e.g., rune stones, tarot, astrology. Despite this desire and the ability to predict the future the past and present situations offer indispensable reference points. Frederick Levine, in *Body, Mind and Spirit*, has written about this subject as follows:

> The real value of learning about the future lies in putting it into the context of the present. Therefore, a good psychic will tell you more about yourself as you are now than as you will be in several months' time. Where the future enters the equation is in knowing whether the way you are running your life right now will have positive ramifications in the future. Where you are going in your life is always based on where you have come from, and in this way predictions can be powerful tools to help you now.

For example, one of my regular clients wanted to know what he could expect by planning to becoming a full time song writer-publisher over the next five years. While he made his living as a drug rehabilitation counselor, he had managed to devote several hours a week to his music. He had produced some original music, built his own recording studio, and his jazz quartet played at local clubs on a part time basis. When this issue came up in one of our sessions I instructed him to relax, close his eyes, and ask, "Based on my present status and career plan (full time song writing-publishing) what can I expect over the next five years if I fully pursue this course now?" He wanted to know what his efforts would amount to; he wanted to know the future. Following my request, he saw himself in an empty warehouse without doors. In discussing his mental picture we concluded that this plan would not give him what he wanted. From his perspective the big warehouse without doors described his fear that he would not be able to create or produce enough music for the audience he wanted to reach. He was able to see that his thinking was unrealistic.

To resolve this dilemma I suggested that he could stay with his plans if he stretched-out his time table, or adjusted them toward a new target. Without getting specific, I asked him to relax and use his inner eyes to answer the question, "How can I resolve my problem?" Upon seeing the image of an archer hitting nearby target while missing distant targets, he sat back and began to mumble about what was realistic. He then concluded by identifying some smaller targets: developing his inventory of demonstration tapes, working with an agent, working alone rather than through his quartet. He enjoyed working with his quartet, but he felt a sense of relief and control over the prospect of working alone.

Numbers

The use of clairvoyance to visualize numerical outcomes has several applications. While it is not possible to predict numbers with consistent accuracy in the quantitative sense, most sincere attempts yield useful insights. In my experience the most stable applications include seeing when future events will occur, estimating income or sales volume (for existing endeavors), group size and related measurements. Whereas these applications tend to yield helpful insights others such as gambling, predicting natural disasters, and estimating incomes for new endeavors, often miss the mark.

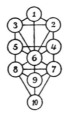

What happens when we look for insights about numbers based on literal rather than symbolic meanings? What we do more often than not, and usually out of ignorance, is to ignore it. Rather than look for meanings that go beyond our present level of thinking we often miss it completely. We tend to expend energy defending our limited view of what numbers mean, and to denounce other meanings as false. Sadly, people spend much energy holding on to their view of the world rather than revising it and learning from the deeper mind.

What the conscious mind does not see, it does not consider. Without changing your consciousness, what you consider, there is no awareness but the awareness you have. Is it possible that clairvoyant insights will take you to a level of consciousness at which not knowing what is going on is diminished? In general, and in the cases that follow, the answer is yes and no. The more clearly you see the reality of your situation and its projected futures the better equipped you are to deal with the world and the possibility of change.

The less clearly you see the reality of your situation the less able you will be to determine correct courses of action and to make wise decisions.

For instance, one woman had moved to a section in Washington state where meeting "good" men seemed impossible. She wanted to get married again or to have a close relationship. She thought it might help to know what to expect and when to expect it. I always have doubts about the usefulness of such information, but as usual I set them aside and tried help. I centered my mind, looked for a time line extending two years into the future, and then scanned it for a date. I saw her meeting a man about eighteen months later and sitting down with him in her house. Things turned out as predicted in this case. She met this man within a week of my predicted date and invited him to live with her the following week. Their live-in relationship lasted just over a year and they remain friends to this day. As far as I can tell, my assistance helped this woman to adjust her expectations and put her energies into other concerns until the unconscious could fulfill her wishes. She waited for the "right man" because she greatly valued previous insights and trusted our counselor-client relationship.

Another woman wanted to know if I could tell her when she would meet her future husband, the date. Several years ago an astrologer in India told her that she would get married in 1988, the next year. She wanted a second opinion from me. In my mind I saw the date March 12. Unlike the woman just mentioned, this one had never been engaged or married or in a serious relationship. Because she was thirty-five I figured that this date was more a question than an answer. But, what did it mean? Was there something significant about the numbers 3 and 12, 3 x 12 or 312? To keep matters simple I told her that something about this man or the marriage question related to March 12. I added that I couldn't tell if she would meet her future husband on that date. Although she didn't reveal it at the time, the next day she called to tell me something interesting. She found out that the man's birthday fell on March 12. While I never saw her again, she was quite moved at this possibility.

In responding to a similar question I told a man that I saw him meeting his future wife on the 4th of May in the following year. While nothing showed up on that date, two days later his mother told him about her dream on the evening of the 4th of May. She had dreamt that a young woman (whom she and her son thought highly of years ago) told her that she planned to marry her son. While we didn't think much of his mother's dream at the time, it made sense some two years later. Then, in a counseling session, he told me that his only close contacts with women over the last twelve years consisted of short-time sexual encounters. It was as if the unconscious was reaching out to him through his mother to look for the "right" woman. Beyond this, I have no way to evaluate the role of these insights. To this day, four years later, the man remains single.

In addition to seeing the future through mental imagery, the I Ching helps to keep our interpretations honest. This happens because mental pictures are perceptions by nature and often difficult to judge in terms of exact meaning. They call for an open mind to potential meanings without judgment. By contrast, the I Ching tends to shut off perceptions and arrive at a fairly specific verdict. It offers fairly precise judgments on a scale of "easy to difficult" in its limited language of the sixty-four hexagrams.

Mental pictures that suggest favorable or unfavorable future incomes become meaningful when integrated with the I Ching and past income data. (I mention the I Ching here because it is designed to integrate past, present and future.) Our personal experiences shape the meaning of our predictions about future, just as history serves as a bench mark for judging the future. For instance, income estimates for the first year of a new business would not be as realistic in terms of expected results as a one-year projection for an existing business. The following two examples will serve to get these points across.

The owner-manager of one of my business clients, a shoe store chain, asked me to project the demand for stockings at their stores over the fall and winter months. This estimate was an aid to setting inventory levels. Before attempting an estimate the manager gave me potential ranges to evaluate: 20, 35 and 50 percent increases in demand over the last year. He expected an increase in the thirty to forty percent range and hoped I could pin it down. In my image I saw a strong man add ten pounds to a hundred-fifty pound weight and then lift it over his head. In my thinking it seemed to represent a sixty percent increase over the last year. To verify this I consulted the I Ching on the question, "What could the store expect by planning for a sixty percent increase in demand for stockings?" Upon getting Hexagram 2 (Fulfillment) I concluded that planning for this figure would produce the best result.

As in other cases, these symbolic estimates provided a view of reality that allowed them to master the terrain of the next year. With this information or road map they generally knew where they were, what to expect, and generally how to get there. The actual demand for stockings turned out to be sixty-five percent over the last year, slightly above the sixty percent increase they planned.

In my business I find it useful to make clairvoyant income estimates on a quarterly and annual basis. Even though these estimates miss the mark in terms of exact dollar amounts, they tend to explain trends with great precision. The following example of images from my counseling practice in the period June 87 through May 88 will serve as an example. The symbolic estimates for the quarters June-August, September-November, December-February, and March-May follow:

- First quarter image: I ride an ascending elevator.
- Second quarter image: I see myself walking in the rain with an umbrella.
- Third quarter image: I see two ladders leaning against the opposite sides of a tower.
- Fourth quarter image: I see fireworks on the Golden Gate Bridge to celebrate its 50th anniversary.

Imagery and Intuition   89

    These mental pictures went beyond income projections alone. They brought into focus the integrated whole of the year and what experiences I could expect. They told me something about the coming year's income trends, but dimly and just in pieces. But the actual monthly-quarterly figures (see graph) speak for themselves.

    The first quarter rises like an ascending elevator. The second falls like rain. The third goes up and down like two ladders leaning against opposite sided of a tower. Compared to quarters one, two and three, the quantum leap in the fourth quarter calls for a celebration.

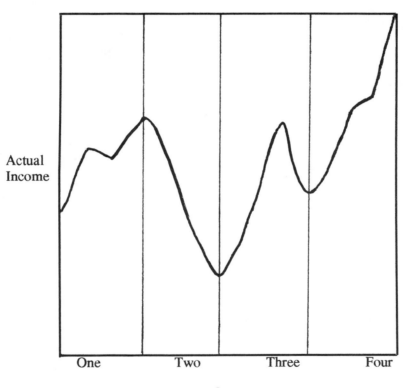

5

Elements of the I Ching

*In the midst of winter
I finally learned that there
was in me an invincible summer.*

Albert Camus

The I Ching or Book of Changes is a perennial philosophy that reveals the wisdom of God or the Self within through the complementary interplay of two polar opposites, Yang and Yin. Though this was the plan of China's great spiritual thinkers who gave us the I Ching, many users of the I Ching fail to recognize that this duality presupposes a uniting principle, namely God, that is the source and support of the opposites emerging from it. In Chinese philosophy it is the Tao that allows Yang and Yin. The Tao means the "way" of the inner teacher or unconscious that nobody knows with certainty. By viewing the Tao as a conscious way or method to bring separated elements together we are close to the psychological meaning of the concept. [1]

In searching for an understanding of God and the unity of all life in our universe, we get little from the usual Western philosophies. It appears that the rapid rise in the popularity of the I Ching is in part because it presents an "objective way" in which the experience of oneness is available to all. [2] The Ten Wings, or articles on the Changes explain how the Book of Changes does this, and why it does it.

The logic of the sixty-four hexagrams relies upon the logic of numbers and elements obtained by chance to determine the situations and relations among them. While the I Ching sets up no order or ranking of numbers, it does make a distribution of values of the various situations portrayed, which in themselves are equal to one another. They serve as coordinates for the events and actions in our unique situation. The system of numbers behind the I Ching offers a rational and abstract tool for grasping the confusing diversity of our inner and outer world. In linking these numbers to the elements and to statements of truth about the human condition they serve as a more perfect expression of thought than written expressions.

The sixty-four hexagrams of the I Ching *are the instrument by which the meaning of sixty-four different yet typical situations can be determined.*
C.G. Jung

The I Ching *insist upon self-knowledge throughout.*
C.G. Jung

The Book of Changes reveals the wisdom of the inner Self. It is an attempt to clarify universal problems whose reflection in other cultures has lead to the insights expressed in their various religions and mythologies. It is an attempt to provide a channel of expression for God. The language of the I Ching's holy scriptures, commonly known as hexagrams, is connected with our instinctual, unconscious energies and is very remote from the world of rational, differentiated human thought. Although the hexagrams appear to be objective, most interpretations require the use of intuition.

Used primarily as an oracle in the West, the Book of Changes has equally great significance as a book of wisdom or history, like the Bible. The fundamental concept of the Changes, the eight trigrams, was first conceived as images of all that happens in the conscious and unconscious realms; they are images that are constantly undergoing change. Since ancient times they have been in a state of continual transition, one changing into another, just as transitions from one phenomenon to another are always taking place in the outer world. According to the Ten Wings of the Book of Changes, whoever has realized what the Changes have to offer, be he a philosopher, a psychologist, a member of the clergy, a social reformer, or a pragmatic statesman, even an empire builder, will not be able to live without the Changes again. [3] In describing the psychological basis for using the I Ching as an oracle Wilhelm comments on Chapter X of the Ten Wings.

> The person consulting the oracle formulates his problem precisely in words, and regardless of whether it concerns something distant or near, secret or profound, he receives—as though it were an echo—the appropriate oracle, which enables him to know the future. This rests on the assumption that the conscious and the supraconscious enter into relationship. The conscious process stops with the formulation of the question. The unconscious process begins with the division of the yarrow stalks, and when we compare the result of this division with the text of the book, we obtain the oracle.

The Book of Changes has attracted an ever widening circle of seekers that has recently grown considerably. In his book, *I Ching*, John Blofeld elaborates:

> There are already numerous English translations of Eastern works whose authors devoted most of their lives to self-conquest and self-understanding; for books such as these, the Book of Change (I Ching, pronounced Yee Jing) is not a substitute, since it has a specialized function; but its worth is incalculable in that, besides being permeated with the highest spiritual values, it enables any reasonable un-

selfish person who is capable of fulfilling a few simple conditions both to foresee and to CONTROL the course of future events!

Some ten thousand years ago the eight trigrams were known and used as symbolic pictures to explain the outer physical world. The Ten Wings, the sixty-four hexagrams, trigram and line interpretations, and the present form of divination has been around for three thousand years. In this period, divination was seen as a bridge between the inner and outer worlds. To this day this bridge explains how to practice inner spirituality in the outer world, and how to solve outer world problems through guidance from the inner world.

Generally, you can understand the I Ching through prolonged reflection and meditation along one of two paths as follows:

1. Through an in-depth study of life's meaning based on what the mystics have taught, including the Ten Wings. Ideally, this study is followed by continued and prolonged use of the Changes as an oracle. This means consulting the Changes and being guided by its pronouncements.

2. The second path begins with consulting the I Ching in concert with analysis, experimentation and intuition, and then following its guidance over the long-run. This course is then followed by an in-depth study of what the mystics have taught, including the Ten Wings.

I dare to say that an awareness without spiritual foundation is like a stool with only two legs.
W. Brugh Joy

The first path begins with the goals of mysticism followed by the use of divination. The second path reverses the order, becoming with divination as a tool on the path to mysticism. As already mentioned in the chapter on mysticism, all the great mystics recommend the first way. Although mystics tend to depreciate occult tools, regarding them as questionable and distractions to true spiritual growth, the I Ching occupies an elevated place.

Although this book presents the I Ching as an oracle rather than a historical document, the primary difference between them may be summarized as follows:

The Book of Changes	*The Book of History*
Lao Tzu (540-460B.C.) Father of Taoism	Confucius (551-479 B.C.) Father of Confucianism
Taoist Religion (600B.C.-present)	Confucianism (600B.C.-present)
Chinese Buddhism 400B.C.-present)	The Ten Wings (221B.C.-1700A.D.) (Ten philosophy article to explain the I Ching—see Wilhelm)

The Book of Changes	*The Book of History*
Various Schools 300B.C.-200A.D.)	1st & 2nd Wings, *Judgement*
Diplomatists Schools	3rd & 4th Wings, *The Image*
Militarist Schools	5th & 6th Wings, *The Great Treatise*
Legalist Schools	7th Wing, *Words of the Text*
	8th Wing, *Discussion of Trigrams*
	9th Wing, *The Sequent of Hexagrams*
Zen School of Buddhism (200B.C.-1900A.D.)	10th Wing, *Miscellaneous Notes on the Hexagrams*

> *In view of the* I Ching's *extreme age and its Chinese origin, I cannot consider its archaic, symbolic, and flowery language abnormal.*
>
> **C.G. Jung**

The I Ching is a work that represents thousands of years of slow organic spiritual growth. It embraces the "occult" and mysticism in that it allows its users to gain access to its wisdom from either direction. There are many benefits in using the I Ching as an occult tool for divination. However its great philosophical depth and wisdom take it beyond this level; its place in history compares to the Bible. Out of its wisdom come the religions, philosophy, and mystical teachings of Taoism, Chinese Buddhism and Zen Buddhism on the one hand, and Confucianism on the other.

Until the beginning of the twentieth century the I Ching was still a mystery in the Western world. Some ninetieth century translations were made but while they were qualified in language, they were ignorant of the unconscious and the philosophy of the Changes. In short they failed to understand the reasons for its importance. Richard Wilhelm, a Christian missionary, was the first to study it from the standpoint of the Chinese themselves. His translation appeared in German in 1924, in English in 1950, and made it possible for Westerners to use the Book of Changes as used throughout the East. The importance of the I Ching on a worldwide basis is still in its beginnings and it has already met with great favor. Its influence is mainly due to Wilhelm's work, and to the great attention given it by Jung and the Jungian school of psychoanalysis.

The pages that follow give insights into the I Ching's language of hexagrams, trigram elements and lines to make it useful in self-development, self-therapy, and in solving important life problems. These insights come out of my personal experience and spiritual. Consequently, they reflect the path I have followed and where it leads. I have found that if our attitude is not in harmony with the great harmony of the cosmos, the Self within, the I Ching will reflect this. If forthcoming events may threaten your inner equilibrium, the I Ching will give you a warning, so you will not lose the way. In situations where you are carried away from your inner truth the I Ching points the way back to the center.

The I Ching As Defined by Itself

The philosophy unveiled through the I Ching is simple and consistent: If you relate correctly, keeping yourself in tune with the universe, things work out beneficially for all concerned. The I Ching acts as a lantern, your line of communication from God and, like dreams or mental images it is guides you through the unconscious. One way of describing the Changes is to ask the I Ching to define itself. The response I got upon asking this question was Hexagram 49 (Changing) changing to Hexagram 51 (Earthquake). In summary, this means the I Ching restores order, makes the appropriate changes, and puts its users in touch with new trends. It gives power and influence to those who follow its advice and takes nothing from those who don't use it.

The first hexagram deals with renovation of character and resolving situations that are in conflict. It brings the awareness of how and when to make changes in our situation. The I Ching advises that changing should be avoided in most cases. This is an ironic fact about the I Ching: it is about changes, but cautions against making them. The I Ching cautions us to make changes in our lives gradually, improvement by improvement. It calls for timing and effort to bring the elements in our external world into accord with the new change or transformation. In short, changes should not be made until they are already taking place. This is advantageous on a practical level because it places you at the leading edge of the new change. If you attempt to change too early, you over-shoot the mark, and if you refuse to change you are left behind.

From Hexagram 51 we learn that the Book of Changes deals with powerful yet natural forces that lead to the growth and fruition of everything. Unless the activity behind these forces is untimely, they are beneficial. This hexagram tells us that changes made as a result of following the I Ching's judgments may be so abrupt that the people affected by our actions may feel threatened.

In describing the I Ching based on clairvoyance, I saw the following inner movie:

> An individual mops up the ground floor of a tall office building. After a while, this person opens the shades, lets in the sunlight, and begins to make himself comfortable. This person then takes a fast elevator to the top floor. Intermediate floors get cleaned on the way up. Upon arriving at the top floor the person looks out with a pair of binoculars to survey the entire countryside. He then aims a gun (with rubber bullets attached to the gun by strings) and shoots at appropriate targets and people below. After this "catch," he pulls these targets to the office building.

The I Ching *does not offer itself with proofs and results; it does not vaunt itself, nor is it easy to approach.*

C.G. Jung

According to this image, the I Ching operates by connecting its users to their foundations. After making this connection, the task of working on your foundation begins. This effort is not complete until you (the user) can answer the questions, "What am I becoming? What is my purpose in life?" If you sincerely seek answers to these questions, more light shines on your unique foundation, calling or destiny. Armed with this essential information, the Changes guides you up the elevator of your personal building, to the heights of your potential.

Through this image we see that following insights through the I Ching helps us to make the right connections with the items relevant to our purposes. Unlike the Changes, we tend to be poor at relating our personal experiences to our highest purpose in life. This is not a problem for the I Ching as its message is always tied to the inner teacher, and therefore to your purpose for being. When you forget your foundation, points of reference, identity, or purpose, advice from the Changes misses the mark. But, when you know your place it makes a great deal of sense.

The I Ching also takes its users on a journey of achievement, increased power, and awareness. Through the Changes we learn to overcome our tendency to remain on the outside or at the ground floor of our unique purpose. While it takes time to understand the unconscious, and to reach the heights of our potential, the payoff is worth it. Although the I Ching tends to have limited uses in the beginning, its vast and perhaps infinite uses become apparent as you ascend to the heights of your potential.

Divining and Sampling

The method [I Ching], like all divinatory or intuitive techniques is based on an acausal or synchronistic connective principle.
      C.G. Jung

As already mentioned the I Ching, as well as clairvoyance, work in a way that is analogous to how modern sampling works to aid us in understanding unknowns about the universe. In both sampling and divination we have the capacity, due to our ability to use basic laws of the universe, to reduce uncertainties and reveal what is hidden in the outer and inner world. Although sampling and divining share the goals of increasing our awareness of the unknown, explaining the whole, and allowing us to know in advance what will happen, they go about it in the different ways shown here.

Elements of the I Ching

Sampling	*Divining*
Applied to outer physical-world	Applied to inner psychic-world
Favors thinking, sensing and the right-brain	Favors intuition, feeling and the left-brain
Realm of chance	Realm of synchronicity
Realm of estimating, forecasting, and prediction	Realm of foretelling, prophesy, prognostication
Realm of the natural and physical	Realm of the supernatural and metaphysical
Inferred from facts, data, probabilities, certainties	Inferred from signs, symbols, potentialities, uncertainties
Quantitative models of outer-world phenomena	Qualitative models uniting inner and outer-world phenomena
Scientific and non-scientific	Non-scientific
Examples—opinion polling, market testing, counting	Examples—tarot cards, I Ching, mental images, dreams

In the case of sampling, a natural law, a small part of the whole shows the nature of whole. With divination, a different application of the sampling law, inner and outer events appear to be connected but have no logical causal relationship.

Talking to the Unconscious

It is well-known that the unconscious stores more information than is readily available to consciousness. Psychoanalysis, dream work, and mental imagery are key methods by which the West attempts to reveal the inner Self. Many people in the West also attempt to "program" the unconscious in various ways to assist them in fulfilling their personal needs. For example, we see this in the positive mental attitude movement, autosuggestion and in various forms of affirmation. These methods work well for affirming what we know about the truth and creating what we want. However, the I Ching happens to be the East's most reliable method of working with the inner psychic world.

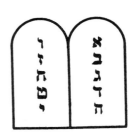

Although both East and West realize that the unconscious is where things really happen in influencing a person's life, the East's idea is a bit more involved. Unlike the West, the East does not think in terms of cause and effect relationships. While people of the West tend to think they are planning their own lives, and some people actually do, people of the East tend to think in terms of being swept along by the great trends and currents of circumstances beyond our

What may appear to the outer mind to be desturctive may appear to the Unconscious to be rectifying and healing.
W. Brugh Joy

control. If the laws of cause and effect really govern everything to the extent generally assumed in the West, then there is little room for synchronicity, intuition or divination. Foretelling the future becomes a matter of noting the past and assuming that given similar causes, similar results will occur.

According to traditional Eastern thinking, when people accept "the way" and live in harmony with its trends and currents, they enjoy serenity and their schemes are apt to prosper. When individuals swim against the currents of their own nature their plans inevitably fail, and they suffer stress, disappointment, frustration and hardships along the way.

As Blofeld points out, it is no accident that the most frequently encountered word in the I Ching is *shun,* meaning peaceful or glad acceptance of what has been, what is, and what will be. [4] The East supposes that the everything and every situation that makes up our present state of consciousness and outer physical reality grows out of the world of the unconscious. The West has only considered this notion of the unconscious since the ninetieth century. We hear about it through countless mystics, gurus, and some psychologists who tell us about our connection to God and the oneness of life.

Hexagram Elements

In relation to hexagrams the elements tell us how we affect others, how we understand or view our situation, and the patterns of self-other relationships within our inquiry. As already discussed, the elements are both extroverted and introverted. Although these are opposing orientations, both can be present in a single hexagram.

In terms of human behavior the introverted hexagram, identified by a broken line on top or in the sixth position, normally points to a hesitant, reflective, cautious response that tends to keep to itself, shrinks from objects, is always slightly on the defensive and often remains in the background. With introversion our situation and intended course of action do not readily fit in the outer physical world.

The extroverted hexagram, identified by a solid line on top or in the sixth position, normally points to an outgoing, candid, and accommodating response that tends to adapt itself easily, quickly forming attachments and, setting aside any possible misgivings, often ventures out with careless confidence into unknown situations. With extroversion the subjective inner world may be suppressed, thus causing a denial of the inner Self and genuine self-expression.

Our comprehension of the four elements, including extroversion and introversion, can make an enormous difference in understanding the various hexagrams. In theory, however, an interpretation of hexagrams based on the elements may be only half true. This happens because only one or two elements show up in hexagrams, one in the lower trigram and one in the upper. For instance, Hexagram 49

(Changing) includes the fire and air elements but omits earth and water, and Hexagram 51 (Earthquake) includes only the air element. Our command of the tenets relevant to the four elements is useful for something more than rational evaluation of the hexagram and our relationship to the situation it describes.

An understanding of the hexagram elements provides a focused and fairly objective psychological critique. The hexagram elements give us an overview of the key trends or currents that both assist and impinge upon us. This knowledge may enlarge the number of possible perspectives that can help us understand what is going on, how to respond to it, and what to expect. For objective clarity and evaluation, the use of elements to understand hexagrams and therefore our situation may be unsurpassed. But the choice of method for interpreting particular hexagrams depends on the kind of information we need and the kind of decision we have to make.

The Eight Trigrams

The eight trigrams are structures composed of yang, yin and the four elements. This trinity represents all the cosmic and physical conditions in the inner and outer worlds. Before the hexagrams were created the trigrams were used in early forms of divination.

The basic attributes of each trigram is followed by a brief description.

Heaven: strength, power, firmness, awareness, creativeness, excitement, external intuition.

The heaven trigram suggests faith in one's vision. Those who get it are often too independent and individualistic to be a conformist. Heaven has the potential force of creation behind it but lacks the experience to manifest this energy on a practical level. The person influenced by heaven will find it very difficult to take orders and as a result it tries to maneuver itself into a position of leadership.

Lake: happiness, openness, vision, excess, inner peace, wisdom, internal intuition.

Lake describes the ability to translate abstract teachings and concepts into terms that can be understood by all. Lake serves as the channel of communication for the Self within and the giver of moral standards. Those influenced by lake tend to trust their insights as to the true relationships and meanings of things regardless of established authority or popular beliefs.

Fire: clearness, illumination, dependence, attachment, objective thinking, sociable, external analysis.

Fire describes the ability to organize facts, situations and operations well in advance, and to make systematic efforts to reach planned objectives on schedule. Those influenced by fire tend to be strong in communication and sociable, but often loose themselves in the ideas and desires of other people. Preferring to work with others fire is seldom found in an isolating environment or situation.

Thunder: shock, excitement, movement, vitality, investigation, internal analysis.

When subjected to strong pressure of any sort, those influenced by thunder will simply change. Thunder is an intellectual trigram as well as the potential transmitter of universal ideas. When it comes up the ideas upon which the soul of humanity will develop and grow are chosen. Those influenced by thunder are often surprised because they are not aware that there are deeper aspects of reality that are not immediately explained by logic and rational analysis.

Wind: small efforts, gentle influence, sensitivity, people-oriented, friendly, external concern.

Wind symbolizes the need for emotional security, for feeling that your environment will support your existence, and for feeling nurtured by those around it. It suggests the need to support and nurture others, giving to others what you have received. Wind is essential to the social good and values human contacts. It describes people and places that are warm both physically and emotionally.

Water: uncertainty, mystery, profoundness, dangerous, emotional depth, internal concern.

Getting water suggests that you are open to the temptations of your lower nature and to the glory of the unconscious. As both an end and a beginning water signifies transformation. It symbolizes the most difficult stage of human evolution, the transcendence of self or letting go. Those influenced by water care more about manipulating and molding others than being seen and recognized by the others.

Mountain: standing still, resting, reliability, business-like, meditating, external control.

Mountain represents the kind of slow growth that increases its stature over a long period of time. Those influenced by mountain are most comfortable when they do not have to function from a personal context. Mountain tends to accept what society considers real and sets out to be effective in practical terms. It takes the established order and moves it, intact, into another stage of evolution.

Earth: submissive, devoted, yielding, serving, perfectionism, factual, internal control.

Earth approaches the physical and social universes as a framework through which it can learn to be effective and a reality that must be served. Earth justifies its existence by how effective it is in getting along in the world and making the best of it. With respect to behavior, those influenced by earth conform under social pressure. Earth tends to be good at analysis but not at getting the grand view.

The Lower Trigram

The lower or inner trigram indicates what you are consciously striving to express, the personal quality you are trying to develop and project. Through this trigram, energies from the self are made manifest to the not-self. In other words, this is the trigram of self-manifestation. It relates to the future, to promise, and potential. The inner trigram describes your personal style, manner, and speech. This trigram represents the inner world of your thoughts, your personal orientation, and where you are coming from. It characterizes your approach as well as the way other people receive their first impression of you. It represents the mode of expressing your entire self in action in the world, a natural and spontaneous way of immediately confronting life outside yourself. It is the door through which you express and make active your inner motivations and psychological needs in the immediate environment.

This trigram shows your initial thoughts and the steps you need to take. This is not an easy task because most trigrams will oppose our preferred mode and element of expression in some way. For example, if my preferred element and mode of expression is introverted fire, the earth and water trigrams, and the extroverted fire and air trigrams (six out of the eight trigrams) present some degree of opposition. As already mentioned extroversion opposes introversion, earth opposes fire, and water is in conflict with fire. Compared to the outer trigram, the inner trigram describes your beginning, your microcosm and thoughts on the situation before you.

In addition, the lower trigram points to the correct answer or approach needed to be in harmony with what is becoming visible. It serves as the missing link to our mystery or paradox in that it explains how to reach ultimate conclusions.

Know the personal, yet keep to the impersonal: accept the world as it is.
Tao Te Ching

The Upper Trigram

The upper or inner trigram signifies the "personality" of the outer world, what you expect from the situation and other people, especially those close to you. Just as the lower trigram describes your experience of self on an intimate level, the upper trigram is your experience of the outside world on an intimate level. It represents the style or way in which other people introduce themselves to you. As well as the spatial opposite of the inner trigram, it relates to the kind of impression the not-self makes upon the self or the effect of the immediate environment upon you. To put it more precisely, the outer trigram relates to your experience of others and the outside world. Even more precisely, it describes those aspects of yourself that you experience through relationships with others.

Like carpenters building a log cabins, the upper trigram deals with building forms that call for teamwork or some cooperative endeavor. The top trigram represents the basic "building blocks" or outer structure of the situation being investigated. It signifies the character of the physical world and your relationship to it. It spells out the kind of activity that the inner trigram must adjust to in dealing with other people's differences. The outer trigram reveals the type of activity that you must focus on to improve your relationship with outer circumstances.

The top trigram describes the form of the hexagram as a whole. It represents the situation or condition through which you must learn to assimilate what you have felt, seen or heard into a new level of consciousness and behavior. Through this trigram you have an opportunity to bring your ideas down to reality and to share your personal experiences with others.

The Six Hexagram Lines

Of the various hexagram components that give meaning in this book the lines are least significant. While this book explains the sixty-four hexagrams it does not interpret the 384 individual lines—the six lines in each hexagram. Rather it gives the basic meanings of the six hexagram lines from the viewpoint of what they have in common. On one hand, this book simplifies the meaning of changing lines and the I Ching and on the other, it increases the scope and flexibility of interpretations.

As seen in the Ten Wings described by Wilhelm the hexagram's meaning begins with the first line and is summed up in line six [5]. Individual hexagram lines explain the nature of changes taking place in your situation. According to the Ten Wings the lines indicate where you are and where you are going; their sequence contains additional meaning about your particular situation. The character of each line can be understood as well through the language of elements.

According to the elements and the Ten Wings, the movement of lines is inward or outward; lines one and four, two and five, and three and six have a natural correspondence. The first three lines represent the personal quality you are projecting, and the top three represent your experience of the outside world.

Line 1: The first or bottom line describes the hexagram's cause and how things are beginning to develop. It represents the most significant personal direction within the entire hexagram and therefore subject matter at hand. A yang line here refers to expanding or acting upon some new possibility. A yin line represents introversion, consolidation, or pursuing an established order or idea. Yang expresses the active elements of fire or air, while yin expresses the passive elements of earth or water.

From the Ten Wings we see that this line refers to something hidden from view, either conscious or unconscious:

> The beginning line is difficult to understand. Top line is easy to understand. For they stand in the relationship of cause and effect. The judgment on the first line is tentative, but at the last line everything has attained completion.

The first line depicts a idea or beginning, personal thoughts or desires, and seed potential that has yet to appear in the outer world. When this line changes you are thinking about some new endeavor. It stands as a symbol of initiating some new personal experience.

Line 2: The second line refines the first line into one of the four elements. The fire element (two yang lines) points to excitement, promotion, risk taking, and independence. The air element (yang followed by yin) refers to thought, analysis, and relatedness. The earth element (two yin lines) refers to control, convention, and the established order. Finally, the water element represents feelings, sensitivity, and support. The second line describes the element through which your intentions express. Again, a yang or yin line here can be understood in relation to the first line.

The idea of seeing the "great man" is a common theme for this line. This statement refers to finding a third party or source of knowledge or principle that can help you in the situation at hand. Although your position is that of a subordinate here there is always someone who knows how to help you.

As seen in the Ten Wings, the second line usually carries a favorable judgment and the fourth a warning as follows:

> The second and the fourth place correspond in their work but are differentiated by their positions. They do not correspond as regards the degree to which they are good. The second is usually praised, the fourth is usually warned, because it stands near the ruler. The meaning of the yielding is that it is not favorable for it to be far away.

In Chinese tradition line two is related yet subordinate to the superior fifth line in the following way: manager to executive, prince to king, and follower to leader. This line calls for working behind the scenes to support the hexagram's meaning (which is summed up in the fifth line).

Line 3: This line describes your way of dealing with the outer world. An extroverted line (yang) reveals an outgoing orientation, taking the lead, and optimism toward other people. An introverted third line (yin) suggests a private, reflective, and caution response to the outer world. The firm third line points to personal achievement and anticipation of the future. The yielding third line suggests

---

The one yin [inside the fire trigram] concentrates on pursuing experience, while the one yang [inside the water trigram] concentrates on reversing and withdrawing the senses themselves.

The Secret of the Golden Flower

an emphasis on personal security.

Among the six lines the third one is the most unfortunate because it represents the point at which your intention or influence moves from the lower to the upper trigram. This line advises caution because you are taking our first step into the outside world. In his translation of the Ten Wings Wilhelm describes this line in the following way:

> .....it is an insecure position on the boundary between two trigrams. Therein, as well as in its lower rank, lie elements of weakness that in most situations show the place to be endangered.

Line 4: The fourth line, like the first, is the trigram's foundation. As in the first line, yang refers a new beginning or cause, while yin in this position signifies consolidation or following an established order. Unlike line one, this line refers to your experience of energies from other people and the outside world. A yang line here suggests an experience of something new and dynamic from the world outside (defined by the hexagram as a whole). This may be unfortunate if such activity tends to usurp rather than support the fifth line. A yielding fourth line suggests an experience of something well-defined and regulated.

In Chinese tradition the fourth line refers to a subordinate minister, adviser, or consultant to the fifth line. Line 4 deals with the fears tied to pursuing any new activity or course in the outer world. It serves as a message to proceed with caution in taking your first steps, e.g., in advising others, doing something for the first time, or putting yourself at risk.

Line 5: The fifth line describes the element of the world around you. When combined with the fourth line it describes the impression or effect made upon you by other people. The primary difference between this line and line two is that this one defines the element of your immediate outer environment.

This line is the natural ruler of the hexagram. As such it implies merit, good fortune, and attaining the best possible outcome. It serves as a message that your position is in harmony with the wisdom imparted by the hexagram. A yang line in this position refers to an outgoing, active, and enthusiastic response. A yin line signifies an adaptable, receptive, and obedient response.

Line 6: The top line describes the hexagram's effect or result. It shows your ultimate experience of the entire hexagram. The extroverted top line (yang) or the introverted top line (yin) has much in common with the third line. However, unlike the third line, this one describes the style or way in which you experience other people and the situation before you.

According to the Ten Wings this line represents danger because you have gone too far. This comes about when we have achieved all you can, yet look for more without knowing what you want. "What comes next?" is the relevant question. The top line may be seen as the wise counselor or mystic who remains open to new problems that lay beyond or outside the hexagram and therefore the situation at hand. The following summary gives the attributes of the six lines in relation to trigrams.

Upper trigram	Top line	Consciousness	Wisdom
Interpersonal	Fifth line	Consciousness	Authority
	Fourth line	The individual	Social contact
Lower trigram	Third line	The individual	Personal action
Personal	Second line	The unconscious	Learning
	Bottom line	The unconscious	Instincts

The following hypothetical case gives an example of interpreting each changing lines. Lets suppose a young man consulted the I Ching and got Hexagram 1(Creation) as the answer to his question, "What can I expect by pursuing a date with this young woman?" Although he as seen her around he knows little about her. In line one the young man, seeing the young woman around, is aware of his interest in her. At this point this interest in hidden, known only to him. This line advises him to wait before expressing his intentions until he learns how to express them. Line two tells the young man that he can improve his chances by finding someone who knows how to help him. This might take place by talking to others or working behind the scenes to find out what he and the young woman have in common.

The third line warns the young man about the risk, being accepted or rejected, in inviting the young woman out for the first time. Line three serves as a question, "Are you ready to be accepted or rejected?" The fourth line advises the young man to exercise caution, to keep his ego in check, whether the young woman goes out with him or turns him down. Line four tells him that his intention is making it first contact with the outer world. In the fifth line the young man may expect to win approval, go out on his first date, and thereby achieve his goal. Line six warns him about the risks in taking the next step. Like the third line this line serves to ask questions of morality such as, "What are your real intentions?" "What do you want?" "What are you going to next, e.g., meet her parents, play around, get serious, let her go?"

Finding the Most Important Changing Line

The presence of two or more changing lines tends to complicate how we interpret the lines. To avoid confusion you should find the most important line. *The I Ching for Beginners* (written by China's great philosopher Chu Hsi, 1130-1200AD) provides some excellent guidelines for hexagrams with changing lines. I have adapted these guidelines from lecture notes given in Dr. Yi Wu's class titled "The I Ching" at the California Institute of Integral Studies in San Francisco, Fall 1990:

1. One changing line. Examine the meaning of this line in the first hexagram.
2. Two changing lines. Examine both lines, but the higher line (being more evolved) ought to be given first priority.
3. Three changing lines. Ignore the lines and study the meaning of both hexagrams as a whole.
4. Four changing lines. Examine the two lines in the second hexagram that correspond to the two non-changing lines in the first hexagram. The higher line (being more evolved) ought to be given first priority.
5. Five changing lines. Examine the line in the second hexagram that corresponds to the non-changing line in the first hexagram.
6. Six changing lines. Ignore the first hexagram and study the meaning of the second hexagram as a whole.
7. No changing lines. Study the hexagram as a whole.

Hexagram Stability

Stable hexagrams, those without changing lines, depict firmly established situations and outcomes rooted in the past. The stable hexagram serves as a message to cultivate your existing garden instead of planting new ones. It suggests that the way is clear for natural growth and nourishment. Its form suggests dependable and consistent results, whether favorable or unfavorable. The keynotes for stable hexagrams are steadfastness and permanence.

Unstable hexagrams, those with three or more changing lines, refer to situations or outcomes likely to change of fluctuate quickly. Unstable hexagrams are unsteady and marked by emotional instability. The future or second hexagram is so different from the first hexagram that you can expect some form of shock. These hexagrams point to big changes, e.g., extroversion to introversion, fire to earth, air to water, or vice versa. With unstable hexagrams you can expect the future,"for better or worse," to be completely unlike the present.

Grading Hexagrams

The hexagram grades appear after the hexagram summaries and represent my observations on the degree of ease or difficulty in experiencing the hexagram. The grades, A through F, attempt to rate or measure varying degrees of tension (positive and negative stress) associated with the hexagram. These ratings correspond roughly with the hexagrams "stress level." They don't describe hexagram outcomes in themselves. Each grade is represented by a single hexagram that personifies the path. These definitions follow:

A	Increase	Hexagram	42	Easy
B	Progress	Hexagram	35	•
C +	Correction	Hexagram	18	•
C -	Limitations	Hexagram	60	•
D	Danger	Hexagram	29	•
F	Obstacles	Hexagram	39	Difficulty

An interpretation of hexagrams based only on the grades gives a limited but reliable judgement of the hexagram's outcome. While these grades or paths are no panacea they are an excellent aid for decision-making queries.

While forty percent of the hexagrams belong to grades A and B, individuals with limited experience may find the I Ching lacking in positive outcomes. This comes about because it is human nature to always expect that which is positive, beneficial and easy. Since the likelihood of getting the other less desired grades is at least two in three, it is no wonder why those who use the Changes will find its guidance rather sobering.

As already discussed, extroverted hexagrams are identified by a yang line on top and introverted hexagrams by a yin line. Even though the I Ching consists of thirty-two extroverted and thirty-two introverted hexagrams, the introverts are nearly twice as favorable as the extroverts. In particular, grades A and B consist of nine extroverted hexagrams, i.e., 1, 13, 14, 27, 35, 37, 42, 50 and 53, and sixteen introverted hexagrams, i.e., 2, 8, 11, 15, 16, 19, 24, 32, 34, 40, 45, 46, 48, 49, 55 and 58. The difficult D and F grades consist seven extroverts, i.e., 6, 21, 23, 33, 38, 41 and 44, and five introverts, i.e., 7, 28, 29, 39 and 47. Because people of the East tend to prefer introversion to extroversion, just the opposite of people of the West, it is perhaps no mystery that the hexagrams favor an inner attitude.

Methods of Interpretation

There are several layers of hexagram interpretation. These layers or methods fall into two basic categories: outside and inside.

The easiest outside method calls for the rating of hexagrams from the "easy," positive, and ego-expressive (grades A and B) to the "difficult," negative, and ego-repressive (grades D and F). The next outside methods call for an interpretation of the hexagram's title, the hexagram's summary, or time permitting, the hexagram's trigram elements (upper and lower). Outside interpretations based upon analyzing the hexagram's text and line meanings are the most in-depth.

The inside methods call for the use of clairvoyance to expand the meaning of the hexagram and to provide a context for its interpretation. The straightforward method is to consult the I Ching and then use clairvoyance to see how the result applies to your situation. While your images will be tied to the hexagram this rather modest limitation still lets you visualize what's going on. The next method, which takes more time, uses clairvoyance first and then the I Ching. I have found that this method gives greater depth and insights about the questions you ask.

By integrating clairvoyant images and hexagrams from the I Ching you can rise above the limited interpretations found in books on either subject. When these tools come together we have combine perception and judgment; we give the unconscious a much richer language to explain itself than either tool can offer alone. Although both tools reflect non-rational functions clairvoyance has much more to do with sudden, lightening-like comprehension, whereas the I Ching draws upon subtle factors that come into being at no particular point, seeming rather to have always existed.

Whereas clairvoyant insights tend to be expansive, uplifting and ego-centered like the element of fire, those from the I Ching tend to sink and penetrate like the element of water. Although images see what can be and what may be the I Ching sees realities and relates everything to our place in life. The language of hexagrams is finite, stressing partnership and closeness with other human beings; the language of imagery is infinite, stressing leadership, independence, and the individual uniqueness in every situation. In short, Clairvoyance shows the lay of the land with map-like precision while the I Ching adds the heights and depths of the lands mountains and valleys.

Neither clairvoyance or the I Ching is "better" as far as telling you what the teacher within has to say. By themselves, neither the inside nor the outside methods are "better" as far as telling us what the hexagram is saying. The method of choice depends on the kind of information you need, the kind of decision you have to make and the time or cost of the assessment requested. For dealing with number of individual factors or consultations, or a limited time or budget, the outside methods are best. A combination of inside and outside methods is probably best if you require high-accuracy inferences about a few people or places or situations. The inside methods provide the depth and richness of the inner world, while the outside methods provide a check against the more radical conclusions to which the inside methods are prone.

Outside methods will appeal to beginners and to those who are eager to reach a level of precision and objectivity through shortcuts. While this approach does not ignore the inner world, it tends to gloss over its nuances of meaning. These methods aim for reliable description of the hexagram's meaning and hope to find the underlying principles that govern various outcomes.

Inside methods assume that the inner world is a more significant indicator of the hexagram's true meaning. The inside approach to evaluating the hexagram's meaning in your situation should help you to construct a portrait of your inner world. This methods helps you to see things as you feel them and to find out which motives guide your behavior and the behavior of other people. Inside methods are more demanding and time-consuming than the outside methods because more information has be be collected and related to your situation. Even though you have to feel your way along without ranking numbers, elements, summary themes, trigrams and hexagram texts of the outside methods, the payoff is always greater.

Inside methods produce greater insights and potentials for controlling situations than outside methods. Inside methods give you a working overview of the hidden dynamics at work. The inside and outside methods of evaluating hexagrams are both right. Each method reveals a different aspect of human nature and each uses the best avenue for its purposes.

When we enter into to communion with Thee, we are never sure of the Voice that speaks within us.
Howard Thurman

6

Counseling or Psychotherapy

*If we do not have, in some measure,
an understanding of the nature of God,
we will be inclined to relate to circumstances
as we perceive them.*

Roy Eugene Davis

The field of personal counseling includes hundreds of traditional and not so traditional psychotherapies. It includes many forms of psychic or intuitive counseling based on clairvoyance, astrology, tarot cards, the I Ching, and so forth, to enhance the growth of its clients. We can understand the nature of psychic counseling by placing the various styles of counseling into one of two realities. In his book *The Medium, The Mystic, and The Physicist*, Lawrence LeShan has provided a useful definition of these two realities. In Sensory Reality, one gains information through the senses; in the Clairvoyant Reality, one gains information through ESP. [1]

In this work, the Clairvoyant Reality contains counseling and therapy styles rooted in visualization methods, the I Ching, and other intuitive disciplines. The Sensory Reality contains counseling and therapy approaches rooted in science. In the first group information is gained through psychic means: the therapist or counselor perceives how all things (including people and events) relate to themselves, and then to the other individual or client. Because everything is part of everything else those who gain information in this manner understand it in the same way they understand themselves: through self-observation. In the second group information is gained through the ordinary means (through the senses), and the therapist perceives the unique characteristics of each thing (people and events), and then proceeds to its relationship with other things. The counselor or therapist uses his sense organs to listen and examine things and then proceeds to apply his intelligence, philosophy and scientific methods to gain an understanding.

Many volumes, both profound and superficial exist on the various instruments, vehicles, or tools of awareness in the Clairvoyant Reality. Although these experiences in conscious awareness often

appear external to the Self within, all experiences originate within the individual. With the exception of visualization, these outer physical aids offer the opportunity to integrate into one's experience of Self that which at first seems to be external to the Self. LeShan describes how such techniques help make the external, internal and the internal, external in this way:

> Historically, certain techniques seem to have been evolved to help individuals living in the Sensory Reality to attain some of the information obtainable in the Clairvoyant Reality without losing the security and values of their everyday Weltanschauung. These include astrology, numerology, the I Ching, and tarot cards.
> These techniques appear to function in a definite manner, although this is frequently hidden and overlaid by extra and distorting attributes. Through the use of a structured setting in which the individual is oriented to a strong expectation and mental set for results, plus an enforced passivity of action and will (one has to *wait* to see how the cards fall, and it is out of his control), the person is placed in a conscious psychological situation closely allied to that of the sensitive. The unstructured data (the I Ching paragraphs, for instance, have no exact or precise meaning) let a possibility arise for the conscious perception of unconscious material....it appears to the individual as if his information is coming from objective data rather than from unconscious paranormal sources. Under these conditions, some Clairvoyant Reality perceptions are occasionally likely to take place and to be interpreted as if they were Sensory Reality perceptions.

Both the Sensory and Clairvoyant approach to counseling aim to help their clients observe the relationships of external events to changing internal perspectives, but there are major differences in technique, involvement and responsibility. Generally, counseling tends to proceed in one of three ways: therapy that requires frequent visits over a long time and the development of a genuine relationship with the client, counseling which requires frequent visits over a somewhat intermediate period and the development of an interpersonal exchange, or one-time consultations and readings in which the consultant provides some specific service to a largely inactive participant. The degrees to which these approaches can assist in the healing process depend on a host of factors including the counselor's training and experience, and client's readiness. While board-certified training is important, a psychiatrist is not necessarily any better than a psychologist, a social worker, a minister, or psychic, or even as good. In reality, a therapist's or counselor's ability bears little relationship to any credentials he or she might have.

In this book, the terms psychic or intuitive counseling and counseling refer to a dialogue between counselor and client, whereas a psychic reading or one-time consultation tends to be one-way from counselor to client. What happens in the one-time consultation varies widely from client to client. Whether the client seeks insights for the first time and has no sense of what questions to ask or has great understanding of the process, each person, counselor and client are unique. The best counselor for one person may not be the best for another. At worst, clients may approach the session by asking, "What can you tell me about myself? What do you pick up about me?" or "What do you see?" and come away with limited insights. In this case the client may listen passively or not at all, and have little or no commitment to his or her personal growth. At best, the client may ask the right questions and come away with invaluable insights. The session may be a dialogue between counselor and clients and may facilitate long-needed changes and the impetus to express the Self within.

For instance, one woman who was uncertain about her next career move asked for a psychic reading to choose a course consistent with her heart. She came into the session feeling pressured by her husband and son to work full time. She had been off her teaching job for about a year due to a stress-related disability. Her questions were direct. They were: "Should I return to full-time teaching? Should I opt for part-time teaching as a substitute? Should I devote more time to my part time interior decorating business?" After exploring each option through clairvoyance and the I Ching, as if it were my choice, my response was, "Take it easy, take up part-time teaching." I suggested this course of action because the insights that came up were overwhelming in this direction.

When well-developed intuitives (sometimes also referred to a sensitives or psychics) give a "reading," they are reflecting patterns in the deep psyche.
W. Brugh Joy

Psychic or Intuitive Counseling

Most forms of counseling aim to identify and lead out an already existing capacity in reasonably competent individuals, not the expert manipulation of a somewhat passive personality. The success of counseling or therapy (whether it falls in the Sensory or Clairvoyant Reality), depends upon the client's belief that his or her problems will be resolved. [2] Therapy aims to help clients bring many of their previously unconscious thoughts, trends, conflicts, and problems into the light of day. Counseling on the other hand provides help with the expected problems and stresses in life, such as marital discord, career difficulty, facing a tough decision, planning the future, or understanding other people.

Intuitive counseling is a general term for psychic counseling. This kind of counseling is similar to psychotherapy in that it works to uncover how someone has a hand in creating his or her own problem. As in psychotherapy, psychic counseling can offer an opportunity for clients to learn how they relate to themselves and what they are doing to themselves to interfere with their own improvement. In both cases we aim to get behind what the problem looks like on the surface.

Whereas psychotherapy tends to deal with bigger problems over the long-term, counseling tends to be short-term, more direct and less serious than psychotherapy. Psychotherapy tends to help clients who express problems such as "Nothing works, nothing helps, nothing makes me feel better, I am depressed and can't get around it." Psychic counseling on the other hand helps for problems such as "What if I pursue this career or job option? What is the nature of my problem or conflict and how can I resolve it? I have some ideas but can't make up my mind." In both approaches one gains valuable insights about oneself, one's relationships, and other people.

Psychotherapists and counselors use a broad variety of methods to help individuals. Some use one particular approach such as visualization or dream work while others draw upon many methods. In my own work I have borrowed many ideas from one of the leading humanistic psychologists, Carl Rogers. He preferred the term "counseling" rather than "therapy," and the term "client" rather than "patient." He labels his style of psychotherapy "client-centered" because the client sets the direction for the therapy. By encouraging independence and discarding the past, Rogers helps the client to gain insights into his or her present situation.

As in humanistic psychology, psychic counseling is based on the premise that the real world is what we believe it to be. I have also borrowed some ideas from the oldest form of psychotherapy, Sigmund Freud's method of psychoanalysis, in that I attempt to dialogue with the inner psychic world, to uncover its unconscious material. Like psychoanalysts, psychic counselors see our outward behavior as the tip of an iceberg, and that beneath our conscious outward behavior is a vast unconscious, the hidden portion of the iceberg.

This brings us to the need to differentiate between the psychic and psychotherapy approaches. The typical psychotherapy client feels troubled by his or her behavior and is willing to work through the painful process of internal change. As a result, psychotherapy tends to be long-term and intense, and aims to modify deep attitudes and behaviors that involve the whole person such as shyness, arrogance, helplessness, insensitivity, and so on.

Generally, psychotherapy demands a commitment in its attempt to help change a person's internal structure. By contrast, psychic counseling attempts to help us understand and improve our outlook toward the future and specific immediate life situations without requiring the commitment to significant internal change.

Counseling tends to be short-term and often centers on clarifying unconscious attitudes, trends, needs, and relationships for the client. Because counseling tends to work on the conscious aspect of a situation, as perceived by the client, the effort to make changes at the depth-psychological level may not occur. In those cases where psychic counseling goes beyond five to ten sessions there is a gradual area of transition between counseling and psychotherapy where the boundaries become blurred.

In all forms of counseling no single approach is appropriate to all participants. Psychic counselors work with detachment in that they rarely challenge the client's defenses. Psychotherapists on the other hand tend to confront client's defenses when clients resist change or fail to look at their own contributions to their problems. However, some psychotherapists take a formal, detached stance to reduce the threat to the intimacy in the relationship. In either case the counselor-client relationship must fit the client's current situation. As with psychotherapists, the psychic's success in relating effectively to the widest range of clients will rest upon flexibility and breath of knowledge, skills and life experience.

For example, one woman, a regular client for psychic counseling called for a telephone session. To start this session she asked a general, rather awkward question, "What is the nature of my growing depression?" I called her back at the time we agreed upon and gave her the two mental images I saw; we then discussed their meaning. In the first image I saw her look into a clouded mirror—she was trying to dress up and look good, but could not see her self. In the second image she tried to climb a small hill but could not as the mountainside kept sliding down like a descending escalator. These inner pictures were direct and suggested an effort to advance her self-image and socioeconomic status in spite of the obstacles. My images and interpretations came as no surprise. She knew what they meant because she had been living with her situation and knew enough about it to understand what was going on. Upon hearing them she remarked, "You just told me what I already knew but couldn't see." While her response is not uncommon, some new clients expect to hear things they know nothing about. But this is unrealistic for two reasons. First, clairvoyants can only see what is there even

Life, at its best, is a flowing, changing process in which nothing is fixed.
Carl R. Rogers

People grieve and bemoan themselves, but it is not half so bad with them as they say.
Ralph Waldo Emerson

though the person may want to believe or hear something totally different. Second, unfamiliar images, e.g., insights about the distant future or life-altering outcomes that have not been considered, are often confusing and misleading.

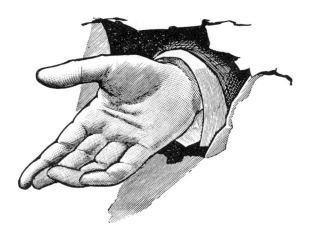

Being of Help

Once the initial judgement is made either to seek or to give help, further exploration is necessary to determine the relevance of this help to the client's concern. For example, does the issue have broad or very specific ramifications? How does it relate to the problems the person is having in daily life? Is it possible for the person to keep his commitments and follow the wisdom of his heart? Is the client seeking something that he or she does not already have, such as knowledge or some possession? Such questions go beyond mere curiosity or the desire for more information; rather, they help to clarify, for both the counselor and client, relevant issues, experience, and realistic expectations.

Genuine psychotherapy is a legitimate shortcut to personal growth which is often ignored.
M. Scott Peck

The process of counseling (helping another) is not an experience in which one person does something to another. Rather, it is a complex interaction between two or more people with the ultimate aim of facilitating the attainment of some beneficial and specific goals. Despite the client's immediate response, the effects of healing insights seldom show up immediately. As a result, the counselor may feel discouraged or frustrated. This situation is less stressful when the counselor can abandon the need to "cure" or "do-something to the client," and the need to accomplish some breakthrough or tangible result for the client. As long as the counselor tells the truth and the client takes the responsibly for his or her own growth, the relationship will be productive.

Yet, there is no solid evidence that any one technique or factor in counseling or therapy is superior to all others. However, the individual skill of each counselor and the counselor-client relationship are perhaps more important factors. Another important factor in helping others is the development of a plan to guide the counselor-client relationship. Although the client's goals should set the stage for planning, all forms of counseling include practical factors such as clarifying the client's problem, the amount of time and money clients can spend, the frequency of sessions, and the client's desire and readiness to work with the counselor or vise versa. Because these factors lay outside the structure of counseling and often intrude in disturbing ways, seeing clients on a continuing basis is seldom possible to achieve.

In view of these real issues it is necessary to understand what techniques to teach clients. Then, when financial, geographical or other reasons become obstacles, the client can at least continue independent of the counselor, even in a limited way. For this reason, the technique chosen must be safe for use by the client alone. In addition, the client must have progressed to a level that will enable him or her to use the technique with some degree of mastery.

The teaching of techniques to the client occurs naturally over time although people vary in their motivation to learn and ability to work alone with sufficient confidence. Encouraging clients or students to do independent inner work through the I Ching or tarot cards or astrology and perhaps mental imagery is a fundamental part to accelerating the expansion of awareness. In this way their self development takes on a life of its own, with its unlimited possibilities of growth and self-realization.

To be effective, all counselors or therapists or gurus should think in terms of the client's needs and what services they can provide to help the client. In addition to giving information, guidance and wisdom, they should elicit information, guidance and wisdom from the client. The counselor should ask the client, "How can I help you? What do you expect to get by working with me? Tell me about your problems, yourself, your relationships, your career, etc."

This brings us to the question "What guidelines should psychic counselors follow to proceed in the direction from the single visit to counseling on a continuing basis, and beyond short-term counseling?" This question is not easy to answer but Bernard Rosenblum, M.D. provides some excellent guidelines in his book *The Astrologer's Guide to Counseling*, adapted as follows:

- What is the client really looking for?
- What is the client ready to hear?
- Why is the client coming to see me at this point in his or her life?
- What is the best way to use inner psychic information to help the client develop her or his sense of initiative, responsibility, and participation in life?

We believe in any method which produces results, for each has its place in the Whole.
Ernest Holmes

- What is the appropriate kind and degree of exploration to be done of this client's life and psyche?
- Does the client really need psychotherapy or psychic counseling? If so, what is the appropriate way of offering that opinion?
- Does the client challenge any sore spots of my own?
- What are my strengths and weaknesses and training as a counselor?
- Do I see my role as a teacher, counselor, or therapist? What is it I'm really doing?
- Am I expecting that I will be able to change this client's life? Is this expectation realizable? Am I looking for too-rapid change?

Levels of Knowledge and Attachment

I have found that when I have trusted some inner non-intellectual sensing, I have discovered wisdom in the move.

Carl R. Rogers

Most individuals and the issues that interest them lend themselves to being assisted by some form of intuitive counseling. For example, when someone wants my help in finding the "best" solution, i.e., one in alignment with that person's inner Self, I may ask, "What are your options, where do you feel stuck, or what do you want to know?" These questions define the level of knowledge available to support and interpret the images that come up from the deeper mind. They also explain the degree of attachment or desire for present wants.

The use of visualization methods and the I Ching by individuals themselves, or by counselors or therapists with their clients, is most helpful when they meet two conditions. First, the individual is open-minded and unattached to specific outcomes; and second, the individual has sufficient history with or knowledge of the issue being investigated. If the person seeking guidance from the inner teacher has too little knowledge of the issue being addressed, the process is difficult. This happens because we have a limited frame of reference for interpreting what comes up. The more we desire some specific outcome, the more our rational mind fails to see the truth.

One's level of knowledge and attachment may be understood in terms of the following chart. First, the deeper one's self knowledge, the deeper one's relationship to the world of the unconscious. Second, the greater one's attachment to desired outcomes, the greater one's dishonesty. The chart given here present the possible relationships between knowledge and attachment. It help us to examine how these dimensions interact. The results of the possible relationships appear in the results and chart given here:

Outcomes

	Low	High
High Attachment	Excessive hoping wishing, dependence	Excessive analysis, mistrust, stubbornness
Low Attachment	Shallowness, triteness detachment	All the benefits

Knowledge

Since these four possibilities create different degrees of honesty and clarity, it is helpful to find out how we can set up our relationship to the Self within so that it can be as clear and honest as possible. To create this ideal relationship the spotlight is on how the individual operates in his or her head. When we know how to succeed within ourselves, we tend to do things right. It is only our narrow views of reality that stand between us and the continuous flow of reliable insights.

In the case of *high knowledge* with *high attachment* the client or person seeking help has a deep involvement with the subject matter. In this case emotion-backed demands tend to cloud the individual's ability to "see" how the insights from the deep Self fit his or her ideal outcome. This state lends itself to mistrust, excessive analysis, and tends to block the truth. In this state people tend to be happy when information from the inner world matches their preconceived expectations, and unhappy when it does not match. In this phase the use of intuitive tools is highly conditional. It's like saying, "I'll accept what I'm seeing if it meets my desires, but reject it otherwise." While excessive analysis and mistrust can create a feeling of security at times, it overshadows the genuine insights.

What happens in the case of *low knowledge* and *high attachment?* In this state individuals want something to happen without effort. Here the person wants some kind of miracle. *Low knowledge* means that the person has spent little or no time to learn about his or her subject matter, but is still attached to specific results. *Low knowledge* with high desire leads to self-deception, disillusionment, cynicism, anger, and resentment. This state of affairs comes about through the desire to get something for nothing. Although wishing and hoping require little effort or commitment, it is empty and unrealistic.

The third situation involves *low knowledge* with *low attachment*. Individuals in this state keep their true ideas about self-fulfillment and problem resolution to themselves. They tend to see insights from the unconscious as unclear and irrelevant for their situation. This phase includes those attitudes that tend to be shallow and trite. Since *low knowledge* means little if any objective experience, there is little foundation for interpreting insights.

It is the forth state that gives all the benefits of an honest relationship to the deeper Self and none of the limitations found in states one, two, or three. This state implies high knowledge and low attachment. In it the individual enjoys his or her relationship to the unconscious, sees what is going on, and realistically understands it. By having significant prior knowledge and no attachment (complete openness) one has the greatest opportunity for being assisted by wisdom from the unconscious. By minimizing our attachments to specific outcomes, we avoid distorting the here-and-now with emotion-backed demands that misinterpret what the inner world is trying to say.

In this ideal state, one's relationship to the inner world is less and less conditional. There is more emphasis on getting at the truth and less on the outcome. We cooperate with the unconscious in the great mystery of life and nurture our own well-being.

A Personal Comment

Mankind is slow to realize that there is simply no way to salvation except by changing one's consciousness, which means trying to do the Will of God consistently in every department of life.
Emmet Fox

My feelings about my work in counseling have changed with my experiences over the past decade. During the first half of this period I would compare my role to one of the gardener trimming a large institution's lawn with a pair of hand clippers. My role seemed endless, thankless, without status, and incomplete. Since that time my view has changed. I see my role with clients as one of a spiritual guide. I work with more and more clients on an ongoing basis. I now teach more and more people to expand and train their intuition. What has remained constant over the years is that my clients come from a wide diversity of places in mind, culture, and geography. Many of these people live out of state and have not met me in person. Many have great needs—impossible to meet. And some have well defined questions or issues which lead to clear solutions. My capacity to deal with them is limited just as often as it seems unlimited. Even though major steps get taken and the right questions often come up, most steps are small ones.

In my early years as a psychic counselor I was an outsider, and as such, I played my role by going from door-to-door, searching for entry into another's inner life. With my shovel and pick in hand I spent five years digging clients out of the asphalt and building relationships. I see this outsider as a teacher with a following of students who want to learn. I am surrounded by a larger community of people who recognize my presence and maturity.

So what has remained constant in my experience as a psychic counselor? With the exception of my ability to perceive another's difficulties and opportunities, and reveal them accordingly, I find that I am not in control of a single thing. Despite the diversity of individual clients and issues that come to me (mainly professional women between thirty and fifty years old with career and relationship concerns), most issues tend to be similar. Through intuitive tools I work with clients to clarify and resolve their uncertainties. To put it more precisely, we work at finding what their heart or inner teacher has to say about the problem. My premise is always the same: Each person already has the answer as soon as the problem emerges. As I once heard, "If theres no solution, theres no problem."

In my work with clients (using clairvoyance, the I Ching, the element survey, tarot cards, astrology, religious science, and other tools as appropriate) it has become evident to me that significant spiritual growth comes about by very subtle and subjective experiences. Clients attracted to psychic counseling tend to avoid the more conventional paths of psychological and religious aspirations because they cannot bear to see life imprisoned by such realities. With the aid of intuitive approaches many people become increasingly integrated and effective, and continually seek opportunities for growth.

Even though I have introduced the psychic approach to a large sampling of our population, I find it a very elusive thing to extract from these experiences the meaning that seems genuinely inherent in them. That is, I realize how ridiculous these experiences, which have much value to my clients, would seem to most people. Nevertheless, I will present a few key observations that have come to me. Those involved in long-term counseling appear to move away from a state in which their inner world is unrecognized, unowned, and unexpressed. They learn about themselves and the intuitive tools which help them to communicate with the deeper mind. They move toward a state in which the ever-changing inner world is experienced knowingly and acceptingly in the moment, and may be accurately expressed. Generally, they move toward fluidity, a high level of trust and knowingness, certainty of feelings and intuitions, acceptance of reality, and closeness to their inner life. Initially, most people see intuitive and psychic counseling as tools for self discovery and for getting at the truth. Those who use it over the long-run soon discover that what takes place is relevant to, and has implications for, every area of life.

Often more difficult than to accept our fact is to learn to deal with our fact.
Howard Thurman

7

Applications

We limit ourselves when we try to fix accurately before hand the particular form of good that we shall produce. We should aim not so much at having or making some particular thing as at expressing all that we are.

Thomas Troward

While mastery of the outer world is central to western thinking, Eastern thought tells us that this is not the only possible relation to it. As a whole the west attempts to control the unconscious, while the east calls for the opposite, being receptive to it. To benefit from its wisdom the individual must be patient, refrain from taking action and be receptive to the voice within. To make use of the I Ching and visualization, avenues for reaching for the inner teacher, one must be able to listen without prejudging, anticipating, classifying, evaluating, approving or disapproving, without dueling with what has been presented, without concentrating on what is being revealed to the degree that succeeding portions are not heard at all. This concept is easy to understand in theory but difficult to attain in practice.

The perceptions of suchness of the "way things are" is more Eastern, and passive than is the Western attitude of achievement of integration and abstraction. But this does not mean that the perception of things is the only active task. More precisely, it is the non-interfering willingness for things to be themselves. It is the ability to wait patiently for the inner structure or hexagram message or image to reveal itself to us—a finding and acceptance of order rather than ordering. For example, in trying to understand another person it is most efficient in the longrun to give up active concentration and striving to understand quickly. When you call upon the inner teacher to perceive what is going on, you should avoid striving, concentrating and focusing of attention upon what seems reasonable.

Since we in the West often accept a receptive, non-interfering attitude in certain areas of life such as breathing, meditation, and sleep, we can at least understand what it feels like to observe and to

Adopt the peace of nature her secret is patience.
Ralph Waldo Emerson

absorb receptively. However, because of our extroverted orientation, we avoid the receptive strategy of knowing; we don't regard it as a scientific technique. This is unfortunate because there are many areas of knowledge for which such an attitude is essential. For instance, the receptive strategy is widely used in the fields of clinical psychology, physics, astronomy, ecology, and in principle in any field dealing with large masses of data of any kind.

In this century, and especially over the last four decades or so people in the West are learning to integrate being active and receptive. This change rejects the traditional conviction that orthodox science is the only reliable path to knowledge. This conventional view is philosophically, socially, and psychologically naive. This movement toward human potential is part of a larger and more inclusive world view—a movement toward rediscovering human needs potentials, and capacities. The importance of these human potentials is well on its way to being restored to religion, to industry, and to our social and political arenas.

Getting Acquainted

The authors of the I Ching imply that those who use it are themselves part of the nature they observe. As in mental imagery, the I Ching aims to make its users fit in, to belong to and to be at home with themselves and the object being observed. Those who use it are part of the scene rather than a spectator. These techniques allow users to study the universe from within the universe in the same way that an infant would study its mother from within its mother's arm.

Applications

The I Ching offers an understanding of the nature of the present and the potentiality of the future. It also opens the possibility of effecting a total transformation in the individual, group, and society. However, if the individual interpreting the hexagrams does not possess the honesty of mind and purpose to see things are they really are, regardless of consequences, will follow then the message of the inner teacher is blocked and the patterns of the present will continue to unfold into the future.

As already discussed, divination in general and the Book of Changes in particular reveal the essence of the present and contain the seeds of the future. Throughout this book I have attempted to show how psychic tools, clairvoyance and the I Ching, reflect the whole of nature and society and include within them the observer. In the Book of Changes the inner psychic and outer physical worlds are no longer perceived as a duality, but in their essential unity. And, the potential of the moment is revealed in the pattern of the hexagrams. The act of creating and then interpreting hexagrams, divining, adds many insights about the information that acts upon the inner and outer to give it form.

Since I do most of my counseling with ongoing and referral clients, they are receptive to my style of working with imagery and the I Ching. Although most new clients accept clairvoyance without question, some are nervous and skeptical when it comes to I Ching. In such cases I may attempt to discern how they view the world, their situation within it, and how I can help them dispel such fears. In other cases I simply avoid the I Ching during their first visit or until I have gained their trust.

I have been working with Robin, a financial analyst in her mid-forties for four years. She first came to me through an ad in the yellow pages. In the early part of our first session I made it a point, at her request, to explain how I worked and the rationale for my approach. Even though she mailed me a two-page letter of the issues she wanted to work on I started by explaining my approach. I drew a two-dimensional box on my blackboard. I then pointed to the box and said, "Under ordinary circumstances people live in this kind of box out of habit, familiarity, their attachment to what they know, and their past experiences. The larger area outside the box represents the unknown, the unfamiliar, future potentials, and the unconscious Self." When I explained this idea a bit further she blurted out, "I see your point, the box describes me." I then explained that my goal was to help her step out of the box and access the unconscious. At this point I was prepared to start the session by clarifying her questions and expectations. However she asked, "How will do you that?" I responded, "Are you somewhat familiar with clairvoyance or mental imagery and the I Ching?" "Imagery somewhat," she said, "but how does the I Ching work?" With a skeptical tone, she then asked "Does the I Ching have any scientific basis?"

Before answering I thought to myself, "I doubt that this client will come back." I then asked, "Are you familiar with sampling?"

The habit of analytical thought is fatal to the intuitions of integral thinking, wether on the "psychic" or the spiritual level.

Aldous Huxley

"Of course," Robin answered.

"Are you familiar with nonscientific or nonprobability sampling?"

"Yes. But what does sampling have to do with the I Ching?"

"Its not the same thing but it is a close analogy."

"Hum," she relaxed a bit and asked, "how?"

"Well lets look at an example. Suppose we were going to market a new product but knew nothing about the consumer demand for it. What little we knew would be in the box whereas the unconscious or potential market demand would be outside the box. One approach would be to write down all potential characteristics of the marketplace on pieces of paper, place them in a hat and then draw out some pieces at random."

"You mean take out a sample?"

"That's right," I replied. "The I Ching like the hat has all potential characteristics about the universe in it. To use it we simply draw out a sample of hexagram."

"I see where you're going with that but I'm still not sure."

I scratched my head and responded, "The I Ching represents the whole blackboard (I paused), the person consulting stands in the box, reaches out without looking, and grabs a sample hexagram (I looked for her OK before going on). That person brings the sample back, examines it and makes an estimate of what is going on outside the box." I continued, "We could say that sampling, foretelling and prophesy are one and the same thing."

"Oh, you mean the I Ching is used to predict?" Robin asked.

"Without going into greater detail, that's about it," I answered. I then set my blackboard aside and started clarifying Robin's issues.

In my counseling experiences over the years clients often report that insights from the I Ching, and to some degree clairvoyance, bring them out of their comfort zone. Michele, a struggling, self-employed technical writer, in her late twenties remarked, "The I Ching is a challenge, somewhat unsettling, and involves taking risks. The hexagrams I seem to get are often both disturbing and empowering. But I'll continue to seek its wisdom until I find something more reliable." This comment came after

working with me for nine months. Her comments describe what most of my long-term clients seem to experience. When new clients ask me to consult the I Ching or look at some problem, I often point out that their inner teacher, not I, will show the way. I may add that my methods are mere bridges, to and from their inner teacher. In this way I feel no need to produce the desired outcome or catharsis with each consultation. There is no need for me to manipulate or please clients by toning down what the images or hexagrams reveal. Those who use my assistance on a regular basis, i.e., daily, weekly, monthly, quarterly or annually as desired, grow at their own pace. They are free to come and go as they please.

Slowly and painfully those who look to the unconscious for wisdom learn to become good observers. They learn to wait and watch and listen patiently, to keep their hands off, to refrain from being too active, too impatient, and too controlling. Perhaps the most important lessons in trying to understand the way things are may be summarized as follows: keep your mouth shut and your eyes and ears wide open.

In the remaining pages of this chapter I will share some of my counseling experiences by following two of my long-term clients from how they were before encountering the techniques outlined in this book, how they affected them, and what their life was like afterwards. It is my aim here to outline how effective these methods can be for a great number of people. I will also present some ads and workshop fliers that highlight my applications of psychic counseling. This material represents my attempts to present in an understandable and acceptable way this often misunderstood subject. It has been useful in reaching some people who simply wanted to learn and improve their lives, who don't have any major problems, as well as those with mild disturbances or problems, and those with major issues.

The Case of Sarah

Sarah was strictly business in our first session. She walked into my home office carrying her attaché case, wearing thick glasses, and navy blue business suit for her Saturday morning appointment. I felt a bit awkward meeting her in my chi pants, sandals and sweatshirt.

I asked, "Are you coming from or going to work?"

"No. Why do you ask?" she replied.

"Your outfit looks nice, like you're ready to do business."

Because Sarah came to me through her friend and former client, she had a sense of what to expect. Without delay we agreed to investigate the following issues: staying or leaving her present job as a Program Director of Computer Education for a large firm, and coming to terms with her confusion about her wonderful and difficult long-distance relationship.

Sarah had moved to California from New York two years earlier to take her present job. For most of those two years she felt that she wanted to move back. However, during her recent ten-day vacation in New York she realized that she would love to put down roots and settle here in California. What was her working environment like now? Her department got reorganized about four months ago. She now reported to someone who was her peer instead of reporting to a vice president.

"How do you like the job itself?" I asked.

"My job put me in a position of national importance and offers an excellent platform for disseminating ideas. I am pretty much a workaholic but have yet to develop an extensive network here in California. I am not at ease with my company's fast-paced, competitive style and don't know realistically what is possible for me here. I have no sense of job security."

Sarah felt on good terms and was recently in touch with her old boss.

"What are the pros and cons?" I inquired.

"Its a much smaller company—a software company and returning would require me to move back to New York, something which I am reluctant to do. The plus would be the potential to put down professional roots with a growing company and working with terrific people."

Because of Sarah's uncertainty about the future of her present job I suggested that we do a forecast of her situation over the next year through imagery and the Book of Changes. I added, "Give me a minute to tune in and then I'll share my insights." She agreed. I relaxed, closed my eyes for a moment and shared my images of her next year on the job.

"This is how things look to me," I said, "I see a picture of you fighting to make an opening from behind some curtains and clouds. After a while you appear to give up and go in the opposite direction."

No problem can be solved until an individual assumes the responsibility for solving it.

M. Scott Peck

I paused and then interpreted this image. "Over the year I think you'll try to move ahead within your present job or company, but there are no clear openings. In time I think you'll turn toward another job or company out of frustration. But perhaps you'll accept whatever happens, rather than make plans for change." I then said to her, "Do you see how this image might apply to your situation?"

Sarah replied, "Yes in a way. Interesting. But if we had not discussed it, would this forecast still apply? If I refuse to believe it would things turn out different?"

"Well, its like predicting the weather. If we do it we can make certain plans ahead of time. Whether you believe the prediction or not will affect how you think and act toward it, but not the projected outcome. In fact, we know very little and we ignore many things; however, that doesn't change the potentials within them—those potentials are for us to discover. As the year unfolds the potentials spelled out by this image ought to become clear. You should be able to expand my interpretation in light of your experience."

I then handed Sarah my pouch of I Ching stones and asked her to pull out six of them at random. I explained that this exercise would allow us to examine the I Ching's assessment of the coming year as well. As Sarah drew out each colored stone I recorded its meaning by saying, "Yang. Yin. Changing yang. Yin. Yin. Changing yang." I explained the meaning of the six stones and resulting hexagram as follows.

Hexagrams: Decoration(22) changing to Renewal(24)

I said to her, "From the perspective of the I Ching, your next year on the job is described by two themes. Starting with the present, and continuing for the next several months your situation is represented by the theme of Decoration. Decoration suggests an emphasis on outward appearances, ideals, and attachments to forms. Based on the mental image my sense is that your attempt to move forward in your company will be motivated by what looks good on the surface instead of genuine inner fulfillment. Decoration deals with the package instead of the contents. Since Decoration becomes Renewal by the second half of the year it seems to me that your interests will gradually shift toward another job, something completely different. I suspect that your current direction and thinking will give way to something new and vital. This new direction will present itself in spite of your efforts."

I asked if she felt complete about this forecast. She nodded yes and asked if she could sit on the floor. When I said of course, Sarah kicked off her shoes and sat on the floor, I could tell that she was finally at ease with the session.

I then said, "Lets take a look at your question: staying with your present job versus going back to your old job in New York, OK." "OK," she answered. I pointed to the pouch of stones and said, "Pull out six stones like you did before. But this time the question is, what can I expect by planning to stay with my present job?" As she drew out the stones, one by one, I wrote down her hexagram.

Hexagram: Solution(40) no changing lines

"As the title suggests, this hexagram points to an emotional release or solution from an obstacle or moral dilemma. I would give this plan a B path or grade," I said. "Hum," Sarah responded. "Select six stones again and lets see what comes up for planning to go back to your old job. As soon as you do this we can compare results." She drew out six stones as follows.

Hexagram: Excess Yin(62) no changing lines

After commenting that Excess Yin implies dealing with details and gaining more awareness of some aspect of a larger endeavor, I paused for a moment and said, "What do you think?"

Sarah looked at the two hexagrams, frowned a bit, and mumbled, "I guess the B grade for staying is better than the C+ grade for leaving. Is that your reading?"

"Pretty much, but your choices are close," I replied. "Based on the B for staying and the C+ for going I think I would stay put. Both hexagrams are better than average. You could go either way and meet with little difficulty. Since both hexagrams are stable you have a solid foundation and good historical basis for either decision."

Sarah looked over the hexagrams with a puzzled expression. I asked, "Would you like to see something in writing on the meaning of these hexagrams." She nodded yes. I got up and pulled out *The I Ching Workbook* by R.L. Wing from my bookshelf. I sat down, opened the book to Hexagram 40, and set it down before her. Her face lit up as she read over its meaning. She then turned to Hexagram 62, read most of it, and said, "I see what you mean, Hexagram 40 seems better."

In the second half of this session I helped Sarah to examine her relationship to her boyfriend, John. I suggested that we look at what potential was present of the short- and long-run in her relationship. Unlike the first part of our session I asked her to select tarot cards. I suggested this because she had several detailed questions that didn't require in-depth insights. Most of her questions had to do with the up-coming weekend she had planned with John.

I shuffled the deck of cards and spread them out face down. She had had tarot readings in the past and generally knew what to expect. The cards Sarah drew to the question she asked suggested less than an ideal relationship in the short-run, but good communications over the long-run. After discussing these insights I suggested that she select cards to look at what she expected from John and then, what he expected from her. This result was a real eye-opener. According to the cards, Sarah expected great things from John, an abundance of loving feelings toward her. And, he expected as much, if not more from her. I pursued this inquiry to get at the subconscious potential between Sarah and John. I wanted Sarah to think about what seeds were present in the unconscious, and which seeds she wanted to nurture. As we talked about the meaning of the cards she drew I could sense her growing excitement about John. She then told me that John would be in town from New York for a week-long visit, and asked, "What can I look forward to in this visit?" I suggested that she ask: "How will I experience John?" and then "How will John experience me?" "Does this sound OK."

She said, "Yes."

At this point I reshuffled the complete deck. She then pulled two cards, one for each question. In each case the cards referred to unexpressed emotions and a tendency toward negative thinking. Sarah was not surprised. She understood how these insights applied based on her experience with John. Sarah asked another question: "What can I do to make things better during John's visit? Specifically, how can I minimize my negative thinking?"

I looked toward the deck and said, "Lets try it again."

After pulling the first card on this issue Sarah responded, "Interesting, I hadn't realized how much time I spend thinking that this relationship won't work."

Ten days later Sarah called to tell me she wanted to work with me in the future. She then said, "I played the tape you recorded of our session and talked about everything with John—things shifted for the better between us. I'm glad I found out about your services. I felt up in the air before the session but you really brought me down to earth."

About three months later Sarah called to schedule her second session. As we started, she recalled her experience of our first meeting. She made it a point to talk about the results and how she applied them to her job situation. She looked relaxed and sincere. I had her full respect. Among the four issues we agreed to look into, one dealt with making some decision about an immediate job opportunity with her former employer, a lateral move to another department. Another issue dealt with two investment options, real estate and precious metals on margin.

When Sarah told me about her opportunity to change jobs I asked her to outline the pros and cons. "What would you gain?" I asked. She was con-sidering a move from her administrative-type position to sales and marketing. It seemed like a big change to me, but that was secondary to getting at the truth.

"What is your impression, your evaluation," she asked.

I sat back in my chair, closed my eyes for a moment, relaxed and said, "This is what I see, You're trying to move a large rock aside with a small crowbar." I started to interpret, but Sarah interrupted saying, "That's all right, it can't be too good."

I agreed but explained that since this was a big decision she should reserve judgment until consulting the I Ching as well. I then said, "By combining what the image and the hexagram tells us, overall insights are more reliable."

I handed her my pouch of stones and recorded the ones she drew out. Sarah got Hexagram 35 changing to Hexagram 62, Progress becoming Excess Yin. She looked up and asked, "What does this mean?"

I said to her, "In the language of the hexagrams, you can expect some progress and forward movement and excitement. But this movement would be minor."

"What do you mean?"

"Well, from my experience, these hexagrams suggest that you have big expectations for this sales. I think they greatly exceed what is possible. It's as if you expect a mountain but end up with a mole hill."

The reality you seek is the reality you have.
Howard Thurman

Despite Sarah's apparent irritation with this insight she went on to the next issue. She asked me to take a look at a real estate deal that had come her way. Sarah had several thousand dollars and wanted to invest part of it by buying some houses in Phoenix, Arizona. She had picked up from her sources that as a Taurus she could make lots of money in real estate. I responded, "I've heard that too, but that information is wrong. It takes much more than that to make money." In spite of this she assured me that this investment proposal came from a reliable investment counselor. I said, "OK," and proceeded to relax.

With my eyes closed I immediately saw an image. I then looked at her with my head slightly lowered and said, "I see you driving your car in the dark with no light on. I also see you trying to lift up this manhole cover from a sewer, but someone under its surface tries to keep the lid down."

Since the meaning of this scenery needed no interpretation I suggested, without further comment, that she consult the I Ching as well. One by one she pulled six stones out of the pouch to answer the question: "What can I expect by buying the two homes in Phoenix?" Her result?

Hexagrams: Inner Truth(61) changing to Obstacles (39)

"What do these hexagrams say?" Sarah asked.

I cleared my throat and said, "The first one, Inner Truth, tells me that you have intuitive knowledge about this deal, but you are presently operating in the dark. Your situation is like one of counting inventory with a blindfold on. The four changing lines point to lots of instability. This means that the difference between now and the future is like night and day. The second hexagram, Obstacles, refers to something that stands in the way of your progress. Its like a wall that you want to get beyond but can't."

Applications

"This sounds like your image," Sarah replied.

"That's right, but the image is usually more graphic than the hexagram."

"I've noticed that. Why?"

"Well, hexagrams are finite and limited, only sixty-four of them, whereas mental images have no limits. When the unconscious speaks through hexagrams, its message is restricted by this structure and never changes. When it speaks through imagery, its natural tongue, there is no structure. Its message is free to express, unrestrained or infinite so-to-speak."

"Tell me," Sarah, asked, "why do the images you get and the hexagrams I get say about the same things?"

I paused and said, "The simplest answer is this. There is only one mind, one unconscious, one universe, one inner teacher, one God. And when two or more people are receptive to this fact, they tend to see and hear the same thing." I then asked, "How long have you had this idea?"

"About two months. Why?"

"Because I wondered how attached you were." "From my experience, when we get too attached, insights from the unconscious have little value."

"You don't think much of this idea, do you?"

"Well, this investment could work, but based on these hexagrams I wouldn't recommend it. I think you'll lose money and regret it in the long-run."

"Sarah then asked me to look at her investment in precious metals on margin. I thought to myself, does she really want to know? I said, "OK, but what's going on? Do you want to look at the future of precious metals in general or a specific deal? Do you want to make some decision? What time should I examine? Can you be specific about what you want me to look into?"

"Oh, how about looking at how my particular investment looks in the short-run. Should I cut my losses now and sell or keep things as they are for at least three months as recommended by my financial adviser?"

With this clarity I relaxed, cleared my mind and asked for an assessment of the short-term outcome. Over the next few seconds I saw a locomotive going up a steep hill. When the locomotive stopped and reversed its upward motion before reaching the top I thought to myself, when does it stop? Six weeks came to mind. I then told Sarah what I saw and added, "I think it means this. Things are going up for now, but will turn downward in about six-weeks. If I were you I'd consult the I Ching about two questions to zero-in a bit further: First, what can I expect by cutting my losses and selling within six-weeks? And second, what can I expect by keeping my investment intact for at least three months?"

In the next few minutes Sarah wrote down the first question and consulted the oracle. She got the following hexagrams for selling her precious metals with six weeks.

Hexagrams: Influence(31) changing to Ascending (46)

She took the next five minutes or so to read about these hexagrams. She appeared to smile as she closed the workbook. I told her to consult about her second question and then compare insights. Again she wrote out her question, "What can I expect by keeping my investment as it is for at least three months?" Slowly, with this question in mind, Sarah pulled out six stones. I had the sense that she expected better hexagrams, what I call Path A hexagrams. Although one's conscious wish for getting certain hexagrams won't create those hexagrams, many new clients continue to think so. What hexagram did Sarah get?

Hexagram: Waiting (5) no changing lines

I let her review the meaning of this hexagram in silence for the next five minutes. Afterwards I said to her, "Sarah, what conclusion would you draw?"

"I think its better to cut my losses and sell. Is that your reading as well?"

I nodded my head to say yes, but added, "It looks good to stay with it for another four to six weeks."

About four months passed until I heard from Sarah again. She called and asked for an afternoon session. As we got underway I said, "Give me an update on the last four months. What's been going on with you? I'd like to hear about the results of our last visit."

She collected her thoughts and said, "I'm still in the same job. It's much better than before. I decided not to pursue the sales and marketing position. I bought the two houses in Arizona, and so far I'm happy with this deal. I held on to my investment in precious metals until last month. But I should have sold within six weeks because I ended up losing about seven out of the twenty-two thousand I had invested. My financial adviser kept telling me he expected things to pick up. I remembered your image of the train stalling on the hill and then rolling back down, but felt that my adviser had more experience."

"What shall we look at in this session," I asked.

"I have two or three big issues to go over. I'd like to take a six-month leave of absence from my job to study sanskrit in Pennsylvania or India. This course is coming up in about six months and I need to start making plans now. I want to know whether I should take this course or let it go until next time around. My former company in New York offered me a job as director of research for a branch they're starting in the Bay Area. Is this a good move for me? And, what kind of relationship would I have to the president?"

Over the next hour I assisted Sarah in looking into these issues. She concluded that it was best to put off the sanskrit course. While her relationship to the president of her former company looked good, taking the job of research director would not improve her situation. She came to this conclusion after discussing the hexagrams and images for staying with her present job versus taking the job with her former employer. Since neither outcome looked ideal, Sarah decided to stay put. She reasoned that it didn't make sense to change jobs unless the new one looked better. I agreed with her reasoning saying, "that's what I'd do." I could sense that she felt at ease about these insights. I felt as if her confidence in the I Ching and in me had increased since our last meeting. As this session ended, I asked "What shifted for you regarding the way we've been working? I notice that your belief or attitude toward this way of working, looking at inner potentials and the future, seems to have shifted."

She replied, "Two things. First, I feel good about our results. And second, I have talked with two colleagues that think highly of the I Ching and use it on a regular basis."

This session marked the turning point in my work with Sarah. Since this session I have assisted her on a frequent and continuous basis. Slowly, starting with our next session a month later, and for many, many sessions from then on, her major issues in life emerged for resolution, piece by piece. The scope of our work widened greatly. Over the next two years her main issues dealt with hiring the right candidates to work in her new department and buying the right home. Sarah had many issues, including her dying mother, child adoption, finding ways to minimize her losses on the Arizona houses, romantic and professional relationships, and selecting the right forms of therapy as well as therapists. However, I will only review our work on two issues.

Much of my work with Sarah's concern about hiring the right people centered on her trouble in expressing and responding to feelings. Despite her avoidance of astrology she made it a point to justify this problem by saying, "I'm all earth. I have no planets in water signs. I have a history of poor judgment in personnel matters. I am often insensitive and sometimes too sensitive." What was the nature of this poor judgment? How was it that she had not been able to express her true feelings? How could I help her turn things around? Sarah and I have worked on this for the past few years. Practically all of this work relied upon using the I Ching, and often imagery, to evaluate and select candidates for the numerous job openings in her department.

As soon as Sarah found herself in the position of finding the right people she was afraid of selecting the wrong person and afraid of hiring people on a trial-and-error basis. Her position was difficult. Being fully aware of her poor judgment until now, she decided to put her faith in my work with the I Ching. I reminded her that the I Ching is God's means of communication and that if she followed its guidance she would do well. Since the I Ching had no problems with feeling, getting at the truth, etc., she would inherit these benefits.

Those who take time in their self-development have the deepest roots.
David K. Reynolds

Sarah increasingly put her faith in the I Ching rather than follow her own feelings because she had the strength of an ally in me, because she had come to feel that I could help and had her interests at heart. This alliance in faith such as she and I had constructed is a prerequisite for all successful counseling.

Sarah's first hiring decision was that of selecting an office manager-executive secretary. After three weeks of searching and combing through resumes and getting recommendations from her colleagues she called, at my suggestion, and presented me with the names of four applicants, the top four. This session marked the beginning of my telephone consultations with Sarah. From this point forward about ninety percent of my work with her has been over the telephone. I evaluated the potential for each candidate as follows.

Assessment of Nancy S.

>Image: Nancy looks on at a distance as you (Sarah) work with Jackhammer. She has long delicate fingernails and appears to be doing light cleaning work.
>
>Hexagrams: Duration(32) changing to The Army(7)

Assessment of Kerry

>Image: Kerry attempts to carry water in her cupped hands, but it leaks through her fingers. In the background someone shakes their head as if to say "No, she's not the one."
>
>Hexagrams: Contemplation(20) changing to Splitting Apart(23)

Assessment of Elizabeth

>Image: Elizabeth sits on a chariot that is pulled by a team of horses. As she races by, several papers fly about.
>
>Hexagrams: Youthful Ignorance (4) changing to Exhaustion (47)

Assessment of Nancy T.

>Image: Nancy tries to remain seated at the center of a revolving phonograph record, but is thrown off by its by its circular motion.
>
>Hexagrams: Meeting of Opposites(44) changing to An Outsider(54)

About an hour later I called Sarah back and gave her the results of my assessments. I could sense her disappointment. She had interviewed three of the top four candidates, and two of those were referred by colleagues she respected. She felt obligated to make some decision but held off in view of my insights. The people around her had advised her to hire someone from within the company. However, the pool of good inside applicants dried up with these four. Sarah called back about two weeks later and gave me the names of two new applicants to evaluate. They were the top two outside candidates. "Are these candidates somewhat suitable to my needs and personality?" Sarah asked. How did this assessment turn out?

We must transcend the appearance, even though we admit it as a fact.
Ernest Holmes

Assessment of Allison
Image: Allison cleans and organizes everything in an office with a smile. She then sits down to proofread some letters, but overlooks some typing errors.

Hexagrams: Ascending(46) changing to Assistance(8)

Assessment of Carolyn
Image: Carolyn works to gather up spoiled fruit that fell off a tree some time ago.

Hexagrams: Shocking (51) changing to Nourishing (27)

After reporting this assessment, I said "either Allison or Carolyn would be acceptable. Both of them would be better than average employees." Sarah let out a sigh of relief and then commented on my image of Allison. She told me that Allison had a long and solid history of secretarial work but that her resume had a couple of typing errors in it.

"Does your image suggest that I can expect more of this?" she asked.

I replied, "It's hard to know for certain but my guess is that Allison will tend to make small typing errors and to gloss over details. You'll have to decide on how important this is, and how to deal with it if you hire her."

Since this was Sarah's first hiring decision with the I Ching we spent more time than usual discussing what the oracle had to say about Allison and Carolyn. Even though both candidates were fairly equal, Allison's hexagrams were slight better. What about my image of Carolyn? What did it mean? I saw it as a message that Carolyn would have a tendency to waste time on projects or activities of fairly low priority.

I added, "The scene of gathering spoiled fruit suggested bad timing."

With this, Sarah interrupted, "I see what you mean, I think I'll go with Allison. But what weight would you give to the images? Is it more or less important than the hexagrams?"

"Mental imagery is always more descriptive, personal and flexible than hexagrams but has more potential for bias, and for being colored by the image maker's lack of experience and awareness about symbols. When it comes to decision-making I would put more weight on the hexagrams. When it comes to describing how something is likely to take place, to be felt and experienced, I would put more weight on imagery."

With this decision behind her, Sarah felt better about consulting the Book of Changes before making her personnel decisions. Actually, her relationship to this way of working is still in its early stages. The serious day-to-day issues and decisions still lay ahead, the challenge of allowing herself to truly manifest in a thousand little ways. Over the next couple of years I assisted Sarah in using the I Ching to build-up and reorganize her entire department. We used its assistance to hire every individual from secretary to engineers, project director, legal advisers and a host of outside consultants. Recognizing the fact that her poor judgment had dominated her ability to hire good people and make wise management decisions, Sarah let go of her judgments in favor of gaining access to the unconscious, a power much greater than herself. Later, Sarah was to say, "I really wouldn't trade places for anything with the person I used to be. I think I've found a lifetime ally in the I Ching. My life is much easier now. At least in a way."

Now that things were on course with her department, Sarah decided to consult the Book of Changes for buying a home. Although she had planned to buy some place as her primary residence within three months the whole searching process took about twelve months. Why did this take so long? In the first part of this search Sarah looked at three houses in the $250,000 range in Palo Alto. One evaluation after another, nothing looked favorable. I suggested that she consider other south Bay Area cities. She thought this was a good idea but wanted to consult the I Ching about that. Her outcome? The Cauldron (Hexagram 50) changing to Ascending (Hexagram 46). With this result Sarah expanded her search for the right home.

Over the next several months Sarah called me on numerous occasions to address home buying. With me she agonized over the innumerable small but independent decisions she had to make about the house she would someday buy. During this time we looked into partnership arrangements or joint ownership versus sole ownerships (Sarah is single). We covered home buying as an investment versus personal residence, fixed versus variable rate mortgage, evaluating three additional cities and four mortgage companies and various real estate brokers. We got into other issues as well: whether to buy a condominium, duplex or single family home, size, etc. While it was not apparent to me at the time the string of unfavorable hexagrams revealed that Sarah's uncertainty about her interests and the housing market were substantial. When she began to limit her search to one real estate broker, the city of San Jose, and three bedroom houses in the $200,000 range, her hexagrams shifted. Within the next six weeks she came to discover and accept an excellent deal. Although the I Ching was an excellent guide, its insights were limited to her awareness, inexperience, and ability to ask certain questions.

I have described Sarah's case at some length to give readers an understanding of the value and ways of working with the I Ching. I have worked with many Sarah's I suspect there are thousands who would find an ally in the Book of Changes as she did.

After about two more years, Sarah asked if she could work successfully with the I Ching, independently of me. Although it took her four years to get to this point some clients never learn, and others become independent much sooner. I said of course, but suggested that she consult the Book about her relationship to it and what she could expect by doing so. Upon doing so, she got Great Power (Hexagram 34) changing to The Cauldron (Hexagram 50). On my urging she began to rely upon the oracle for many of her issues. In this way she built up her trust in the unconscious and her own judgments, and discovered what works best for her. She continues to work with me on significant personal and professional issues, particularly those requiring greater insights. However, our work has reached a plateau in that she is more independent than before in her ability to listen to the unconscious.

The Case of Ralph

Ralph was the most perplexing client I have ever seen. He was about thirty-five years old when I first met him. He was very intelligent and overweight by his own judgment. Throughout most of the first visit he kept on his overcoat and folded his arms over his chest. I invited him to relax and explained the message of his body language. With this his arms dropped down to his lap. Although he kept on his coat he took it off for the second visit.

Initially Ralph came in for one consultation then another about a week later. At the time I didn't think much about our work. I figured him to be a one visit client. I came to this conclusion for two reasons. Because he was unemployed and living with his mother I assumed he couldn't afford my services. In addition, he scattered his problems over a wide spectrum. In the space of two hours he asked for my insights about ten different women whom he knew through personal relationships, several educational and career plans, and his astrological chart. While I gave him my intuitive impressions these initial sessions only scratched the surface. My comments were necessarily brief because of the many questions he raised. While I sensed much pain behind his questions I did not discuss this.

Two years went by before I saw Ralph again. During this time he worked for about a year in two different part time jobs—first as laundromat manager, and then telemarketing salesman. He also started acting classes at a community college but dropped out when he broke his hip in an accident that put him on long term disability. He told me that he could only afford one session because he had no money. He ended up having two more sessions on credit. While it slipped my mind at the time, his questions in this session were exactly the same as those raised two years earlier. He wanted my insights on his relationships with several women, career possibilities, etc. I have found that recurring questions and themes is common among ongoing clients.

My typical sessions went like this. Ralph would start by asking two or more questions. I might clarify these questions or paraphrase them or suggest additional relevant questions or issues raised by his questions. Once he explained his questions and we both agreed on them I would make use of the I Ching, tarot, mental imagery (in that order) to flush out answers. The insights gathered through these tools assisted me in explaining to Ralph where the unconscious and his inner teacher appeared to be guiding him. My aim was to help him get as many useful insights as possible and to put him in touch with his inner teacher. He would often raise the subject of astrology by asking for my interpretations of various transits in his chart. While he had a habit of relating most of his issues to his astrology chart I discouraged this. We talked less and less about astrology as our work progressed. Although he never stopped talking about the subject, he conceded that he was overdoing this one-sided approach to self-analysis.

Problems do not go away. They must be worked through or else they remain, forever a barrier to growth and development of the spirit.
M. Scott Peck

Again, two years went by before I saw Ralph. Over this period he continued to live with his mother and draw disability payments. I asked him if his life had changed and suggested that he consider using my services on a more frequent basis to help him. He agreed. Gradually at first and then quickly over the next year I worked with Ralph. We worked by telephone since our first few visits. This was great for him because his hip injury made it painful for him to move about.

In the early stages of this work, Ralph's interest was squarely on his relationships with women, mainly prostitutes. We looked into well over sixty relationships. The questions he raised were these:

"What can you tell me about the romantic potential between me and her?"

"How does she feel about being a prostitute."

"How does it look to pursue a sexual relationship with her?"

"How was sex for us in the past and how will it be in the future? How was sex between her an other men in the past and how will it be in the future?"

"How does she really feel about me? How do I really feel about her? What do we have in common? What is my attraction to her?"

"What kind of sexual experience can I have with this one or that one?" "What did she think about sex with me?"

"What is the nature of her personality? How does she see herself?" "How does she see me?"

One by one, we looked into these questions. For three months there was little variation in Ralph's interest and view of his relationships with women? Since high school his only close relationships with women had been the services of prostitutes. As he came to ask these questions, one after another, I began to question how helpful I could be and came close to telling him that his problems were beyond my ability. He should be seeing a psychotherapist I thought. I continued to work with him because he was open to my suggestions about what was important, and my advice (insights from the inner teacher) on how to heal his relationships.

My work with Ralph took a sudden change for the better when I told him that he was really sick. I wanted him to come to this conclusion on his own but I could no longer wait for him to see it. Until this time many issues from Ralph in counseling were somewhat painful for me to see. I added that he would never attract a "normal" relationship unless he changed his thinking about women. The central element leading to this change was the trust and closeness of the relationship we were able to make with each other. From then on about once every other week for the next three months Ralph would ask new questions to probe into his feelings about women.

Initially he asked the questions, "What is my past, present and future relationship to prostitutes as a whole?"

He soon asked,"How should I go about creating the right relationship for me?" "When will this happen?"

The Tao doesn't take sides; it gives birth to both good and evil.

Lao Tzu

"What prevents me from creating good relationships? And how can I overcome this obstacle?"

"What can I expect by becoming celibate indefinitely, or until I meet the right woman for me?"

"What was my lesson with prostitutes, what were they teaching me, and what did I learn?"

"How did I relate to women in prior incarnations, my past-lives?"

"What types of non-prostitutes am I attracted to, and what types are attracted to me? Where and how can I find them?" A few weeks after covering these topics Ralph said his attitude toward women really changed. I asked, "What happened to change things?"

He said, "You know, I'm through with prostitutes. Even though I still know a lot of them and have friends that will try to fix me up with dates, I have reached the point of no return. The whole world of women just looks very different now. Thanks to you I see where I've come from and have a sense of where I going. Until a few weeks ago I had no sense of what I was doing or the pain I was in. Now I see how much. I know the prostitutes are there and I know I've been a part of that world. But this part of me seems to have really died."

Through five months of regular counseling, mainly by telephone once or twice a week for two hours, Ralph moved from a position where he rejected the notion of creating normal loving relationships to one where it was becoming quite meaningful for him. In the process of understanding and transforming his attitudes his interest in exploring loving relationships and other aspects of his life grew. Even though Ralph retains his interest in sex, his dream of a loving relationship has become his first priority. His discussed his interest in pursuing pure sex with increasing rareness. Dramatic changes took place in his thinking about women and relationships. His whole emphasis shifted to women he knew where not prostitutes. He raised questions like, "What do I need to complete or resolve in this relationship? What is the potential for friendship, and for romantic relationship with her? What can I expect by pursuing this relationship in this way or that way? How does she experience me? How do I experience her? What do I really need and yearn to get regarding romantic love? What stops me? What is my true relationship to women and to love relationships." Before this turning point his awareness of women and much of his life, was stuck back at a time when he was eighteen and leaving high school. In this area of his life Ralph never outgrew his teenage years.

I have outlined Ralph's case to show a very different example of how to apply the subject matter of this book. My comments in this case have centered on his attitudes toward women and relationships. However, a significant part of my work with him dealt with issues around his low self-esteem, health, and career planning. Although our work does not fit the neat package that I have described here this rather brief summary does give an accounting of what took place.

Advertising and Education

In my own business new and first-time clients account for twenty-five percent of my income. I am presenting a sampling of some advertising aids and educational announcements to show how psychic counseling and intuitive training may be introduced. Although most people have opinions about psychic practioners and the people that use them, a great deal of mystery surrounds the subject. Unlike the widespread acceptance of "board certified" psychologies and therapies, there are few standards and limited acceptance of psychic counseling. The main reason is that professionals who work in these fields, and our society as a whole, tend to identify psychic counseling with art and certified therapies with science.

With the exception of psychic fairs, new age forums, and events such as the whole life expo, ads for psychic counseling rarely appear in the well-established, traditional directories. For example, Bay Area telephone directories had no listings for "psychic consulting and healing" until 1990. While the term "intuitive counseling" sounds more acceptable than "psychic counseling" it does not tell us what it is or what the counselor does. Generally, those who advertise this service in local telephone books do so under the title of "spiritual consultants." I like telephone directories because they work. While I advertise in four sections I should mention that most of my calls from the ads under "career and vocational conseling" and "astrologers" as a psychic-astrologer. In the case of career counseling I always add a comment to tell potential clients that my approach is psychic-based. When people do call they have some idea of what I do.

Getting referrals from satisfied customers is the best source of advertising. Its free. It takes no time to educate these clients about what I can do for them and less time to establish a rapport with them than clients from telephone directories. Most referral clients are sold on what I do for them from a friend with firsthand experience.

There are many non-traditional sources for advertising psychic counseling as well as the more alternative or "new age" psychotherapies. For instance, many ads for psychic consulting may be found in free directories such as *Common Ground* (under the heading "Psychic Arts and Intuitive Sciences") and *Open Education Exchange* under the heading "Psychic and Metaphysics"). While these directories are of great value to psychics and those who use psychic services, I stopped using them several years ago when I switched to telephone books.

The promotional pieces that follow include the informational side of my small brochure, a reprinted newspaper article from *The Daily California* (originally dated July 11, 1990), and a workshop flier. While the brochure speaks for itself, the article provides an example of how the general public tends to measure my work. As an advertising aid, the newspaper article drew and continues to draw many new clients. I use it in conjunction with workshop fliers and other announcements about my availability.

Without any intentional, fancy way of adjusting yourself, to express yourself as you are is the most important thing.
Shunryu Suzuki

Psychic Counseling and Consulting

My speciality aims to help clients understand and alter subconscious patterns. My approach is rooted in experience with mental imagery (clairvoyance), the I Ching, the Science of Mind, tarot cards, dreamwork and astrology. If you are not already familiar with these right-brain intuitive methods, you will find them remarkably precise, practical and accessible. Typical counseling and consulting topics deal with career/life planning, problem solving and decision making, current and potential relationships, personality assessments, behavior patterns and prediction. Topics are only limited by one's interests and questions.

Follow-up/Ongoing Assistance

Follow-up assistance is available to address those problems that cannot be solved with our current level of awareness. Through ongoing assistance clients remain on course and become liberated from unhealthy behavior patterns. In time, the right questions emerge and the right actions/results manifest. Typical follow-up issues: expanded psychic reading/training, spiritual direction and clarity, self-healing and mastery, forward planning, financial planning, business decision making, personal goal setting and evaluation, and, in general, discovering the meaning of one's life.

Background

Dr. Allen David Young is a personal counselor, spiritual consultant and one of the nation's leading psychics. He founded the Aquarian Institute and was professor and Associate Dean for the School of Business at California State University, Hayward. Allen is also professor of psychology and management for two bay area universities, and author of "Numbers and Change: A New East-West Psychology of Spiritual Growth."

THE DAILY CALIFORNIAN

Reprint From

Jobhunting? Psychic Consultant Counsels Clients

By Suzanne Snyder

Berkeley consultant Allen Young helped his client Harold Gordon decide whether to take a job at The East Bay Investment Company.

Young advised Gordon not to take the job because as a psychic he "saw" that the company would soon be going out of business. Three months later it did just that.

"The things (Young) has done for me have been accurate," said Gordon, a client of Young since 1985. "He helps me to understand what I need to do."

For 15 years Young said he has been using his psychic powers to help his clients resolve problems with their relationships, careers or money matters.

For example, Young said a couple asked him whether they should buy a house that was in good condition, in a convenient location, and selling for a reasonable price.

Young told the couple not to buy it since he saw something wrong with its foundations, which his clients did not notice even on a second look. The couple took the consultant's advice, and last year's Oct. 17 earthquake ruined the house's foundations.

Working out of his office on 2113 Prince St., Young said he helps about three people a day.

For $65 an hour, at a half hour minimum, a client may receive advice over the phone or in person. When a potential client calls, Young said he assesses the persons expectations to determine whether his psychic ability can be useful.

"I don't deal with raving manacs—mentally ill people," he said. "I deal with people that are normal, people that want to get ahead in life."

He said he will not tell clients how to rob a bank or profit in the stock market.

If he decides he can help, Young said he sets an appointment to use his psychic skills.

Initially, Young said he became interested in the psychic world because he wanted to help himself. At age 29, he said, his marriage was falling apart, a business college he owned went bankrupt and he lost an election for Oakland City Council member.

Meanwhile he was busy working as the Associate Dean of the Business School at Cal State Hayward.

"I overextended myself in the business world." Young said that a friend recommended he consult a known psychic to obtain some insight into his life.

Young said he was "semi-resistant" his friend's advice but went to the psychic anyway. He said the insight that this stranger had into his life inspired him to learn more about psychic phenomena.

In a psychic skills development course, Young said he accidentally discovered latent psychic abilities. The instructor asked him to describe the likes, dislikes, fears and interests of a fellow student—a stranger to Young.

Young said he concentrated on the subject, closed his eyes and started saying anything that came to his mind about this student.

"I thought I was saying bullshit," Young said, but it turned out that everything was true.

Young attributed this experience and many other similar ones to a faith in his psychic ability which led to his change from a career as a business professor to a psychic counselor.

More than half of Young's clients find him through other clients, while others find him through advertisements in magazines and in the Pacific Bell Yellow Pages under the headings of "Spiritual Consultants," "Career & Vocational Counseling" or "Management Consultants."

The clients, whose average ages are in the 30s and 40s, vary from business owners to anyone who wants "input as to what his or her inner self is saying."

While Young said he usually

succeeds in assisting people through psychic means, some people dispute the validity of his practice.

"The psychic world doesn't fit into the nice, neat little packages that psychology has been using for the last 100 years," said Beth Hedva, who received her doctorate in parapsychology from Columbia-Pacific University and now works as a psychic consultant in Oakland.

"It is the read herring," Hedva said. "What we psychics are really up against is a domain of experience which contradicts any explanation."

Young responds to skeptics with the line that "there are certain things you can't prove but that doesn't mean they're not true."

Allen David Young, Ph.D.

Counseling and Consulting
Career • Relationship • Personal

2113 Prince Street
Berkeley, CA 94705
843-1299

WEDNESDAY, JULY 11, 1990

"EXPANDING YOUR INTUITION"
AT
THE FIRST CHURCH OF RELIGIOUS SCIENCE, OAKLAND

SATURDAY	**WORKSHOP by**
June 29	DR. ALLEN DAVID YOUNG
10am - 5:30pm	Fee: $45 per person

Learn how to listen to your heart and see beyond the outer vision of "situations" and "things." This workshop teaches techniques that enable you to develop intuitive skills to understand the unconscious and make better decisions. Participants learn how to ask the right questions and read answers from the deeper mind through practical techniques using mental imagery (clairvoyance and visioning) and the I Ching (Book of Changes). I will show participants how to work with these symbolic tools and explain, using real life examples, how their intuitive insights can foretell major events, assess the present or past, and assist in making decisions from the heart.

Using lecture, discussion, and individual and group exercises, this workshop focuses on helping you to clarify and resolve current and future problems (in mind), for yourself and others. To do this you participate in a variety of personal exercises that expand and develop your intuition. In the process you will learn about the various levels of intuitive knowing and conditions that both impede and nurture intuition. The workshop includes psychic models and a survey to measure your element(s), way of being in the world and intuitive style. (Bring an example or two of some problem or situation or decision in your life that you would like to resolve.)

• • • •

Allen David Young, Ph.D., has been doing psychic counseling, management consulting, and intuitive mastery workshops for more than ten years. Over the past twenty years he has taught psychology and management at Holy Names College, U.C. Berkeley, Cal State Hayward, and Lincoln University. He is author of *Practical Innerwork*, a book containing many of the techniques used in this workshop.

- -

Workshop registration at
First Church of Religious Science
5000 Clarewood Drive
Oakland, CA 94618
(415) 547-1979

NAME_____PHONE_____
ADDRESS_____

Part Three

Consulting the I Ching

>*Between the idea
>And the reality
>Between the motion
>And the act
>Falls the shadow.*
>
>**T.S. Eliot,**
>*"The Hollow Men" in
>Collected Poems*

8

Consulting the I Ching

This medicine is not a material thing; it is the light of essence, which is none other than the the primal true energy. It is necessary to attain great concentration before you see it.

The Secret of the Golden Flower

The I Ching is like "medicine." Consulting the I Ching, is a process of communicating with the unconscious to integrate two levels of reality. The first is the transpersonal reality—the inner teacher or Self within. This process leads to the second type of reality, the interpersonal and social—the self-other or self-environment.

The I Ching can only serve as a "translator" for the deeper mind—a channel of expression articulated through the language of sixty-four symbolic pictures known as hexagrams. Even though any one can gain wisdom by asking questions through the I Ching and then interpreting hexagrams, it is necessary to accept and work within the confines of its language. Generally, questions that begin with "who," "where" and "when" seem to make less sense than questions beginning with "what," "how" ănd "why." Questions like "What can I expect by making this decision or taking that course of action?" are appropriate for two reasons. First, they at least give the impression that we have considered this decision and thought about its effects. Second, they are specific (for instance, the questions "Who has what I am looking for?" or "Where is it?" are too general). Others such as "When or where will something occur" call for specific time-space answers that are alien to the sixty-four hexagrams.

The process of writing down questions or requests for advice is an essential part of consulting the oracle. The act of spelling out what we are looking for will tend to center us, make us receptive and, at the same time, focus our attention on the Self within. In addition by discovering what it is we really wish to know, we learn something of our true feeling. For instance, we may inquire about the possibility of taking a major course of action, but in wording the question and applying a time factor to it, e.g., its significance to the

The method of the I Ching *does indeed take into account the hidden individual quality in things and men, and in one's own unconscious self as well.*
C.G. Jung

present, the future, or the whole of our life, we may discover that we do not imagine this event extending endlessly into our future, but see it more as a thing of the present, or vice versa. The following list of sample inquiries should prove helpful.

- What is the nature of this letter or paper, or article, or book (complete document, or draft, or outline)?
- What guidance should I follow in working with this client, or customer, or coworker, or employee, or superior?
- Investigating through an unlimited series of "what if" questions?
- What can I expect by taking or pursuing this job, or design, or course of action, or goal?
- Making decisions based on "what if.....?" or "what effect will taking or not taking action A, B, or C have?"
- Evaluating the feasibility of ideas which come from brain-storming sessions by asking questions such as "What can I expect by pursuing this idea?"
- What is the nature of this activity, or event, or time period (past, or present, or future)?
- How would you (the teacher within) describe this situation, or idea, or event, or thing?

As a rule, the wording of specific questions leads to specific responses. Profound and rare questions such as "What is my mission in life?" "What is my relationship to the unconscious?" "What can I do to make my life more rewarding?" or "What can I do to make the most money?" may be asked as well as simpler questions or indepth predictions and forecasts.

Since the inner teacher, the unconscious, will answer almost any question that you ask with sincerity, you might ask, what are insincere questions. That is to say, how do you know when not to ask or what questions to avoid. While there are no firm answers the following four techniques tend to work.

First, after formulating your question or series of questions, cup three coins in your hand, shake them, and drop them in a random fashion to request permission from your inner teacher to consult about your specific question. If two or three heads turn up you have permission to consult about that question, but if two or three tails turn up, you do not have it. Here, two heads signifies an OK and three suggests an important question, a definite yes. Conversely, two tails tells you it is not OK to ask while three make a stronger statement, definitely no.

The next technique that tends to ensure a good relationship to the Self within is to ask, "What does my inner teacher think about my relationship to it?" This question helps you to be psychologically honest, and to understand things about yourself that you may prefer not to see. Everyone should ask it at some point, and ask again if your relationship to your spiritual path seems to change.

Another way that helps you to understand what the inner teacher is saying through the I Ching is to get someone else (a friend, counselor, teacher, or perhaps your therapist) to interpret your result. Their opinion will tend to keep you honest and may bring a fresh insight or clearer understanding. As a rule, whenever two or more people come together, permission to work with the inner Self by consulting the I Ching seems to be implicit.

The final technique calls for being centered. Simply relax, after formulating your question(s), by taking ten deep breaths. You can do this with opened or closed eyes. After consulting the I Ching, relax, take ten deep breaths again, and then interpret your results. This little process has a way of clearing the air or lines of communication between you and the teacher within.

Again, once you formulate your question or inquiry and write it down with a date, you should ask permission to consult before proceeding. I will outline two methods of obtaining wisdom from the unconscious through the I Ching. The first is a one-coin version (no changing lines allowed) for generating hexagram answers to more mundane issues than those addressed by the three-coin (changing lines allowed) method. But for those who are just beginning, one of the oldest, simplest, and more popular methods is the three-coin method. Other methods exist and some readers will have different ways of generating random hexagrams.

The deep psyche is that part of the individual's unconscious which transcends the personal and blends with the universal collective.
W. Brugh J o y

The One-coin Method

The use of one coin to generate one hexagram is the most elementary and direct method of consulting the I Ching. Cup one coin in your hands and shake it (or toss or flip it with one hand) six times, and then allow it to fall in a random fashion. The first toss represents the bottom line of the hexagram; the second toss represents the second line; the third toss represents the third line, and so forth. The coins should be read as follows:

Coin face	Type of line	Probability
Heads =	———— (Yang)	1/2
Tails =	— — (Yin)	1/2

By tossing or flipping the coin and recording the six lines, you build your hexagram. The bottom, second and third lines make up the lower trigram; the fourth, fifth and sixth lines make up the upper trigram; and the six lines together represent the completed hexagram.

By looking up the upper and lower trigram patterns in the "Table of Elements, Trigrams and Hexagrams" we can determine the hexagram's number and then its meaning. To do this find the lower and upper trigram patterns in the table that match the hexagram you have generated, and then note the number of the hexagram where the two meet. Unlike the in-depth three-coin method the one coin method is uncomplicated and best suited to mundane inquiries. By omitting changing lines, the inner teacher reveals its message through one hexagram.

One-coin Examples

- What is the nature of the I Ching methods presented in this book?

Nourishment

27

As already mentioned, hexagrams may be described in terms of upper and lower trigrams alone as follows.

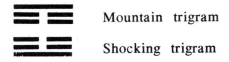

Mountain trigram

Shocking trigram

- How would you (the teacher within) describe the one-coin method of using the I Ching?

Radiance

30

The Three-coin Method

For the three-coin method use three pennies or any three coins of the same size. Cup the three coins in your hand, shake them, and drop them in a random fashion. The first fall of coins represents the bottom line of the hexagram. The second fall represents the second line, and so forth. Although heads can be used to denote the presence of yang or yin it makes more sense to use heads for yang and tails for yin for two reasons. First, the word yang means "young" and the word yin means "old". Second, yang is more symbolic of the seasons of spring and summer than yin. And these seasons come before the yin seasons of autumn and winter. With this in mind the coins should be read as follows:

Coin Group		**Type of Line**	**Probability**
Head, Head, Tail (2 heads, 1 tail)	=	———————— Yang	3/8ths
Head, Head, Head (3 heads)	=	——————— • changing Yang	1/8th
Tail, Tail, Head (2 tails, 1 head)	=	——— ——— Yin	3/8ths
Tail, Tail, Tail (3 tails)	=	——— ——— • changing Yin	1/8th

After the coins have been tossed and the six lines recorded, you have built your hexagram. The bottom, second and third lines make up the lower trigram; the fourth, fifth and top lines make up the upper trigram; and the six lines together represent the complete hexagram.

Three-coin Example

- This example, taken from the previous chapter, answers the question, "How does the I Ching describe itself?"

Looking at the upper trigram, compare it with the one like it in the "Table of Elements, Trigrams and Hexagrams." Then find the lower trigram on the left side of this table. Where the two meet in the table, the number of the hexagram is indicated. This is the hexagram you have drawn from the unconscious. Changing and unchanging lines and hexagrams are not distinguished in the table.

The movement of lines from changing yang to yin and from changing yin to yang is analogous to the natural progression of the four seasons. In symbolic terms, yang may be represented by spring and summer, and yin by autumn and winter in the following way. The airy nature of spring (yang) gathers outer strength as this season progresses to summer. Summer (changing yang) sheds its fiery nature as it changes to autumn (yin). The watery nature of autumn gathers inner strength as it progresses to winter. The cycle is complete when winter (changing yin) sheds its earthy nature by moving into spring.

The Shorthand Yarrow-stalk Method

The ratio of lines in the yarrow-stalk method is one-three-five-seven, representing changing yin, changing yang, yang and yin [1]. As I have outlined above, the coins reflect the ratios of two-two-six-six for changing yang, changing yin, yang and yin respectively. Unlike the yarrow-stalk method, the coin method makes no distinction between the unchanging and changing forms of yang and yin. In the yarrow-stalk method, the hexagram takes on a brand new perspective. Since hexagrams are merely sixfold accumulations of individual lines, and certain lines are more probable than others, it follows that certain hexagrams are also more probable [2]. In the yarrow-stalk method, yang lines are three times as likely to change as yin lines. And, the appearance of hexagrams dominated by yin lines (four or more) is more than twice as likely as hexagrams dominated by yang lines.

To use the short version of the yarrow-stalk method, we need sixteen colored marbles, beads, buttons or equal-size objects in four different hues, reflecting the ratios one-three-five-seven. These marbles must be hidden from view (perhaps in a pouch) and then mixed up to ensure a random selection. The first marble is then selected, recorded as representing the first line, replaced, and then mixed in with other marbles. This process of random selection with replacement is repeated five more times until we build a complete hexagram from the bottom up. The selection of marbles should be read as follows:

Marble Groups	Type of Line	Probability
Group 1 (5 marbles)	Yang	5/16ths
Group (3 marbles)	changing Yang	3/16ths
Group 2 (7 marbles)	Yin	7/16ths
Group 4 (1 marble)	changing Yin	1/16th

You can use any four hues for the marbles or other objects. The colors I uses are black (one), white (three), dark blue (seven), and yellow (five). If small beads are used, you may want to use thirty-two or forty-eight (as long as the same ratio is maintained). It should be noted that the "Table of Elements, Trigrams and Hexagrams" applies to this method as well as the one and three coin methods. This use has already been explained.

The full yarrow-stalk method takes about twenty-five minutes, and is considered the oldest and most traditional way of consulting the oracle. All that is reasonably known is that this method is far older and certainty more soundly based than the three coin method. Although the yarrow-stalk method may be more aesthetic, there is no numerical difference between it and the shorthand method described above. A detailed description of the yarrow-stalk method can be found in the *I Ching* by John Blofeld [3].

Creating Elements and Trigrams

As mentioned earlier the hexagrams are made up of trigrams and trigrams are made up of the elements. Creating elements and trigrams by divination may be of more use than creating hexagrams. Why? Because they offer an excellent way to study what's happening at the most basic level. While answers expressed in the language of elements and trigrams are limited this limitation allows you to grasp the meaning of the elements in general and the elements at work in your situation in particular. You can also interpret hexagrams solely on the basis of the trigrams within them as follows.

Lower Trigram: your position, where you are coming from, what you are striving to express.
Upper Trigram: the position of others, where the outer world is coming from, what other people are trying to express.

By using the one- and three-coin methods to create elements or trigrams you can ask the inner teacher to answer questions in a way that allows you to study the parts of whole situations, including complex hexagrams. You can divine elements by creating two random lines, and trigrams by creating three random lines in the following way. (The examples that follow are part of the examples just given in that they represent their lower elements and trigrams.)

One-coin Examples

- What is the nature of the I Ching methods presented in this book? (Element created by flipping one coin two times. First for the bottom line, and then the top line.)

   Air element

- What is the nature of the I Ching methods presented in this book? (Trigram created by flipping one coin three times, from line one on the bottom to three line three on top.)

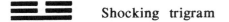   Shocking trigram

- How would you (inner teacher) describe the one-coin method of using the I Ching?

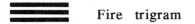   Fire trigram

Consulting the I Ching 157

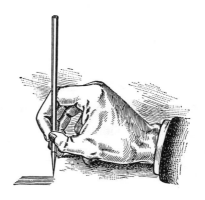

Three-coin Examples

- How does the I Ching describe itself (as an element)?

    ▬▬ ▬▬   Air element (no changing lines)

- How does the I Ching describe itself (as a trigram)?

    ▬▬▬▬▬ ▬ ▬   Shocking trigram (no changing lines)

The Sixty-four Hexagram Titles and Grades

	Hexagram Titles	Grade
1,	Creation (The Creative)	A
2,	Fulfillment (The Receptive)	A
3,	Initial Difficulty (Difficulty at the Beginning)	C-
4,	Youthful Ignorance (Youthful Folly)	C-
5,	Waiting (Nourishment)	C-
6,	Conflict (Litigation)	F
7,	The Army	D
8,	Holding Together (Unity, Co-ordination)	B
9,	Minor Accumulation (The Taming Power of the Small)	C+
10,	Conduct (Treading)	C-
11,	Flowering (Peace)	A
12,	Standstill (Stagnation, Obstruction)	C-
13,	Relatives (Fellowship with Men, Friends)	B
14,	Great Possession (Possession in Great Measure)	A
15,	Modesty	A
16,	Enjoyment (Enthusiasm, Repose)	A
17,	Following (According With)	C-
18,	Fixing (Work on What Has Been Spoiled)	C+
19,	Becoming Great (Approach)	A
20,	Contemplation (View, Looking Down)	C+
21,	Biting Through (Gnawing)	F
22,	Decoration (Grace, Elegance)	C+
23,	Splitting Apart (Peeling Off)	D
24,	Renewal (Return, The Turning Point)	B
25,	Innocence (The Unexpected, Integrity)	C+
26,	Major Accumulation (The Taming Power of The Great)	C-
27,	Nourishment (Providing Nourishment)	A
28,	Excess Yang (Preponderance of the Great, Excess)	D
29,	Danger (The Abyss, Water)	D
30,	Radiance (Fire, The Clinging)	C+
31,	Influence (Wooing, Attraction, Sensation)	C-

32,	Duration (The Long Enduring)	B
33,	Retreat (Yielding, Withdrawal)	D
34,	Great Power (The Power of the Great)	A
35,	Progress	B
36,	Defeat of The Light (Injury)	C+
37,	The Family (The Clan)	B
38,	Opposition (Opposites, The Estranged)	D
39,	Obstacles (Obstruction, Trouble)	F
40,	Solution (Deliverance, Release)	B
41,	Decrease (Loss, Reduction)	D
42,	Increase ((Gain)	A
43,	Breakthrough (Resoluteness, Resolution)	C+
44,	Meeting of Opposites (Coming to Meet)	D
45,	Reunion (Gathering Together, Assembling)	A
46,	Ascending (Pushing Upward, Promotion)	A
47,	Exhaustion (Oppression, Adversity)	F
48,	The Well (A Well)	B
49,	Changing (Revolution)	B
50,	The Cauldron (A Sacrificial Vessel)	B
51,	Shocking (Thunder, The Arousing)	C+
52,	Keeping Still (Mountain, Desisting)	C-
53,	Gradual Development (Gradual Progress)	B
54,	An Outsider (The Marrying Maiden)	C-
55,	Abundance (Fullness)	B
56,	Wandering (The Traveller)	C-
57,	Gentle Penetration (Wind, Willing Submission)	C+
58,	Joy (Lake, The Joyous)	B
59,	Breaking Up (Dispersion, Disintegration)	C-
60,	Limitations ((Restraint)	C-
61,	Inner Truth (Inward Confidence)	C+
62,	Excess Yin (Preponderance of the Small)	D
63,	Partial Completion (After Completion)	C+
64,	Before The End (Before Completion)	C-

Table of Trigrams and Hexagrams

UPPER TRIGRAM ▷ / LOWER TRIGRAM ▽	Heaven	Thunder	Water	Mountain	Earth	Wind	Fire	Lake
Heaven	1	34	5	26	11	9	14	43
Thunder	25	51	3	27	24	42	21	17
Water	6	40	29	4	7	59	64	47
Mountain	33	62	39	52	15	53	56	31
Earth	12	16	8	23	2	20	35	45
Wind	44	32	48	18	46	57	50	28
Fire	13	55	63	22	36	37	30	49
Lake	10	54	60	41	19	61	38	58

1

CREATION

Summary: Yang. Increasing in influence. Drawing strength from within oneself. Intuitive insight. Self-expression. Leadership. The beginning of something new and exciting. Inspiration. Unrestrained creativity. Grade: A

Today you are thinking about new and exciting ideas. Stimulated by imagination, you are now capable of great inventions. The symbol of this hexagram is the beautiful dream or illusion. Even though its only in your head, you have the ability now to make it real if you recognize that you must work to make any idea real. Despite the signs of sure success, you are dealing with causes rather than effects, thoughts rather than things, potentials rather than realities, the new and untried rather than the tried and true. You and you alone have control over the visions you create. You are the creator, pioneer, architect or inventor.

The adage "What you can conceive, you can achieve" applies to this hexagram. Its advice is simple: "Do what you love, the money will follow." Your qualifications in the situation at hand are not born of schooling, degrees or the right "political" or business connections, but of natural, intuition and creative talent. However, your actions may not produce practical results.

The time of **CREATION** denotes intuitive potential and wisdom that is visible and powerful. It symbolizes the inner world at work to manifest your thoughts and ideas. It is connected with early spring, new beginnings, progress and vitality. It serves as a message that you are now making the hidden world clear. Because your success has roots in the beginning of some new cycle, your plans and ideas may now become real.

Getting **CREATION** suggests that your intuitive insights should determine your course of action. The archer who takes aim and strikes his desired long-range target captures the essence of your position in the situation at hand. This symbolic picture points to far-sighted vision and intuition instead of rational thinking. It suggests that your consciousness is both expanding and liberating itself from the limits of your immediate environment.

Your place in the path of life is in the driver's seat.
Anonymous

FULFILLMENT

Summary: Yin. Receptiveness. Supporting what is. Getting results. Following the established order or precedent. Yielding. Serving. Devotion. Gentleness. Helping others attain their goals. Receptive to your plan. Grade: A

FULFILLMENT calls for accepting some established order or leadership or system that others have embraced. Now you are facing realities rather than potentials. Your proper course is that of following others rather than taking the lead. If you push ahead now you will deny your natural character and miss the way. Success comes from seeking the tried and true, while failure comes from taking action toward the new and untried.

The reason that this hexagram's title is **FULFILLMENT** is precisely because other people have already invested the required time, energy and hard work. You should now accept the harvest of these prior efforts. This hexagram's advice may sum up in the adage "A bird in the hand is better than two in the bush." Simply put, accept the known and established; let go of the unknown and what may be.

Hexagram 2 completes the action initiated by Hexagram 1. While Creation implies ego-expansion and favors potentials, **FULFILLMENT** implies ego-repression and favors reality. At this time it is best to accept, cooperate, and conform instead of taking the lead. Your efforts must follow an existing idea, inspiration or direction to be successful. You should expect to fail if you attempt an independent course or stand as an equal, side by side, with the established leader.

The conditions represented by this hexagram bring both success and recognition as a result of serving other people. At this time the need for mature preparation and for accepting the responsibility of supporting others is at a high point. By working as the "servant" or "power behind the throne" to established individual or tradition, you may now gain personal **FULFILLMENT** and material success. By assisting others in the situation at hand, you may act as an agent or force in guiding human evolution.

The ability to experience and to flow with what is signals the beginning of the unification of mind, body and spirit.
W. Brugh Joy

INITIAL DIFFICULTY

Summary: A process that begins in difficulty and requires great effort to overcome. Being stationary and firm in the beginning. A condition that requires you to give a lot before growth is evident. Stockpiling your energy. Grade: C-

As of today, you cannot express your good ideas or intentions in a way that will take shape or be understood by others. As the title **INITIAL DIFFICULTY** implies, you now face a new condition or endeavor. This project or situation is almost beyond your ability to handle. You may feel unusually discouraged because your vitality is at a low point. Although the task is far from impossible it requires skill, perseverance, and patience to surmount.

Your plans may be thwarted for now, but you can still move forward by staying on course. While authority figures, such as employers, government officials, parents or those who owe you money may prove difficult to deal with, this trouble is only temporary. You may find that they are untinitionally unreceptive to your efforts. As a result, it is best to work patiently toward bringing them around to your point of view.

Your condition is one of growth beset with an **INITIAL DIFFICULTY**. You should avoid hasty actions because several elements are in motion, and struggling to take form. Since any premature move might bring disaster, it is best to remain stationary and wait for conditions to improve. The situation at hand may be viewed as water in a dam that is unable to move, and therefore accumulates. By stockpiling your resources and getting help from other people you can overcome the obstacles ahead later.

The time of **INITIAL DIFFICULTY** serves as a message to nurture the seedling situation before you. In this way, you can offer the protection and support needed for its future growth. Because your current endeavor is still in the early stages, you must attend to the elements within it until they reach maturity. Giving in to the temptation to complete things in a single sweep will lead to failure.

YOUTHFUL IGNORANCE

Summary: Youthful Folly. Undeveloped. Unguided. Uncivilized. Arrogance combined with mistrust. Assuming you know what to do in spite of your ignorance. Uncultivated Growth. Immaturity. Foolishness. Insincerity. Grade: C-

When they think they know the answers, people are difficult to guide. When they know that they don't know, people can find their own way.

Lao Tzu

This hexagram serves as a message that you lack clarity of mind and experience in the situation at hand. Your true status is marked by limited vision, bewilderment, and confusion. This comes about because your energy is scattered and lacks a unified focus. Although some progress is possible, you must follow your inner teacher and have the right attitude (a receptive frame of mind) to achieve your goals. In short, remain patient and accept your **YOUTHFUL IGNORANCE**.

In times of **YOUTHFUL IGNORANCE** you are not satisfied with your position or relationships. You could use help in the form of patience and endurance. You need a more mature outlook than the one you have now. While you have good intentions, you are limited in vision and unwilling to admit how little you know. If you lose sight of your intended goal, and impatiently concern yourself with immediate and often irrelevant questions, you are likely to fail. At this time you will become mixed up with whatever faulty thinking you dwell upon. The truth is that you are as free from negative circumstances as you refuse to think about them.

You have no practical experience or knowledge of how to proceed in the situation at hand, even though you think you do. This may result in your behaving brashly and acting inappropriately. You may also find yourself pursuing a course that you don't even understand. Without the proper guidance your judgment is poor. Because of your lack of training other people may easily deceive, cheat or dupe you. An important spiritual lesson of this hexagram is that nothing is sure at all in your life until it has been put through the furnace of meeting its oposite.

Getting **YOUTHFUL IGNORANCE** suggests that you have qualities that are appropriate in children but deplorable in adults. You tend to exhibit child-like impatience, undeveloped taste, ignorance or limited mentality. Your professional activities may be somewhat difficult at this time, as others may oppose you whenever you make a proposal. For this reason, it might be best to keep a low profile. At your best you are naive and uneducated; at your worst you are mentally retarded and ridiculous. Generally, you cannot be helped until you learn to listen to your inner voice or a knowledgable teacher.

WAITING

Summary: Waiting for personal nourishment. Feeling held back while expecting some kind of harvest or fulfillment. Calculated inaction. Anticipation. Conditions that require faith, patience, and sincerity.   Grade: C-

Today your eagerness and desire for success comes about because you are **WAITING** for it. If you give in to your impatience and attempt to rush ahead you can expect disaster. However, if you have the courage to pause and accept things as they are, the path that leads to success will present itself at the right time. In short, the nourishment you desire will come in its own time; you must learn to wait for it. Since the present time is not ripe for results, you should learn to relax and make the best of the situation before you.

The hexagram **WAITING** calls for hope and an inner certainty toward reaching your goal. Through good timing and applying just the right amount of effort you can produce the results you desire. The image of someone attempting to climb a steep mountain in the midst of a storm describes the condition of **WAITING**. Your situation is like that of the mountain climber. You are unable to move forward as planned. While you appear to be blocked in your present course the setback is only temporary.

Now, your position is one of **WAITING** while looking forward with anticipation or holding back with expectation. It is likely that you are about to outgrow, restructure, or improve yourself and your environment in a major way. Although you are ready for some desired outcome, it is temporarily held back or unrealized. By taking note of surprises or sudden insights you can understand what is coming up.

The **WAITING** theme of this hexagram serves as a message that you are looking toward some advanced suffering or enjoyment. It implies an actual experience or foretaste of something that will or may come later in full force. Generally, what you get is what you need, and not necessarily what you want or hope will happen. In most cases, it is not what you expect.

True mastery can be gained by letting things go their own way.
      Lao Tzu

6

CONFLICT

Summary: Obstruction despite sincerity. Irreconcilable elements. Unresolved dispute. Litigation. An arguement. An outright opposition. A tug-of-war or struggle. Stalemate. The lose-lose situation of meeting the opposition halfway, otherwise discord. Grade: F

You are now facing an unresolved conflict. You may find that your own inward unconscious drives show up in someone else's actions. The situation goes beyond a simple lack of harmony. It points to an irreconcilability of differences and the kind of competition that shows itself in quarreling, disputing, or controversy. Although the time ahead is one of **CONFLICT**, you may avoid it if your actions are well considered at the beginning.

By nature men are alike. Through practice they have become far apart.
Confucius

The conditions represented by this hexagram often lead to irrational behavior and useless anger. There is a strong tendency to project your ego into situations and make every issue that arises a test of your personal validity. You may find yourself standing up for your point of view and fighting for your rights with complete confidence and little regard for the prospect of success.

CONFLICT comes up now because you feel that your position is right despite an opposing position of equal or greater force. You are entering a time of testing and confrontation which will point out your pressures as well as your positive and strong points. Although you may not be aware of it, your attitude is one of self-justification, self-righteousness, and opposition toward the people around you. Complete agreement is impossible now, but disagreements can be minimized if you are willing to meet the other side halfway. In short, you can settle your dispute if both parties agree on an impartial judge such as a coin flip, disinterested mediator, or unbiased third party. Ultimately, you must choose one side and live with it.

As the title of this hexagram suggests you are dealing with misunderstandings and differences that have no real resolution. Generally, the **CONFLICT** here results from an over-emphasis on external factors that tend to be a small part of the total problem.

7

THE ARMY

Summary: External restraints. Feeling stuck. Under a military-type force. A time of danger and recuperation. Limited opportunity. Limited external influence. The need for self-control, perservance, and discipline. Grade: D

When **THE ARMY** comes up you have no visible or outward influence in the present situation. Although your influence in the outer physical world is limited, you have an inner power like that seen in hidden volcanoes, underground streams, and peacetime military soldiers. Your persistence in the right course, i.e., the course given to you by those in power, will allow you to avoid external danger or battle. Such persistence will serve to nurture and awaken what is now dormant within you.

Your position is now one of external darkness and limited opportunities for self-expression. THE ARMY calls for discipline, concentration, self-control, and at least inner quiet. Consequently, the best course of action is to seek out, and wait for assistance from the inner psychic world or those in power in the outer physical world. Any attempts to struggle against the reality of your situation, or to ascend to the heights will make matters worse.

The time of **THE ARMY** represents an "alienation crisis." It has come up because you have been neglecting yourself or some aspect of the situation before you. The present time or condition lacks vitality or movement; everything seems fixed in place; nothing is subject to change. You may feel alone and disconnected from others, like an alien in the world whom no one else can ever adequately understand. The time may be quite difficult for your personal and domestic life as well. You may feel stuck, lonely, and isolated from others.

You are facing an inherited pattern of thought or action in which your influence is limited. Your success now comes about by facing difficulty, through self-discipline, through toughening your resolve, through your perseverance, and most of all through your ability to remain steady.

The Way is present before our eyes, yet what is before our eyes is hard to understand.
    **The Secret
of the Golden Flower**

8

HOLDING TOGETHER

Summary: Sticking together. Unity. Becoming a center of influence. Assisting or supporting others with joy. Inner-directed leadership. Inner strength. Co-ordination. Consistent and upright fellowship. Close associations.   Grade: B

HOLDING TOGETHER represents the kind of leadership that depends upon inner strength and kindness. At this time you are blessed with a spirit of cooperation, and other people are willing to follow your lead. You may now have an opportunity to guide the people around you, finding in them the complement of your own nature. Your success in the situation at hand will come about through being supported by the strength and cooperation of others. Although the time is one of leadership, you should support the main leader if you are not prepared to take over.

HOLDING TOGETHER brings an opportunity to breathe in the kind of joy that allows you hear the finer voice of nature and see the finer side of all things. While you may well say you would be satisfied if you had this, or that, or the other, this is not true! Happiness is something that must come from the mind within being fed and renewed by the truth of life.

Your mental state is relatively quiet, and you can see objectively what is true for you, what your needs are, and how much you can give and receive from others. This is a good time to plan for the future in all areas of your life, because you are neither foolishly optimistic nor excessively conservative. You can now build your relationships upon reality without neglecting your real needs.

You may now see yourself as the creator of some group or vision in which others are likely to join. The scene of several people marching to the beat of a single drummer describes the theme of **HOLDING TOGETHER**. Your position is that of the single drummer. In the situation at hand, your inner teacher communicates in such a way that the people around you are inspired to follow its course. The call of the drum beat suggests a drive to attract new experiences. This image refers more to being a center of influence within a larger body than leading the larger body.

The present time of **HOLDING TOGETHER** is one of equilibrium. The demands of your environment are in balance with your emotional needs. Emotional maturity and experience have prepared you for this, and now you can put your understanding to work to make your life run more smoothly.

MINOR ACCUMULATION

Summary: Something you expect is not quite ready. A small gathering or accumulation of energy. Achieving your goals with gentle and sensible limits. External refinement. Taming power of the small. Adaptability. Grade: C+

MINOR ACCUMULATION serves as a message to subordinate your ego drives and wait for the signs of sure success. At this time it is best to settle down and wait before initiating anything grand in the outer world. You can do this by getting into a position where you can afford to be unconcerned about results, i.e., assisting others, adopting a wait and see attitude. If you can take the course of detached consciousness, you may learn something about how life works; in fact, you may learn that your own actions have created your difficulties.

As the title of this hexagram suggests, it is necessary to control some of your thoughts and emotions. If you are willing to hold back and proceed slowly, you can accumulate what you need, avoid difficulties and then move forward within limits. The more you perform the task as hand in a thorough and careful manner, the more chance there is that it will succeed. If you are careless you have little hope of success.

Getting **MINOR ACCUMULATION** raises the question, "What is your hurry?" Today you should prepare to accept the tumultuous process of slowing down your schedule of events. You should re-examine your current outer-directed goals and align yourself with the situation at hand. Any actions you take to advance or direct the course of external events at this time will only cause frustration.

The demands of the situation before you may exceed your ability to meet them. You may exert a friendly and restraining influence on the task at hand, but you should avoid sweeping measures to get your way. The time calls for limiting your focus to small endeavors or the refinement of some existing project instead of larger events. It is only through inner determination, gentleness and adaptability that ultimate success can be attained. Consequently, you should work behind the scenes to make small adjustments, to remove psychological obstacles, and to exchange ideas and plans with others.

10

CONDUCT

Summary: Controlling restless desires. Putting low and high in the right place. The power to direct, restrain, and manage. Coercive force. The need to keep one's thoughts to oneself. Making the correct appearance. Behaving with decency and correctness. Grade: C-

The time of **CONDUCT** is often one of challenge because you are bringing together that which is strong and powerful with that which is weak and gentle. Your task is somewhat difficult because this is your first public appearance. You are now facing real differences in elevation or social status; consequently, the attainment of equality is impossible. Although success is possible, the dangers in the task at hand require extreme caution. As a result, this hexagram serves as a message to seek out the "right" balance. Here, the right balance refers to dealing with other elements from higher and lower classes in status or value through humility, moderation, and inner truth.

CONDUCT is often experienced as an identity crisis in which you question what you are doing. Since employers or superiors may sense your hesitation and wonder whether you are the right person for the job you are doing, it is best to express yourself in a controlled manner. In short, you must now act or proceed cautiously and gently.

Rather than make the first move it is better to wait and see.
    Lao Tzu

CONDUCT calls for aiming high-pressured water at a fire. It suggests that your position is one of controlling your intentions and creative impulses. By directing your talents and actions to support others you can guide the growth of new cooperative projects. Through such actions you may guide the growth of new endeavors. The time denotes an opportunity to share your insights with others whose status is often higher than yours. To develop and focus your talents in the midst of other people who don't share your goals, you must act out of self-discipline, purity of motives, and compassion.

CONDUCT calls for coordinating your efforts with the acts and achievements of some group endeavor. Since your difficulties with the outer world at this time are signals about what you should be doing, you should approach this period by examining what is working and what is not.

FLOWERING

Summary: Deep harmony. Peace. Excellent opportunity. A change for the better. Inwardly strong, outwardly weak. Little effort, big reward. Manifesting an idea. Prospering conditions. Great accomplishment or achievement. Grade: A

    FLOWERING denotes a time when your ideas and intentions begin to grow and prosper. At this time the productive and life-affirming elements are increasing. Here, the good elements are in power while the evil elements come under their influence and change for the better. This hexagram is present because the creative conditions in your inner psychic world meet with receptive conditions in your outer physical world. In addition, the inner and outer forces in your sphere come together with one will, and everything is in communion.

    You are now able to take a new experience, see its potential and give it a concrete form in your life. You are able to live within a structure and engage in new and stimulating experiences, which keep you from becoming stale. In short, you are beginning a new phase of internal growth. This growth should proceed quite benevolently and provide you with sudden new opportunities in your work—a chance to work with new approaches or to begin a new enterprise and take off on unbeaten paths.

    The **FLOWERING** hexagram serves as a message to use your personal resources to manifest your inner-directed course. Its presence denotes the manifestation of some new form within the situation before you. You now have the urge to keep on going until you accomplish something solid regarding your intentions. In addition, this urge is still going when the rest of the world has fallen by the wayside. Your current environment is like the beginning of spring. It signals new growth, good times, and conditions that will continue to benefit, even in hard times.

    FLOWERING is an extremely powerful time; it points to powerful internal forces for change colliding with powerful resistance from the external world. It brings to together the old and new in your life, between conservatism and your desire to experiment.

It is not enough that we should have matter, we must also have a single impulse, one shove to launch the mass, and generate the harmony of the centrifugal and centripetal forces.

Ralph Waldo Emerson

12

STANDSTILL

Summary: Congestion. Stagnation. Being misunderstood. Being stuck, blocked or jammed. Outwardly strong, inwardly weak. A breakdown in communications. Big effort, little reward. Weak in faith. Misunderstanding, confusion and disharmony. Grade: C-

Whatever draws you toward it, making you think it can catisfy you, governs you, and is your God.
Emma Curtis Hopkins

This hexagram serves to remind you that there is no relation between your intended direction or message and the result you expect. You may be caught in a tug-of-war between your ego on the one hand and your urge to achieve something tangible on the other. Generally, **STANDSTILL** refers to a time when your behavior tends to be childish and leads you to ignore existing laws. Your expectations about the outer world are over-inflated, and at the same time, you are unrealistic regarding your relationship to other people. If you remain filled with your opinions you will only keep yourself stuck.

Today your relationships may be strained because of some real difference between you and others. Your position is outwardly firm, yet weak within. What is ignorant has power over intelligence. The time of **STANDSTILL** is often one of difficulty in communicating with others, and of problems arising from a serious conflict of viewpoints. Your ideas and opinions as well as your ways of communicating with people may be seriously challenged by others. As a result, there should be no question that giving other people freedom from your ideas will cause them to do right. In your present frame of mind you are incapable of seeing the whole picture, and should avoid making any decisions unless you have to.

In times of **STANDSTILL** your personal interests and plans are of limited interest to the people around you. There is no discussion or understanding with other people. Fruitful efforts on your part are impossible because there is no common ground for agreement. Although your ability to communicate with others is at a low point, your troubles can be minimized if you are faithful to the inner world and withdraw into its seclusion. You can tell when you have true faith by the pleasure you take in seeing others successful and prosperous in their own ways.

While it is human nature to want others to do as you think they ought to do, it is divine to see that their own way is their true way. Practically speaking you will tend to give up your position if you are not secure in your thinking, or look for ways to sever relationships with those who disagree with you. You remember that your troubles are probably more apparent than real, no matter how real they seem.

RELATIVES

Summary: Pursuing common interests. Partnership. Pleasant associations. A community gathering. Organizing others. Gathering with like-minded people. Joining a group with common interests, activities, and purposes. Fellowship. Grade: B

When the hexagram **RELATIVES** comes up, common interests rather than private goals may be found at the center of your present associations. In the situation at hand you are dealing with concerns that are universal. Because you are now surrounded by like-minded people you may gain in health, strength, and other areas. At this time, individual tasks are less significant than group efforts. Through group unity and cooperation with others, your goals may be achieved.

Through **RELATIVES** you work with other people to release water from a dam. Under its influence your position is that of working toward group goals to move beyond obstacles that block the flow of knowledge and human life. This is not the time to strike out as an individual. Instead, you should evaluate your life and goals in view of the community before you. By working within this group and pursuing its interests, you can fulfill your expectations.

At this time you are able to understand and support the needs of other people without losing sight of your own desire for fulfillment. You are likely to be in familiar surroundings now and feel that you have some kind of center or place where you can build a solid base for your activities. Your concerns should be focused upon your personal life and the people who affect it most, your immediate or extended family.

You are now able to make the compromises necessary to get along with others. In the time of **RELATIVES** it should be easy to relate your own interests to the interests of any group you are working with, so that everyone will gain from what you do. Through your relationships, you will come to know yourself better than at most other times. Generally, people will be at ease with you because you are at ease with yourself. In addition, routine discussions, negotiations, and transactions of everyday existence will offer no obstacles.

GREAT POSSESSION

Summary: Being within a center of power and influence. The possession of something great. Inner wealth. Shedding light on a large scale. Gaining in dignity and distinction. Great clarity and understanding. Grade: A

    GREAT POSSESSION brings several important principles or spiritual truths into the foreground. It serves as a message that your strength comes from the teacher within you. Your defense is the protection of the spirit. Your mind is the mind of the spirit. Your voice is the voice of your heart.
    Today signals a time or condition that is good for any endeavor that includes public relations or sales. Professional and business concerns are often in the foreground when it comes up. In dealing with others you are more sensitive and responsive to the general mood and therefore able to control your relationship with the group.
    Getting **GREAT POSSESSION** refers to a time of recognition and fulfillment according to inner and outer laws. It should be seen as a reminder that God is good. If your attitude is one of unassuming modesty you may expect good things and great success. Success is further indicated because your position is one of inner strength and authority. In addition, your strength is the result of striking the proper balance between ego-expression and ego-repression.
    In the time of **GREAT POSSESSION** you are a map maker. You are designing roadways as others look on. This hexagram suggests clarity of mind and gaining recognition from others. Simply put, your role is the wise teacher, guide or wayshower. You may now lay down a path for others to follow. If the maps you define are true and accurate, you will generally know where you are and how others may get there. But, if they are false and sketchy, your view of what is needed will be inaccurate and misleading.
    Although **GREAT POSSESSION** is no guarantee of material wealth, you may attract it through your spouse, close friend, business partner, employer or other institution, without any special effort on your part. As such, your personal life may be on public display more than usual; you may find it difficult to hide certain facts about yourself. If spiritual matters interest you, these interests may be especially great at this time. You may discover that you know things that you weren't aware of knowing.

15

MODESTY

Summary: Modesty despite merit. Humility. Yielding over your opinions to the truth. Meekness. Balanced action. Lowliness. Reticent or reserved in manner. Ego transcendence. Sincerity. Good fortune if you are receptive. Grade: A

MODESTY calls for being humble, earnest, honest, receptive, and submissive. It serves as a message to avoid any signs of arrogance or vanity in the situation at hand. You are now on a course that is lowly and unpretentious rather than proud and haughty. You now have an opportunity to shape your fate by selecting the path of benevolent inner forces rather than destructive outer forces. It is wise to recall that you have the mental quality which can increase faith so that the whole world does as you say.

When **MODESTY** comes up it is wise to acknowledge what you don't know and be willing to accept that there are other truths. You do not have to be super strong or competent to succeed at this time, because the natural flow of energies is with you. If you make the effort to understand the rules of the game you are playing in, your views are stabilized, and you will learn how to play more skillfully. The gains you make at this time are not a stroke of luck, but rather the solid result of good organization.

Your mind is earthbound at this time, but this does not mean that you lack vision and foresight. This is a time to turn your attention to the outward aspects of your life—your career, your role in the larger society and your standing and reputation within the community. You should examine your situation as a whole and see if you are going in the direction you want and making adequate progress. You should proceed with **MODESTY** to manifest your personal interests within a social context. If you don't stand for something you will fall. In the long-run you must know what you have faith in.

The course outlined by **MODESTY** tends to take a long time. However, this course is non-threatening, and it is honored and appreciated by all in the end. The symbolic picture of a slow train moving across the countryside describes this hexagram. Like the slow moving train, your position is powerful, yet modest, old fashioned and traditional. Even though you must cover a lot of territory your motto is 'slow but sure.' Since the course of the train is predetermined by tracks that have already been traveled, it implies straightforward progress. Simply put, your path to success now is unexciting. But, it is well-defined.

Few are those who are calm and serious, rare are those who are sincere and unified.
The Secret of the Golden Flower

16

ENJOYMENT

Summary: Feeling high and enliven. Free and enthusiastic movement. Recognition. Harmony. Inspiration. A mystical experience. Lively interest. Spontaneity. Happiness. Comfort. The absence of restraint. Grade: A

When people and things respond because of your words, because your thoughts, it is to your honor, your credit, your skill, that they have come forth.
Emma Curtis Hopkins

This hexagram represents some celebration in which you may be honored for your past activity or contribution. Your present status is the result of gaining recognition from others, and the power generated by a totally-accepted social activity. Today the ENJOYMENT of your heart may be expressed in a burst of good feelings. In spite of your prior isolation you are now becoming active and moving forward without disturbance. Your new ideas, inventions, and endeavors may now be developed and promoted with success.

As a symbol, **ENJOYMENT** refers to a state of freedom, and as well, an attitude of quiet confidence and righteous action. Your movements are now inspired along the path of least resistance. In addition, you are in harmony with the people and circumstances around you. Because of this harmony, you are able to gain help from others without the fear of opposition. Your situation is one in which things blossom from inactivity to liveliness and prosperity.

You are approaching a time in which your ambitions and efforts should bear their greatest fruit. The main effect of the hexagram **ENJOYMENT** is to put you in the limelight, either on a small or large scale, depending on the normal course of your life. You may be called upon to take over the direction of a task or project in which you would have considerable power, but take note that the responsibility will be equally great. Do not pretend to be something you are not because the truth will eventually come out, and if you have misrepresented yourself, you will be damaged.

In a very real way, the present conditions derive their form and individuality as much from what you cannot do as from what you can do. Your greatest asset at this time is that you can see clearly how various parts of your life are working out. This is also a favorable period for intellectual and spiritual growth.

17

FOLLOWING

Summary: Preparing for rest and recuperation. Adapting to darkness or winter-like conditions. Succeeding or adjusting to another. Compliance. Dealing with resistance or liability. Adhering to circumstances. Flexibility.   Grade: C-

As the title of this hexagram suggests your course is one of adapting to the situation at hand. In the time of **FOLLOWING** your ideas or endeavors will not be progressive until you adhere to the requirements of reality without being aggressive. Arrogance and a strong will on your part will accomplish nothing as the time requires the cooperation of others. If you can accept your inherited status with a gentle, reticent, and open-minded attitude, great achievements are possible.

When **FOLLOWING** comes up you should align your efforts with spiritual insights to gain an inner safeguard over temptations in the outer physical world. At this time you should adapt to the situation at hand and avoid ambitious or so-called quick paths to growth. If you attempt to hurry your plans you only increase the chance of failure. Generally, your situation will not improve until you are able to ask for help, and then show a willingness to be led.

This is not a good time to make demands of other people, if peace and harmony are your goal. You may find it difficult to see any point of view but your own. If this happens it is best to withdraw from others and from confrontations with unfamiliar or strange elements. This is not a negative condition; it arises out of a need to be by yourself for a while and adjust to new circumstances.

In the time of **FOLLOWING** you seek and need comfort from the demands of the outside world. You would do well to retire by yourself to your own private place. Success can be yours if you go inside yourself and look at your attitudes, feelings and emotional orientation toward the world around you. You could do this by trying to bring out into the open those elements of yourself that usually remain hidden within you.

"Acceptance" means recognizing what is. Wishing it were otherwise changes nothing.

David K. Reynolds

FIXING

Summary: Restructuring. Correcting decay. Refurbishing. Work on what has been spoiled. Putting something into a correct and conclusive form. To restore to the proper condition. A condition of inner weakness and outer stillness. Grade: C+

When **FIXING** comes up you should plan to reappraise what you are doing and make adjustments where necessary. While this is not an especially happy or peaceful time, your affairs should run along a somewhat smooth course. If you adopt the steady habit of thinking about spiritual truths and positive thoughts, your presence will be helpful to other people. If, however, you are very unhappy at this time, you had best get in touch with what you are really doing.

You should now be willing to work with others to resolve any difficulties that may arise. Even though your life is directed by your own demands much more than you realize, these demands are often unconscious to you, yet expressed by others. As the title of this hexagram suggests, you may be successful in **FIXING** your world when you can examine what is working and what is not. You will erase errors rapidly or slowly according to your own nature. And, if you are truly conscious of your present situation and objectives, correcting past mistakes is unnecessary.

FIXING serves as a message to correct, restructure, and re-organize the situation before you. It denotes decay as a result of gentle, yet persistent indifference. In the situation at hand, you must first know the cause of past mistakes before you can do away with them. You should know that despite the present corruption there are positive aspects. Your success will depend upon your ability and patience to correct the mistakes, and to salvage what is useful.

An important spiritual truth about getting this hexagram is that if you are in bondage, you have some extreme error about your inner teacher and its relationship to your life. Because **FIXING** refers to building and rebuilding your role is the builder. The bridges you build may be tangible plans or courses of action to get you beyond your present condition. To reach your goal you must now work to make a link between the old and the new. Although the task at hand is difficult to accomplish, it may be of value to many who follow in your footsteps. Your greatest difficulty is the result of losing your perspective and self-worth in the face of unforeseen challenges.

BECOMING GREAT

Summary: The beginning of upward movement. Getting closer. Promotion. Spring-like conditions. Immediate success. Notably above average in amount, size, or scope. Rapid, but short-lived advancement. Grade: A

When **BECOMING GREAT** comes up your views have reached the kind of stability that allows you to act from a consistent position. There is far less ego involvement than usual in your endeavor, so you can take whatever steps are necessary, without your personal affairs getting in the way. You respect the people who have more experience than you have, and you are likely to turn to them for advice. In addition, you feel that there is practical work to be done, and you are willing to devote your attention to getting it done properly.

You now have an opportunity to rise to the occasion and rush ahead of your natural development. **BECOMING GREAT** means riding an elevator to the top of a tall building. You are rising like the elevator. You can expect upward movement or progress according to the rules of an established order. The situation before you is one of accelerated growth, and evokes the possibility of opportunities that are normally premature. Since rapid advancement is indicated, you should make an effort to align yourself to its positive aspects.

BECOMING GREAT serves as a message to get your affairs in order in many areas, especially in work and professional matters. At this time you want everything to be as perfect as possible, so you can plan carefully and work out every detail in advance. In summary, the time is one of rapid progress, upward movement, and greater authority over other people than you have experienced in the past. While this increase may range from an accidental happenstance to well-deserved recognition, it tends to be short in duration. Some success is certain because you are in the right place at the right time.

20

CONTEMPLATION

Summary: A need to look at something more closely. Viewing, study, and further survey. Investigation. You need to think in a new way. Meditation. Concentration or reflecting upon. Introspection. Rising above to consider something carefully. Grade: C+

In the time of **CONTEMPLATION** you should look at your overall goals and see what you must have to achieve them. If you keep yourself open to new opportunities, it will be relatively easy to make changes as necessary. You may now be attempting to act on your plans or make gains in the sphere of material possessions. However, the chances are great that you are not clear about what you need and want.

You should now relax, stand back and look into and behind the facts before you. **CONTEMPLATION** calls meditation and spiritual awareness to understand the underlying or hidden principles in the situation at hand. Although this kind of study is subjective, it tends to provide an intuitive awareness of your immediate and extended environment, as well as your future potentials. Through introspection you can get beyond surface appearances and penetrate to the foundation of what is happening.

On an inner level your values are changing. Your inner need for greater understanding may make your current situation inappropriate. If this happens, you may have to make changes to give yourself room for new growth. But these changes may not be obvious to you on the surface. As a result you should work to predict the future, or seek the services of someone who can.

Getting the **CONTEMPLATION** hexagram serves as a message to investigate the situation before you. It implies that the "whole," visible and invisible, ought to be studied. In fact, greater insights are needed before you can move forward. Additional study should now lead you to a closer involvement and understanding of hidden elements in the situation at hand. In short, **CONTEMPLATION** brings the potential to gain some practical understanding of what lies beyond outer appearances.

When they think they know the answers, people are difficult to guide. When they know that they don't know, people can find their own way.

Lao Tzu

21

BITING THROUGH

Summary: Dealing with difficulty. Reform. Taking decisive action to correct an injustice. Fighting it out or working through conflict. Separating innocence from guilt. Imposing penalties for wrongdoing. Attaining justice. Grade: F

BITING THROUGH calls for taking swift and decisive action against the corruption at hand. You must now make an effort to overcome ignorance, injustice, and wrongdoing. By taking the righteous course you master the life-denying forces, and avoid acting out of revenge. If you act now according to established laws and moral principles you can correct behaviors that undermine your efforts.

There are often two sides to the hexagram **BITING THROUGH**. On the one hand, you may be inclined to keep your opinions to yourself and not communicate them to others, even when you should. On the other hand you may be more in touch with your short-comings than at most other times. The first of these two effects may be inappropriate, but the ability to understand your liabilities can be useful.

You should now gear your efforts to dealing with your destructive traits or habits to move forward. You can do this by learning to recognize and follow the integrating principles at the center of all difficulty, your inner teacher. You should know that solutions from the inner world exist and stand ready to heal the corrupt elements before you. But if you hesitate or deny the possibility of change, you will put yourself in further difficulty. In the end, success is the result of taking tangible steps to correct the chaos at its roots.

At this time you may feel that others will hold anything you say against you. And this may be true. But it is even more likely that what you don't say will be held against you. As a result, is very important in the time of **BITING THROUGH** to say everything that has to be said. In this way you can eliminate all doubt and uncertainty both from other people's minds and from your own. Keeping secrets will only undermine others' confidence in you. If you keep the situation out in the open, it is less likely to work against you. But if you truly feel that silence will bring you peace of mind and be beneficial, of course seek it out.

As long as you are running away from your problem, you will continue to meet it in a new guise at every turn in the road.
Emmet Fox

22

DECORATION

Summary: An aesthetic form. One-dimensional thinking or view. Elegant. Ideal. Pleasant. An ornament. Existing only in theory and not in reality. An appearance of beauty in manner, form, and style. Graceful. Grade: C+

Today you are dealing with the beauty of an external form. Although this kind of form relates to some tradition, and has its own elegance, this form is not the essential or fundamental element. Your position demands greater honesty because what is apparent to you now is not the real things. While **DECORATION** is important for unity, significant issues must be examined with intellectual depth and thoroughness. You should avoid taking action or making decisions that you consider important or crucial. If such decisions are made, you are likely to regret them.

The theme of **DECORATION** is well described by the image of people at a picnic. As suggested by the picnic scene, you are prepared to deal only with the comfortable, positive, and ideal elements in the subject at hand. Your attitude is lighthearted and hopeful toward the fulfillment of your personal desires. While the time must come to get beyond your idealism, the time of this movement is not yet specified. But you should now make an effort to bridge the gap between your "ideal" and "reality."

At this time you may be inclined to identify yourself with what you own and what you value. If you have money or status or material possessions or even a good relationship, you may feel that you are a good person. If you don't, you may feel bad and discouraged quite apart from anything you have accomplished. While you are now acting as if you are what you have, you are not your possessions and such reactions are completely inappropriate.

DECORATION can give you the foolish confidence that anything you do will work out all right. You may take risks or indulge in gambling. In general, you are seeing the world through rose-colored glasses and are unwilling to look at the situation before you in the cold hard manner that is required.

SPLITTING APART

Summary: Inferior people and ideas crowd out the strong and superior. Splintering. Decline. Breaking up. A gradual undermining. Destruction. Deterioration. Breakdown. An increase in that which is inferior or objectionable. Decay. Wasted potential. Grade: D

SPLITTING APART denotes a situation in which the forces of collapse and decline are growing. You are dealing with natural or cyclical conditions instead of wrongdoing. Since it is impossible to avoid or counteract these conditions, you must adapt to them and remain quiet. At this time, it is not cowardice but wisdom to accept the current decline and avoid major actions. Although progress is denied for now, you can avoid real losses if you assist other people in realizing their goals.

In the time of **SPLITTING APART** you should work hard to actualize your ideals and find a concrete way to put your spiritual views into practice in the real world. However, you can expect the real world to put up some resistance to your ideas. No matter how high your vision is, you should not allow it to become an illusion or excuse for not dealing with the world.

During this period you may be impatient with the restrictions imposed by everyday existence, and you may be preoccupied with fantasies or ideas that help you escape the ordinary. You do not see things as they are and tend to think that they are something altogether more beautiful, or you are disgusted with your situation and reject it as unworthy of your full attention.

When **SPLITTING APART** comes up, the predominant forces in your environment emanate from outside and press on you from many sides. Your situation is depressing and your ability to improve it is nil. You may have too many irons in the fire. Although external influence is denied for now, you have an opportunity to pursue the deepest levels of the inner world. It is through this kind of pursuit that you can seek a way out of your dark and confining circumstances. While you should not expect big changes, you may work wonders behind the scenes. With untiring industry, practical ability, patience and clear vision you are bound for success.

Give evil nothing to oppose and it will disappear by itself.
Tao Te Ching

RENEWAL

Summary: Revitalization. Resurrection. Rebirth. An anniversary or return. The turning point from rest to activity. The act of making new or as if new again. Turning away from external confusion, and back to one's inner light. Grade: B

The hexagram **RENEWAL** denotes a time of awakening, and a change in state from "hibernation" to "activity." It marks the beginning of a new cycle in which things begin to grow and prosper. At this time, you are going through a natural change from the winter-like conditions of darkness to the spring-like conditions of sunrise. When it comes up you have passed the low point of a dormant period. Although the coming changes cannot be accelerated, natural improvements are indicated. Here, new growth is successful when it proceeds at its own slow, yet determined pace.

RENEWAL represents a promise of coming prosperity and growth in accordance with the natural order; all that is good in nature and society is on the increase. You may now be advised and perhaps chosen to reveal your new ideas or creative works at a slow but natural rate. This slow unveiling accords with the realistic process of expanding human awareness. It points to your capacity to respond to life's renewals that are always cyclic and predictable.

The overall effect of the hexagram **RENEWAL** is to open your mind to entirely new levels of consciousness. As your consciousness evolves, you will begin to associate with others whose views are similar, so that you can reinforce and strengthen each other's insights. In this way your ideas may be transformed, as well as your intentions and objectives.

This hexagram also denotes a time when emotional contact with friends is very important to you. You may expect contact between yourself and friends to become much deeper than it is now. If your existing friendships do not meet your needs, you will find new ones that do. A related effect of **RENEWAL** is to bring friends or close associates into your life, and in general you should find it easier to get along with them.

The Way is present before our eyes, yet what is before our eyes is hard to understand.
  The Secret of the Golden Flower

25

INNOCENCE

Summary: Simple, with no evil intent. Uninformed action that is free from defects or flaws. Purity. The unexpected or unintentional. Paradise. Faultlessness. Astounding. So remarkable as to elicit disbelief. Grade: C+

INNOCENCE denotes an outcome that is neither controllable nor predictable. It often points to an undesirable external element that is unplanned, unexpected, and unintentional. Although your response to this element may bring good rewards, the magnitude of your reward depends on the rightness of your action. Even actions that are innocent, spontaneous, and simple tend to fail when they are not in accord with the inner world.

This is an ideal time to express your subjective opinions, but it is not so favorable for reasoned logical communication. Your thinking may be so influenced by your feelings that it will be difficult to think through a situation from an objective position. While you might be quite capable of reasoning in the time of INNOCENCE, pure reason and logic alone cannot communicate all you want to express. If you happen to be upset, which is not indicated by this hexagram alone, others will find you very difficult to deal with, because you will be unable to see any position except your own. Consequently, if you have a problem that you cannot solve within yourself, this is a good time to talk it over with someone else or perhaps wash your hands of it altogether.

You now have or may expect to receive some temporary setback that you had not planned to get. While the outcome is uncertain, it is likely to be mysterious and fleeting. In this time of INNOCENCE, matters of great importance to you tend to be evaluated and communicated through feelings and emotions. However, matters that seem very important to you at the moment may be of little real significance. Your relations with others tend to be quite subjective, colored by personal considerations, and factually inaccurate. But by studying the range of what is possible and the extent to which you are prepared to deal with it, the events that follow may be handled with success.

Activity alone isn't enough; the activity must fit the circumstances.
David K. Reynolds

MAJOR ACCUMULATION

Summary: The result of building-up. A great accumulation and control of energy within a narrowly defined area. Potential Energy with no channel for expression. Restricted firmness and strength. Taming Power of The Great. A major restraint. Grade: C+

At this time, several important elements in your life are being centered, controlled, and aimed toward a single objective. This hexagram has much in common with water within a dam, the writing of a book, and pursuing a long-term course of study. Although outward movement is limited for now, **MAJOR ACCUMULATION** does imply being focused on a single goal. Generally, your success depends on being patient, holding steady, and continuing to nourish the same goal.

MAJOR ACCUMULATION denotes a time in which you are more concerned with personal matters and less with the world at large. Because you are wrapped up in your own concerns, you are likely to have a very subjective viewpoint on most matters. For this reason, you may find it difficult to work with others or stay with an established order.

The image of someone carving steps on the side of a mountain explains the nature of **MAJOR ACCUMULATION**. Your position is like the individual carving steps. You are now making a record of what you have learned; you are preparing a path for others to follow. Your task is fairly difficult. It is nothing less than attaining perfection to manifest your vision. The mountain scene also denotes your capacity to prepare for the future, and to use your will and physical strength. Even though progress may be gradual, you should focus on doing what is useful. In this way you can nurture the people around you and gain their respect as well.

This can be an energetic time. You may find that you can assert yourself effectively and accomplish a great deal of work. The problem is that you will be tested all along and forced to demonstrate the validity of what you are doing. You may be challenged either by circumstances or by other persons. Above all be careful that you don't become so wrapped up in your own beliefs that you cannot see which parts are essential and which are not.

27

NOURISHMENT

Summary: Evaluating one's character through observation Being aware that you becoming what you think and do. Following that which sustains the mind or spirit. Giving and receiving nourishment. Grade: A

    Getting **NOURISHMENT** refers to activities that tend to bring contentment, spiritual development, and inner peace. When it comes up your spiritual and material interests must be identified so that you can better evaluate what efforts have your full support. When this is done, you can apply limits and care over the thoughts that enter your mind, and the words that leave your mouth. You should seek the "right" or spiritual nutrition first, and not be tempted by the material elements around you. At this time, your success depends on seeking an inner instead of an outer-directed course.

    NOURISHMENT often indicates a challenge to some of your basic beliefs. This should not be regarded as a threat, however, because the adjustments you must make now could prove quite valuable later on. You can correct your approach to a number of activities without too many difficulties now, while later you may be so committed that you cannot change.

    You are now able to give or receive some kind of food for your advantage. When **NOURISHMENT** comes up you are gathering fruit. This hexagram refers to some kind of harvest. If the fruit is good, your efforts will be fitting; but if the fruit is spoiled your efforts will produce negative results. If your personal interests are subordinate to interests that enhance your spiritual growth, superior **NOURISHMENT** follows.

    At worst this hexagram denotes a maturing experience, but at best it represents an opportunity to transform you into a better human being. This does not necessarily mean that your present nutrition is right or wrong, but that you should reexamine the elements you support. Your position is now one of acting upon or promoting your own growth.

Everyone automatically attracts to himself just what he is....
    Ernest Holmes

28

EXCESS YANG

Summary: Too aggressive. A loss of balance. A condition of going or being beyond what is needed, desired, or appropriate. Overindulgence. An imbalance or excess. Preponderance of The Great. Grade: D

Getting **EXCESS YANG** serves as a message that you are threatened by outside pressures that cannot be overcome with a single sweep. It denotes a condition or situation of intemperance that cannot last; if it is not changed, you can expect failures. All of your problems cannot be solved now, but you can guard against the tensions created by them. At this time, success can be attained by insight and gentle movements toward centrality, harmony and balance.

When this **EXCESS YANG** comes up every little desire to act that you have suppressed is likely to surface and demand your full attention in some way. The old concerns you have within yourself or those accepted from others are no longer acceptable now, and you feel the need to act even if you have to break away from many things that seem important to you. As you change your way of handling the many issues before you, you will become open to experiences that you would never have considered, and you may adopt a whole new outlook. In short, new avenues are beginning to open, and if you allow yourself to receive them, you will gain new directions for your future.

If you keep your mind from judging and aren't led by the senses, your heart will find peace.
Tao Te Ching

In the time of **EXCESS YANG** you are crossing a bridge that can't support you. You are weighted down with too many concerns, either internal or external, and you must let go of something. If you don't let go your journey will come to an end. You should avoid forcible measures to simplify your life; instead, you should help before trying to continue. Since the idea or thing to be given up is too great to be reasonable or acceptable, you must choose what to keep and what to discard.

In addition, the time calls for setting limits, identifying your options, and moving toward specific goals. Generally, you are feeling the need to assert your individuality against all the forces that have been blocking its expression in the past. It is imperative that you establish some priorities and act upon those that are most important.

29

DANGER

Summary: An abysmal situation. Hardship. Something unfathomable. Hidden emotions. Exposure to potential harm, loss, or injury. Engulfed by desires and passions. External difficulty or inner turmoil. Grade: D

At this time you are facing a condition or situation characterized by danger, distress, or annoyance. Getting **DANGER** serves as a message that you are, or will be, surrounded by external or internal difficulties and opposing tendencies that require great effort to overcome. You may be in danger of being engulfed by your desires and passions. Since this condition will not go away you cannot go forward with full inner knowledge, and an objective awareness about what lies ahead. Once you have gained an inner solution, and understand what is natural, your actions will tend to succeed. If you can accept your limitations, all that really counts is going forward instead of being defeated.

At this time there is tension in your life, but it can be used creatively if you are conscious of what you are doing. If you are not, **DANGER** can signify a time of conflicts, especially with those close to you, such as your spouse and others with whom you must cooperate, partners, co-workers, and such. Generally, this is a period of testing and confrontation that will reveal the pressures and tensions in those relationships, as well as the positive and strong points.

When **DANGER** comes up you are pushing your way through a mob. The disorderly crowd suggests that you are dealing with annoying people. You are influenced by excessive enthusiasm, unclear thinking, and aggressive efforts to move ahead of other people. Your advancement is difficult because the people around you tend to oppose your direction and principles. The time points to some kind of power struggle. To be effective you man have to give up your individuality and pursue popular goals. While this action may lead to remarkable progress, the path of the many is almost always centered in material rather than spiritual values.

30

RADIANCE

Summary: Gaining Clarity. Objective thinking. Fire. Brilliance. Being liable for or responsible for another. Discrimination. Related to or dependent upon someone whose intentions are unknown to you. Cooperation. Outer strength, inner weakness. Grade: C+

You are dealing with a time or condition in which your position in relation to others is that of leader or head of household. Your position should be seen as a force like day rather than night, yang rather than yin, creative rather than receptive, etc. In the time of **RADIANCE** your success is the result of partnership activity in which each member or unit is dependent on the role and respect of the other. Because your position depends upon others, you should go beyond the normal expectations to cooperate with them. By examining your role, and making changes where needed, you can eliminate the elements that tend to work against you and support those that tend to nurture the relationship.

The hexagram **RADIANCE** denotes a relationship that is both difficult and cooperative in nature. This happens because the foreground elements attain their definition and prominence from elements in the background. In short, your active and outgoing force is dependent on passive and withdrawn personalities. Consequently, you should not allow your brightness to blind you to the passive nature of others. Although your situation may be less than ideal, you can achieve your aims if the opposing forces before you are made to work in harmony and support one another.

The benefits of **RADIANCE** do not limit themselves to activities with friends. Any situation in which you deal with many people in a group setting, for example a business conference or organization, is favored by this hexagram. This is not a time when you should try to go it alone, nor should you limit yourself to working with one other person. You may need to be with many people; through working with them you can learn a great deal about yourself. Friends may be more than usually supportive and you can make new friends who will prove to be extremely valuable as time goes one. But this will not be a one-way street, for you will help them also.

31

INFLUENCE

Summary: Persuasion. Attraction. Interaction. Courtship. To make an impression upon. Advertisement. The power to produce an effect by indirect means. The act, condition, or effect of exerting force on someone or something. Grade: C-

    At this time you are able to **INFLUENCE** someone or something by indirect means. You now have an interest in forming of some kind of partnership between yourself and another. Although the initiative is yours, you should subordinate your interests and free yourself of personal motives and prejudice. You can achieve your goal with minimal effort if you allow the person or object of your interest to inspire and change you. If you remain centered and seek what is good for you your actions will lead to progress.
    At this time you have the power to **INFLUENCE** people and sway them to your point of view. However, this power is quite limited. If you try to convince other people from a purely self-centered position rather from a real concern for their interests, you may provoke opposition that could lead to defeat. Even if you do not try to coerce others with your ideas, others may attempt to coerce you. In either case, you should recognize whether these motives are egotistical or whether they are helpful.
    You have a strong urge to persuade, effect and change another's thinking about some matter that you are interested in. If you can identify exactly what you are seeking you will soon be on the right tract for finding what you want. At best you may encourage others to follow your lead because of a genuine concern for attaining what is good; at worst you may be stubborn and concerned only with fulfilling your self-interest.
    When **INFLUENCE** comes up your position is one of leading others out of darkness with a flash light. Your position is one of providing leadership and insight to others in spite of their limited awareness about your intentions. To be effective you should use your knowledge to assist those who seek it or those who choose to follow it. This hexagram also refers to mutual attractions through common bonds, principles, and shared visions. While you may now persuade another to follow your lead, your good intentions will be wasted if they are insincere and attached to having the other person follow your lead.

Nothing can come into our experience unless it finds something in us with which it is attuned.
Emmet Fox

DURATION

Summary: Self-contained and self-renewing movement. Constancy. Continuity. Permanence. Made to last. Longevity. Endurance. Persistence. Uninterrupted existence or growth. Unswerving movement toward a single goal. Grade: B

DURATION denotes a time or condition in which your movement is persistent, well organized, and not worn down by obstacles. If allowed to continue, this movement will lead you to success through completion. Your present course is in harmony with your inner teacher, yet aimed at practical and tangible goals. By remaining flexible regarding opportunities to move or remaining still, you can keep abreast of the times and change with them. By staying focused on a single direction, you can avoid the distraction of jumping from one thing to another.

In the time of **DURATION** you may emerge from comparative dormancy, at least in terms of outward success, and begin to move upward and forward to achieve your ambitions. Now is a good time to plan for the future in all areas of your life, because you are neither foolishly optimistic nor excessively conservative. You can adopt a very careful and pragmatic attitude and see what needs to be done.

No matter what you are doing now the presence of this hexagram stimulates you to discover what you need to make your life fulfilling. If you have been successful in your dealings with the outside world, you will continue to be, but now it will have to mean something in terms of your own life and perception. If you have not been successful, you may be inclined to throw out the old and adopt new directions that will better fit your needs.

The theme of this hexagram, and therefore **DURATION**, is well described by the image of a road being built into a new territory. Your position is like the new road builder, a pioneer, a doer. In essence, you are now making a record or steps in a new area that can be used by other people. Generally, this scene denotes endurance and a long-term commitment to attain valuable goals. It suggests that you have a solid foundation and strong roots in the situation at hand. In short, the attainment of significant goals in indicated. While these goals are well-worth waiting for, they cannot be achieved in a single sweep.

If our reliance is upon anything but our own understanding of Truth, our work will cease to be fruitful.
Emmet Fox

RETREAT

Summary: Withdrawal. Backing down. Letting go and letting God. Remain in the background and wait or move forward suffer. Keeping your activities within certain limits. A need to change your position or course of action. Yielding for the present time. Grade: D

This hexagram advises you to **RETREAT** because of an increase in both opposing and inferior forces. At this time the forces that lay ahead of you are so powerful and frustrating that it is best to withdraw before them. Even though falling back will not lead to progress in the short-run, it points to success in the end. Since you will experience difficulties that cannot be resolved in a single forward sweep, it is best to withdraw until they have passed.

When **RETREAT** comes up you are leaving the main road to take a separate path. In this way you can keep your distance from the dangers that lie ahead. Although the time calls for losing ground in the beginning, protection is found in stepping back. This separation or withdrawal should be proud and confident instead of a cowardly fight. After this has been accomplished you can then study the situation and advance when the time is right.

Getting **RETREAT** serves as a message to let go of the past and make plans for a fresh start. You may feel pressure for tremendous changes both in the direction you are going and in the manner of proceeding in that direction. However, it is best to withdraw into yourself and observe and recognize without making judgments or evaluations. In this way you can get more in tune with what is happening.

At this time your power lies on the subjective level, and when you understand how to tap that power, you will be able to attain any goal you set for yourself. As unresolved problems come to the surface it may be necessary to endure some difficult feelings without acting them out. Your efforts to control these tensions as they arise will eventually work to your advantage.

Rather than make the first move it is better to wait and see. Rather than advance an inch it is better to retreat a yard.
Tao Te Ching

34

GREAT POWER

Summary: Great strength. Excessive power. Pride. Going beyond the mean. Being great and right. The state or quality of being strong. A Napoleonic complex. An effective means of influencing, compelling or forcing. Grade: A

GREAT POWER has come up because your inner worth and influence has increased to the point of expressing itself in the outer physical world. Since this increase is already beyond what is needed impulsive moves may be damaging. If you forget what is natural and show off your strength you can expect any rise to the top to be followed by a fall. Success is indicated as long as you accept the responsibilities at hand.

GREAT POWER denotes strong ego tendencies, emotional intensity and strength. But if you hurry you may lose the right course, and your position will be much less than it could have been, if you had taken enough time to find your truth. Because your desire nature is excessive you may experience much pain and suffering if you don't control it. Another danger signaled by getting this hexagram is that you may become so focused on external affairs, e.g., your job, social prestige, partner, status, etc., that you overlook what is happening in your personal life.

At this time you have the greatest opportunity to make an impression upon the world as an individual. In your personal and professional life, you may gain many responsibilities. You may feel that prestige and making money are more important than service. If you are ambitious for leadership, the situation at hand will offer that opportunity as well.

On a deeper level, getting **GREAT POWER** suggests that you are willing to trust your insights about relationships and meaning of things, regardless of established authority. The essence of this hexagram may be described by the image of new grass sprouting on a barren mountain. The mountain may be seen as some kind of established order, obstacle, goal or perhaps a structure. The appearance of new grass suggests that your situation is shifting from the sterile and fruitless to the productive and fruitful. According to this image the situation at hand represents a rebirth that is powerful, growing, and full of energy. It serves as a message that you are now, or soon will be, in a position of great influence over others.

35

PROGRESS

Summary: External progress that fall short of your expectations. Rising. Social advantage. Easy expansion. Stepping forward. Steady improvement or development. Reaching for prosperity, victory or honor. Clarity of mind. Grade: B

In the situation at hand you are extending yourself in some way to raise the awareness of others. **PROGRESS** stands as a symbol of expansion and clarity of vision. At this time your success is dependent upon other people who are willing to follow your lead. It is this kind of partnership that leads to advancement. Real betterment only occurs when external circumstances support the direction of your movement.

Getting this hexagram serves as a message that you are receiving more than you can integrate into your present structure or place in life. The mental picture of a one cup container being filled beyond its limit explains a central dynamic of **PROGRESS**. This scene refers to an excess of insight or recognition or possibilities or even things both received and wasted. Generally, this activity tends to be desirable because those on the receiving end gain something of value even though most of it is wasted. While the benefits represented by this hexagram often look good you may lack the ability to manage them. As a result, you should attempt to distinguish between your intentions or expectations and what is really possible.

At this time your social activities tend to be related in some manner to business and professional affairs. You may feel ambitious for material wealth and status. Generally, **PROGRESS** denotes an enhanced social reputation and increased desire for social prestige and position. This period often coincides with public exposure, personal public appearances, or personal recognition for achievements, even if these are associated with everyday affairs. However, this worldly success can be maintained only when you learn to control your emotions.

DEFEAT OF THE LIGHT

36

Summary: Being surrounded by people with limited vision or knowledge of what you are trying to do. Submitting to censorship. An eclipse. Wounding of the light. A time to conceal your awareness. Grade: C+

DEFEAT OF THE LIGHT refers to situations in which people of limited vision tend to dominate those with wisdom and clarity of mind about their direction. At this time your position is as that of the bright subordinate employed by an ignorant superior. As a result, it is best to remain quiet and accepting in the midst of those who have the power. You should let many things pass as the people in power don't recognize your knowledge. Speaking up at this time will tend to create difficulty and unnecessary pressure.

In the time of **DEFEAT OF THE LIGHT** you should be reticent in expressing your honest feelings and opinions to avoid possible unpleasantness. You may find it necessary to subordinate your desire for self-expression to the needs of the present. To make the best of this time you should be willing to work with others to resolve any difficulties that may arise. In communicating with other people it is best to test out your ideas and see how they react to them.

Getting this hexagram is not a good sign for negotiating any difficult or contentious matters, because you are likely to exercise poor judgment. Even though your ideas may be correct you may experience difficulty in getting them recognized. This is not a time to retreat, but it does indicate a challenge to some of your basic beliefs. This should not be regarded as a threat because the adjustments you must make in your thinking now could prove valuable later on.

DEFEAT OF THE LIGHT calls for an effort to overcome confusion. It points to operating in the dark and attempting to find a way out. Here we see that those in power have a dim view of the future and are likely to make mistakes. Because of these limitations you should not attempt to step forward, but instead wait for better times to return. Although you are surrounded by confusion for the time being, an inner light may be found to assist you in spite of external difficulties. If this light is followed you will not be swept into harms way.

What is a good man but a bad man's teacher? What is a bad man but a good man's teacher?

Lao Tzu

37

THE FAMILY

Summary: Unity and mutual respect between partners in relationship. A satisfying arrangement, agreement or design. Order among opposites. Integration. Harmony between male and female, yang and yin, light and dark, etc. Grade: B

THE FAMILY refers to the integration of opposing and often conflicting natures. As such it suggests a natural state in which the interpersonal elements before come together or adapt to one another in harmony. This pleasing arrangement of differing tendencies expresses the central principle of unity: the integration of opposites. This hexagram points to an important spiritual law: there is no limit to your expansion. It serves as a reminder that all influence and expansion works from within and then widens to include the outer world.

Getting THE FAMILY favors most personal relationships because you are able to negotiate on the basis of your real needs and self-understanding while appreciating the other person's real needs. Since you understand and accept your role in the relationship at hand whatever you choose will be mutually profitable. You may even identify your own objectives with that of the relationship. Generally, you feel secure in yourself and are willing to help those close to you achieve their objective.

The theme of THE FAMILY is well described by the image of symmetrical buildings in an urban setting. It reminds us of traditional forms, stability, and order. The organization of families, groups, or religious institutions can serve as examples for the situation at hand. They all stress the realization and value of harmonious endeavors. This hexagram also brings the negative possibility that too much harmony may be unhealthy and defeat your purpose.

When THE FAMILY comes up, the bonds in personal relationships as well as small groups tend to become stronger. Today it is wise to give thanks to the universe, to your ancestors, to your neighbors, to yourself, and to everything you deal with. By expanding your thoughts to your world and every object in it your idea of God will shift from being abstract to being near at hand as well. Your personal needs will not conflict with the demands of your group or partnership if you base them on a realistic understanding of who you are and what others need from you. In addition, your existing friendships or partnerships will be renewed.

38

OPPOSITION

Summary: Contradictions. Alienation. Feeling distant and perhaps hostile. Antithesis. Duality. Conflict. Two things being diametrically opposed. Unsympathetic. Diverging viewpoints. Differentiation by categories. Grade: D

This can be an extremely confusing hexagram because new information and data may not fit your preconceptions. You should make an extra effort to understand the views of other people. You may learn from them. Because you see and understand facets of life that were never apparent before, this may be an exciting time.

When **OPPOSITION** comes up you may lack a definite position or direction and seek to view things with neutrality. This comes about because whatever you believe, its opposite seems to have just as much validity. Generally, you are involved in a situation where opposing conditions or forces such as yang and yin, optimistic and pessimistic, rich and poor, art and science, etc., tend to neutralize themselves into a stalemate. Yet, despite this divergence small achievements are possible; and these achievements provide the foundation for success.

The time of **OPPOSITION** forces you to look at life in a new way and to see things that you have never seen before, and to communicate with others in new ways. To be successful you must understand those who oppose you and learn to work with views that contradict your view. You will have to give little everyday details the same attention that you previously reserved for exceptionally significant ones. This happens because these details contain the germ of changes that will revolutionize your consciousness if you are willing to let them. If you are not willing and are consciously or unconsciously unwilling to accept what appears to be opposite, everything that happens will upset you.

The symbolic picture of a large building and small shack standing together explains the nature of **OPPOSITION.** This picture describes a condition in which the exalted and the low exist together. It points to the contradictions between what is superior and what is inferior.

39

OBSTACLES

Summary: Obstruction. Trouble. Difficulty. Blockage. Prohibition. Hinderance. A barrier that cannot be overcome in the short-run. A situation that impedes or prevents entry or passage. An inconvenience. A state of uneasiness. Grade: F

Getting **OBSTACLES** will test how well you have put your life together in almost every area, but especially in matters related to finances, relationships and your profession. At this time your opportunities may be curtailed and your freedom of action may be quite limited. Restrictions seem to come from nowhere, and you may have to work very hard just to maintain your accustomed level, let alone improve it.

OBSTACLES denotes something that stands in the way of progress and requires great effort to overcome. It serves as a message that the situation before you is not easy to do, achieve, or master. Yet without this difficulty there can be no achievement or breakthrough. Under the present circumstances, success comes about when you let go of your intended goal, instead of battling the trouble head on. In short, it is best to remain still instead of complicating matters with impatience and struggle.

When this hexagram comes up you should wait until you have acquired the strength and maturity to move forward. Getting **OBSTACLES** advises you to delay the gratification of your current goal until the time of fulfillment has arrived. It serves as a message to examine the problem, and take the time to consider what form of discipline is the most appropriate to your needs. In the longrun, your success depends upon completing the task that faces you.

Because of the course you have chosen you may experience a considerable amount of tension. For a time you may be confused, not quite knowing whether to go backward or forward, to expand or cut back. Generally, it may be best to go off by yourself for a while as other people's advice will be of little value. In order to turn things around you must believe that your inner teacher works through you to will and do some particular mission.

At this time you may learn an important spiritual truth. The moment you see that good things are really coming to you from the Self within, despite appearances, everything looks different to you (better) than it did before. The lesson here is that certain ideas produce certain conditions. If for instance you believe that an **OBSTACLES** prevent you from attaining your goal you will unwittingly give that barrier a great deal of power over you. Recall Jobs cry in the old testament, "The thing that I feared has come upon me."

Problems do not go away. They must be worked through or else they remain, forever a barrier to growth and development of the spirit.
M. Scott Peck

40

SOLUTION

Summary: Deliverance. Liberation. To be set free. Being rescued from inner danger or confinement. Renewed growth. An emotional breakthrough. Submitting to a cause or another person. A position reached after consideration. Grade: B

SOLUTION represents that quality of mind that enables you to face danger or hardship resolutely from a place of inner strength. It points to the power to make choices and set goals, and to act upon them firmly in spite of opposition or difficulty. It may be seen as a message to listen to your inner teacher even if it seems opposite to what you would have thought. Today you have an opportunity to free yourself from something objectionable or undesirable. Although success is indicated, there is danger: You may lose yourself in the joy of liberation. However, if you proceed with caution, until the danger is behind you, true salvation is likely.

Your grasp of what you can and cannot do is being tested now, and it is very important that you accept the actual limitations on your life. Getting **SOLUTION** serves as a test of your grasp of reality and your ability to translate ideals into practice. There is no reason to assume that you will not pass the test, but you do have to be careful. **SOLUTION** serves as a message that the source of your trouble lies more within than outside. It is well described by the image of a mountain climber reducing his load to continue climbing. This image suggests an interest in achievement, maturity, and transcending the ordinary problems in life. It serves as a message that you have the capacity to let go, to transcend and therefore transform your own nature. By reducing your load to continue your present journey you may exhibit an act of the greatest courage.

On another level **SOLUTION** can signify the rather false optimism that makes you take foolish risks; especially with limited resources. You may well be challenged to demonstrate that your ideals are not irrelevant or impractical. You may be called upon to demonstrate that your views depend upon realism rather than the dream world, which is where you may very well be now.

41

DECREASE

Summary: External loss. Sacrifice. To diminish or grow less. A cutback or reduction of that which is excessive. A loss sustained in the accomplishment of, or as a result of trying to build up something. Grade: D

DECREASE refers to an act or process of reducing the length, amount, duration, etc., of some activity or development. It represents the condition of being deprived of what you once had or should have had. This comes about because your external resources are used to support or follow your inner-directed goals. If you fail to accept this decline you can expect serious losses. At this time your success will depend upon shifting and perhaps giving up some of your resources without losing your stability. By drawing upon the strength of your inner attitude you can compensate for what is lacking in your outer physical world.

When **DECREASE** comes up you are settling old debts. It is possible that you are beginning a new phase of growth or completing an old one. Even though something is sure to be diminished in the situation at hand, the seeds of a new way are present as well. This hexagram suggests as well that your external resources have and will be employed for continued self-improvement. To be effective you should make an effort to use your knowledge and resources to air your future growth.

The time of **DECREASE** is best spent in understanding that you are in the midst of a natural cycle in your life. Nothing is gained by fighting it; instead you must learn to flow with it. You are now at the end of an old cycle and the beginning of a new one. If you are patient, opportunities will soon return for success and achievement.

You are not especially happy with what you feel you are facing now. Your job may have fallen into a dull routine, or you may feel caught in some kind of relationship or activity that limits your self-expression. Quite frequently **DECREASE** brings an end to such circumstances. For best results, you should look inward to determine what to give away or make as an offering.

Every phenomenon has two sides. For Everything there is benefit and harm, gaining and losing.

David K. Reynolds

42

INCREASE

Summary: External gain or benefit. Improvement. Good luck. Growth and multiplication. A state of prospering and increases in well-being. Optimism. Generosity. Unexpected improvement. A benevolent influence leading to growth. Grade: A

Getting **INCREASE** means that you are approaching life in the here and now, from moment to moment. Unexpected benefits from grants, insurance, joint finances, corporate money, government funding, and inheritance, along with unusual opportunities for expansion of your affairs, characterize the situation at hand. Because you are open-minded, there is a good possibility of a breakthrough that will enable you to achieve something worthwhile. Your everyday activities should bring new and interesting opportunities for expansion that open up aspects of life that you have not encountered before.

Everyone automatically attracts to himself just what he is....
Ernest Holmes

INCREASE denotes a positive state of health, upswing happiness, enlargement, and success. This has come about because your inner resources or vision is showing up in some outer-directed goal. At this time you have the insight and motivation to correct your faults. Despite difficulty or danger, the inner world alone has the power to help you. The time of **INCREASE** tends to be short-term and contains the seeds of decrease; it must be used while it lasts. Overall, you have an enormous opportunity to broaden yourself and encounter tremendous new experiences that will make your life much more interesting and rewarding.

On a mundane level **INCREASE** favors all forms of business and commercial activity. It is symbolic of the transition from spring to summer. It deals with an improvement in your external influence, and often the experience of generous acts. This hexagram serves as a favorable sign for making progress and moving forward. This is possible because you are approaching adulthood, maturity and a time of harvest. Your personal efforts to gain spiritual and worldly achievements are becoming visible. This is one of the few times in life that can be characterized as lucky. You should experience this time as one of excitement, without pushing the tempo to the point that you can no longer enjoy it.

43

BREAKTHROUGH

Summary: Resoluteness. Going out. Speaking the truth openly. Awakening. Making up one's mind. Making a decision. Advancement through cooperation or teamwork. Resolute action. Grade: C+

Getting **BREAKTHROUGH** signals a change for the better. It denotes a situation in which inferior conditions and ignorance begin to disappear. This accelerates when you follow just and definite rules to deal with your shortcomings. To transcend limited thinking your attitude should be friendly but uncompromising. You cannot fight darkness with evil motives or deception; you must deal with the truth and openly discredit all else. As a rule, it is best to seek out possibilities for growth and expansion instead of accepting limitations. In addition, you should take steps toward what is good instead of engaging your adversaries in battle or by force.

There is a potential here for conflict with people who don't oppose your intentions, but who unknowingly have taken a position that conflicts with yours. This is not the time to assume blindly that you know wherein all truth lies. You may identify your ego with your personal viewpoints to the extent that your ability to perceive reality is distorted.

Generally, **BREAKTHROUGH** serves as a message that you are now able to see the correct answers to problems that have blocked your movement for some time. Today you may solve significant problems and reach desired conclusions, yet the situation still requires attention to details. You must now deal with some paradox or mystery or missing piece of information to the situation before you. To move forward requires cooperation, agreement and perhaps the forming of a new partnership. You should fully communicate with others about your intentions to overcome obstacles.

The time of **BREAKTHROUGH** tends to produce interactions with others that test the clarity of your thinking and force you to prove the validity of what you say. If you have been bottling up pressures in your activities they will become very difficult to bear now, especially if you have not been willing to face them in the recent past.

Prevent trouble before it arises. Put things in order before they exist.
Tao Te Ching

44

MEETING OF OPPOSITES

Summary: A false appearance of reward. A one-sided advance or meeting half-way. A temptation leading to contention and struggle. A risk-taking activity. A confrontation that may lead to danger or greatness. Grade: D

MEETING OF OPPOSITES deals with an effort on your part to expand the awareness of other people within your environment. Today you are prematurely exposing this unknown quantity to others. Because you are acting before thinking you are increasing the potential for contention and struggle. Generally, you are attempting to enlighten others even though your position makes it impossible to do so. While your outreach may touch everyone in time, and serve to influence many, you should begin with step-by-step movement toward your goal.

This hexagram depicts a situation in which evil or inferior elements, after having been eliminated, are unexpectedly placed in a position of power. Although you are dealing with positive and negative interests, **MEETING OF OPPOSITES** comes up when you fail to distinguish between the life denying and life affirming forces in the situation at hand. At the present time your intended course is unfortunate and even dangerous; you are weak or hampered in some way. But if you control your desire for action and rightly use it, significant achievements are possible. If your motives are honest, and you proceed with caution, something great may be accomplished.

When **MEETING OF OPPOSITES** comes up the effects you experience may be either very subtle or very blatant. If you push things, your intentions will create a confrontation, which will force a transformation of some kind in your life. For example, you may encounter some knowledge or person that has a powerful effect upon you and causes you to change.

At this time you may be tempted to take over and run whatever is happening around you. You may work very hard to further your own interests and come on with much more vigor than needed. In the end, your experiences should lead in either great or small ways to transforming how you assert yourself in the world.

When man interferes with the Tao, the sky becomes filthy, the earth becomes depleted, the equilibrium crumbles, creatures become extinct.

Lao Tzu

45

REUNION

Summary: A assembling of those of harmonious spirit. A gathering based on shared bonds or goals. Accumulation. Congregation. Constant movement toward moral goals. A peaceful and happy group meeting. Coming together. Grade: A

Generally, **REUNION** deals with giving and receiving spiritual advice. The image of several people gathered around one teacher describes this hexagram rather well. This symbolic picture depicts the development of understanding and wisdom based on interpersonal and group relationships. It suggests that you are assisting others or being assisted to step beyond the past and limited conditions.

When **REUNION** comes up you may increase your understanding of yourself and your goals, as well as of others and their goals. This is a good time to examine your goals and expectations. How well are you working to attain them? What kind of aid can you enlist from others? While opportunities for assistance are likely at this time, you will have to recognize them and be quick enough to take them.

Getting **REUNION** announces a time to congregate, to move forward, and to be creative. Under its influence, you may have an opportunity to gather diverse energies to accomplish a common goal. At this time you have an opportunity for renewal and for gathering positive forces around you. This gathering could represent involvement with new ideas, social goals, or the ideals of a political movement. When the forces behind the gathering are moral the group tends to be harmonious. But when morals are weak the group tends to be scattered. Even though success is indicated, you should avoid having too many attachments in the situation at hand.

REUNION denotes a time when psychological forces will change your relationship to your inner teacher quite noticeably. You may become attracted to spiritual subjects as a direct result of your own experience. You are more concerned now about the deeper truths hidden behind the appearances of the everyday world. In addition, you may experience an increase in your sensitivity to everything that happens around you, especially to the feelings and moods of others, even their thoughts to some extent.

46

ASCENDING

Summary: Promotion. Pushing upward. Flourishing. All that looks well. Advancing or rising with harmony. Attaining a higher status, rank or condition. The power and ability to begin and follow-through by adapting to obstacles. Grade: A

Getting **ASCENDING** refers to an increase in your personal fame or recognition. It is a sign that you are becoming full of certainty that what seems good is good. Your outlook will remain young if you refuse to be deceived. At this time you are very concerned with form and order and want to incorporate it into your life. This tendency may extend to organizing the people around you as well. You now have an opportunity to know yourself through your relationships and your effect upon your environment.

ASCENDING is a sign of new power and life after a period of sleeping. Today you have the strength of youth and fearlessness. The meaning is this hexagram is summed up in the image of a dead man climbing out of his grave. This image is a sign that conditions have reached a state in which your conscious, rational ego is no longer a controlling factor. When your awareness moves beyond its attachment to past conditions, a new surge of life will eventually emerge. Although progress is often gradual in the beginning, rapid and long-lasting growth is evident in the end.

The presence of **ASCENDING** serves as a message that you are stepping into the limelight, either on a small or a large scale, depending upon the normal course of your life. Everything that happens at this time tells you how you stand toward your premise. Someone may call upon you to take over the direction of a task or project in which you will have considerable power. At this time you do not have to be very strong or competent to succeed, because the natural flow of energies is with you. But you should examine your life as a whole and see if you are going in the direction you want and making adequate progress in your life. Whatever comes up to divert your thoughts, go back again and again to your purpose.

ASCENDING denotes advancement through steady growth. It is a sign of opportunity and rising to prominence through effort. Your intended direction is now supported by the world around you. If you keep your mind on your intentions and avoid being diverted, you can expect fulfillment. This kind of advancement comes about because the forces of expansion are unrestricted in the situation at hand. This outcome strengthens if you learn to bend around any obstacles with modesty and adaptability.

47

EXHAUSTION

Summary: Adversity. Mental and physical tensions. Misfortune. Embarrassment. Spent. Oppression. Entrapment. Unlucky. A stifling situation. Relationship problems. Weariness. A condition of suffering, destitution, or fatigue. Grade: F

EXHAUSTION refers to powerful internal forces for change colliding with powerful resistance from the external world. It comes at a time when your patience is exhausted or at an end. At this time you may take sudden actions to release your self from tensions that the people around you have not anticipated. These actions result from tension gradually building within you. You may suddenly leave a relationship, an oppressive job or your place of residence, without warning anyone. Despite every effort to free yourself, circumstances, duties and obligations seem to hold you back and keep you stuck in an oppressive situation.

In times of EXHAUSTION you may expect limited support or assistance in manifesting your vision or pursuing your goal or completing your work. Today you are weighted down with excessive concerns or attachments of some kind. Generally, your situation is oppressive and signifies the necessity for inner direction or help to avoid complete fatigue. You may be engaged in a struggle with some person or endeavor that is difficult to move or influence. Since you will accomplish nothing through struggle, you should accept the difficulty and seek inner stability. If you find it difficult to work with others or cooperate in teamwork, you may feel that co-workers and friends are getting in your way. They may give you responsibilities that you don't want.

EXHAUSTION denotes a situation in which you are besieged by inner and outer enemies. Your situation is analogous to being on an island surrounded by shark-infested waters. You are surrounded by dangers, but the greater the danger the greater the opportunity for inner growth. Today, you may be denied outward influence because your words and actions have no effect on the people around you. Consequently, it is best to remain private and minimize your dependence upon external circumstances. In this way your inner stability may become the source of later successes.

He who shown firmness in the midst of surging miseries solidifies a firm character.
Emma Curtis Hopkins

48

THE WELL

Summary: A fountain, spring or reservoir to help and nourish all who use it. Self-expression. Consciousness. To emit, originate, or come forth in abundance. An awareness of what constitutes your essential nature. An assertion of individual traits. Grade: B

Getting **THE WELL** serves as a message that the course you are planning reflects your essential nature. It points to an opportunity to fulfill the inborn abilities that constitute your real or ideal self. At this time you are following your intuitive senses instead of pursuing an outer-directed course. You may now avoid the dangers of being inflexible or attached to outside relationships. Even though you tend to intuit the truth and to trust your judgment at this time, you should back them up with solid facts before acting.

At this time the perspective of your life may expand tremendously. You may have opportunities for self-expression, for learning and for teaching others in either a formal or an informal setting. You may have an emotional experience that enriches you, or a business opportunity, or work with aspects of yourself that you do not normally experience, but which help you attain complete self-understanding.

Without any intentional, fancy way of adjusting yourself, to express yourself as you are is the most important thing.
Shunryu Suzuki

When the **THE WELL** comes up you are standing at the center of the universe. It suggests fulfillment, peace of mind, and the nourishing of spiritual growth. Your self-development may now become a source of nourishment when you offer your services to others. The hexagram points to having faith in your inner teacher. Even though no issue is clear or direct you can trust your insights to bring the various components of your situation together.

This is a good time to become involved in a human-potential effort or some other consciousness-raising group. There are many such groups around now, and you should pick the one that seems most suitable for you. **THE WELL** may signify that you are in the public's eye or that you have to deal with large groups of people in some way. You may take a rather paternal attitude toward the people around you, want to protect them and take on their troubles as your own.

49

CHANGING

Summary: Revolution. Transformation. A momentous or sweeping shift. Self-renewal and self-evolution. Changing sides. Overturning. A significant change from the old to the new. Upheaval. A major change in appearance or direction. Grade: B

CHANGING comes at a time when something comes up to challenge you. Can you be yourself and periodically renew your life so that it doesn't become stale? Your goal should now be to create a situation of change in your life so that you don't have to experience a sudden revolution or live with something that doesn't change at all. Don't wait until circumstances have become totally intolerable before you try to reform.

CHANGING refers to natural, yet sweeping changes. It advises you to accept the present transformation instead of resisting the opportunity it brings. You should let go of the old to move toward what is new and right. But if you attempt to advance too soon or hold to the past you will lose your position. Your success will depend on CHANGING at the right time; failure will be the result of either premature or delayed change. While it is difficult to perceive or define what will happen in the immediate future, the present movement relates to your security.

CHANGING announces a sweeping shift between your present position and the future. If you ignore this shift or treat it as irrelevant, your problems will persist and grow larger. It serves as a message that your world has changed or is going to change so much that your original experience of the present situation will no longer have the meaning for you that it once had. As of today your success will no longer lie on the path you have been following.

CHANGING represents a time when your efforts to liberate yourself from unnecessary and inhibiting restrictions start to succeed. This may be a time of unexpected disruptions that test your new way of living. But you can survive this test, if you are aware of what you have been doing and why. You may even find a new opportunity to become more or less structured, but only if you are capable of seeing the possibilities behind the mask of apparent disruption.

If you realize that all things change, there is nothing you will try to hold on to.
Lao Tzu

50

THE CAULDRON

Summary: Nurturing what is holy and virtuous. Transforming a common social arrangement into something precious. An extended spiritual family. A profound insight to bring peace and order. Heartfelt. Grade: B

At this time you should attempt to broaden your horizons in every way possible. This includes study, new and unfamiliar experiences, travel or by meeting people from totally different backgrounds who can reveal another aspect of the world. You should strive to make even the most trivial encounter a positive learning experience. It makes little difference whether you are studying for a practical purpose of for enjoyment that stimulates your intellect and gives you a broader perspective on the universe.

Getting **THE CAULDRON** suggests that you are able to understand your duties and responsibilities for helping other people. In addition to cooperation, unity, harmony, security and stability, it also denotes the newly established order that follows self-renewal. The unity of this time extends from your inner world to your immediate circle, and to the universe at large. This unity brings the kind of enlightenment and true understanding needed for great success. Your success will depend upon joining with others at the right place and the right time. In this way you can add power to your own life.

It is human nature to wish to compel others to do as we think they ought to do. It is divine to see that their own way is their true way.
Emma Curtis Hopkins

THE CAULDRON serves as a reminder to make your life a prayer and to praise all of life. When it comes up it is useful to honor the teacher within by repeating an affirmation like, "I believe only in the clear handwriting of the creator on every part of my mind and body. I am not deceived by the deceptions of the world around me. I recognize that the spirit works through me to do that which ought to be done by me."

The degree to which your spiritual life expresses itself will depend upon the situation and your relationship to it. At this time your intuition may be highly developed, with frequent flashes of inspiration that help to solve problems and understand the future. This may appear as an interest in the larger social order and the laws and traditions that govern it.

THE CAULDRON implies peace and quietude, and a calm mind beyond struggles and victories. When it comes up you should attempt to understand the spirit that moves the social order instead of limiting your focus. This rather spiritual influence reaches into far away places and serves as a guiding light to assist humankind. If you continue to accept your intuition of new possibilities, and therefore the subject at hand, your goals will be well-defined.

51

SHOCKING

Summary: A challenge to your sense of order. An earthquake, alarm or sudden awakening. Being moved or effected deeply. A sudden opportunity. A situation able to cause fear and trembling. An experience beyond all reason. Grade: C+

This can be an extremely upsetting and tense period, particularly if you have allowed your life to crystallize into rigid patterns and you resist change. This can be a time of great tension because your desire for change and new experiences may be thwarted by circumstances or other people. The tension may become so great that you will unexpectedly take very radical actions that you would not have anticipated a short while ago. If you have been putting up with unpleasant conditions in any area of your life, these will become difficult to withstand now.

In the time of **SHOCKING** you will have problems with any relationships that seem to be holding you down too much. Relationships may break up at this time, but not usually those in which you and your partner are open to new and challenging experiences. You may encounter disruptions that make you wonder whether you really understand what is going on around you. You may experience what is happening as a threat to some way of being or some structure that has become routine and comfortable.

The presence of **SHOCKING** serves as a reminder that there is no to change things as they change themselves by your thoughts of spirit. Consequently, you should put aside anything which stands between you and your inner teacher.

SHOCKING may manifest in the people around you, a natural phenomenon, or in your personal life. It serves as a message that matter is the only deceiver. Its presence may stimulate you to put your life in order, as well as the lives of others. At this time you are rarely flattered by those who seek to gain power over you, but rather jolted by those who seek to awaken you. Although most people react with shock, fear, and hysteria when this hexagram comes up, it is possible to accept the present moment without panic.

On one hand **SHOCKING** brings a life-giving quality that produces an advancement and inner quest for truth; on the other, you may experience the sudden letting go of unnecessary activity. You are no longer dealing with ascent or descent, but with natural laws that permit you to move from one natural condition to another.

52

KEEPING STILL

Summary: Coming to a stop before a mountain. To pause or submit quietly. The absence of motion or disturbance. Retreat. To cease trying to accomplish or continue. A situation that impedes or prevents passage. Grade: C-

Do you have the patience to wait till your mud settles and the water is clear? Can you remain unmoving till the right action arises by itself?

Lao Tzu

KEEPING STILL deals with the problem of achieving stillness and rising above external distractions through some kind of meditation or inward turning of the mind. You should stop for the present time, and take action when it is time to act. Although you are prone to activity at this time, such action would be a waste of energy and serve to create unrest. The best form of action is to set limits on taking any action. **KEEPING STILL** does not suggest being inactive, but rather acting correctly in the situation at hand. By holding your thoughts to the present and dispelling illusions of what can or will be, you can avoid worries about the future brings.

At this time you should reflect upon your values and the things that you value. You should examine your relationship to the resources of your life. Do they serve your needs, or do you serve theirs? When **KEEPING STILL** comes up you may need to express yourself through your material and spiritual resources, using them to define yourself and others. More than at other times, you now want to have greater control of your life through the things that you value.

At the unconscious level, an emotional unrest within may disturb your peace of mind as well as your relations with others, especially those that move you to take action. You should be very careful not to be hasty, jump to conclusions or react negatively to anything that others say to you.

KEEPING STILL stands as a symbol of remaining centered and focused. It suggests that your great hopes and excited expectations cannot be sustained without vision. It advises you as well to settle down and develop an understanding of the subject matter at hand. While stillness and activity complement and lend significance to each other, you should now avoid activity and listen for wisdom from your inner voice. By waiting for clear signs from the Self within you can enhance the possibility for growth and progressive movement.

53

GRADUAL DEVELOPMENT

Summary: A stage of Development. Evolution. Steady step-by-step improvement. Slow growth. Tree-like growth that proceeds very slowly by degrees. A progression from a simple form to a more complex one. Grade: B

    GRADUAL DEVELOPMENT refers to steady improvement and slow growth that proceeds in a step-by-step fashion in an unchanging direction. It represents the idea of the traditional and the gradual. Under its influence your success is the result of allowing things to take their proper course. The gradual and unexciting course that lies ahead demands caution and endurance. At this time the main lesson of **GRADUAL DEVELOPMENT** is that hasty action and aggression have no lasting effect. Your endurance will prevent slow progress from dwindling to nothing.
    A significant spiritual truth revealed by this hexagram is that you can discover the truth about what is good for you in your life. This comes about when your expectations are modest, and you are willing to do whatever is necessary to attain them. As of today your energy will express itself in a careful and controlled manner, which will win you the respect of others for your diligence and perseverance. If there is hard and exacting work to do, you can do it better now than at other times.
    When **GRADUAL DEVELOPMENT** comes up you are content to be patient and to work slowly toward your objectives. Endurance and fortitude are your prime virtues. While this is not a glamorous time in your life, your actions may well lead to real and lasting accomplishments. The people around you may find you a formidable opponent because you look at all the alternatives and choose your course of action carefully and methodically
    The meaning of **GRADUAL DEVELOPMENT** is well described by the image of one person watering many plants with one bucket. As a whole this hexagram refers to a gradual expansion of consciousness toward what is good for you. This expansion may reach to the highest levels attained by the intellectual and spiritual leaders of all time. The truth is that all that is good belongs to you and asks nothing of you but to receive its substance. Although your path is routine, gradual improvements and successes are indicated.

54

AN OUTSIDER

Summary: An improper beginning or match. A subordinate or junior. A foreigner. A mistress or second wife. A position of lower class or rank. Starting something new before the present entity has reached its end. Grade: C-

AN OUTSIDER refers to a situation in which you are playing an important subordinate role that is fraught with difficulties. This role is not the result of conscious effort, or being promoted or demoted, but rather of being chosen to serve under those who control the situation you now face. Apart from your meeting certain of their needs, those in control have little concern for what you can offer. Since your value and influence are quite limited, it is better to stay in the background and keep your mouth shut. To avoid the conflict inherent in this hexagram, you should look toward the big picture and choose what is right for you within this framework.

Even though you are not likely to advance to a position of greater power or standing today, your needs may be gratified at a level that most people cannot readily understand. In the world of work you can achieve the most satisfaction simply by doing the work as well as you can and to the highest possible standards. You should be ready to take on even more work if you can, and even though you probably won't be promoted. In this way you can gain the confidence of your superiors and of those under you, which will ultimately put you in a good position.

Getting AN OUTSIDER serves as a message that you are attempting to gain acceptance into another's private life. The mental scene of someone knocking at a door without being admitted gives the essence of this hexagram. It suggests that your position is that of AN OUTSIDER whom the established order has yet to accept. It implies the stirring up of your longing for close partnership or perhaps entry into a love relationship. If you are not ready to accept the limited role of being a subordinate or foreigner, and all that it entails, destruction is inevitable.

God grant me the serenity to accept the things I cannot change, courage to change to things I can, and the wisdom to know the difference.

Anonymous

55

ABUNDANCE

Summary: The attainment of fullness. Plenty. Summit. Climax. The highest possible point. Peak. Maximum. A relative degree of wealth. An overflowing quantity. The joining of intelligence or ignorance and movement. Grade: B

Getting **ABUNDANCE** refers to reaching a climax of ideas and communications on the one hand, and the decline that follows on the other. While the present summit cannot be maintained, you can avoid an immediate decline by sharing what you have instead of holding on to it. At this time your true success is the result of serving the enduring presence of the Self within. Since increase and decrease are as natural as night and day, you should guard against expecting things to get better or worse. You should be neither happy nor unhappy about the present peak, but rather prepare to accept what is.

ABUNDANCE deals with making plans, thinking things over or communicating in any way you can with others. As a sign of mental equilibrium, this hexagram may help you in everything you have to do. This is a good time to get your point across to others, although your primary motive will probably be to communicate rather than score debate points. If you have something important to say, this is a good time to say it.

At this time your intellectual curiosity is great. This may be the right time to begin the study of a new subject. You are able to voice your innermost thoughts at this time, and you should if you feel that something must be said. The presence of **ABUNDANCE** may stimulate the flow of ideas and communication in your life. The time is also favorable for thinking about and reviewing the past as well as for planning and looking toward the future.

The message of **ABUNDANCE** is that you are gaining or have already gained some recognition for your accomplishments, but don't recognize that your peak is already at hand. This hexagram refers to an effort to impress your achievements upon onlookers and the swelling of pride when excellence is displayed.

WANDERING

Summary: Shifting. Changing. Rambling. Floating. Traveling like a stranger. Something present for a limited time. Aimless. Moving from place to place without depth of purpose. Short-term or temporary. Mental preoccupation with an outcome. Grade: C-

WANDERING refers to attitudes that are aimless and therefore temporary in nature. It serves as a message that you are travelling through different places or idea or states of mind. After you visit these places, you will move along to travel elsewhere. At this time you are preoccupied with material rather than intellectual or spiritual concerns. As such it is best to avoid long-term agreements or commitments that may affect your distant future. Despite the temporary nature of the situation at hand, it may bring an opportunity to clarify your goal and to examine the present. Although this is a poor time to impose your way of doing things, you should not lose sight of your larger goals.

When **WANDERING** comes up you are likely, rightly or wrongly, to see change as the only way to get ahead, and to a certain extent this is always true. But the danger here is that you will seek change for its own sake and not take the time to examine carefully which changes will be most effective. Even though recognizing the truth of any matter is important to you now, tolerance and generosity should accompany your dealings with others.

WANDERING may bring an intense release of energy and the desire to attain some specific goal. Its meaning is expressed by the image of someone building a temporary structure in the midst of bad weather. This image may refer to pursuing some course of action under the wrong conditions, a short-lived relationship, or being in the wrong place at the wrong time.

WANDERING refers to increased mental activity and a desire to communicate to others something that you consider to be significant. Whether or not your message is important, you probably think it is. You may be unwilling to listen to criticism, but if you listen and heed what you are told, this can be an excellent time for making decisions, planning, negotiating and concluding deals or agreements.

GENTLE PENETRATION

Summary: Progress through submission and mildness. Affecting. The accumulation of subtle energy. Movement that is free from violence or aggression. An effect produced by gradual and inconspicuous movement. Grade: C+

When **GENTLE PENETRATION** comes up you are involved in a gradual and inconspicuous influence that never lapses. Progress is indicated for those who are patient and submit to the established order. Even though progress is certain, it is not striking; but in the longrun it is significant. Any actions that you take before making the proper preparations will only frighten and repel the people you intend to help. Any attempts to get emotionally involved or take the lead will dissipate your influence; consequently, you should remain in the background and avoid direct action.

GENTLE PENETRATION marks the beginning of a period of gradual but profound changes within yourself. These changes will make your life more solid and dependable. Whether it is necessary, you are now able to get along with very little in the way of material goods.

You are adding drops of water one after another when **GENTLE PENETRATION** comes up. It suggests slow, peaceful improvement. It represents gentleness, ease, softness, and patience instead of swift achievements. The idea of drops of water signify the gentle-hearted approach and serve as a good sign for teaching and advising. Because this hexagram represent the greatest effect of personal development you can expect the kind of development that accumulates, develops, and reinforces itself in the process of thinking and doing.

When **GENTLE PENETRATION** comes up you can expect to make very profound changes and create structures that will last a long time. You should work with great patience because you are not working for today only. You are working for tomorrow as well. At this time you have great endurance, which enables you to work over a long period to eliminate those elements that have become unnecessary and limiting, replacing them with structures that are more relevant to the present.

The changing of one's consciousness is really very hard work, calling for constant unceasing vigilance and a breaking of mental habits which is sure to be very troublesome for a time.
Emmet Fox

58

JOY

Summary: A cheerful mood. Giving and receiving encouragement. Being centered and calm. Inspiration. Inner and outer harmony. Inner peace. Happiness. Motivation. Well-being. A feeling of extreme gratification. Something bright and confidence. Grade: B

When **JOY** comes up, your energy tends to be centered; external circumstances don't affect you. With this centering, your quiet, untroubled nature gives solace and hope to others. At this time you have an opportunity to communicate more deeply than ever before. Whether you seek to improve your situation or to serve others, you should take the time to share your sense of well-being.

The presence of **JOY** may inspire you to think about your goals and expectations in life. You may be inclined to examine your ideals to find out exactly how well they have served you and to what extent you have attained them. At this time it is worth your while to think about whether your goals are really yours or whether they are in part other people's goals that you are trying to adopt for yourself.

The realization of truth consist in the ability to translate symbols.
Thomas Troward

The image of one individual sharing their personal library with the public describes the meaning of **JOY**. According to this mental picture you have an opportunity to reveal your deepest feelings and to share your most persistent and unexpressed private knowledge. Are you ready to share your personal knowledge with other people? If you are not ready to assume the role of teacher your experience may degenerate into false optimism. If you are ready to assume this role, you should look for the thread of truth that connects all things. By remaining at the center you can communicate with others through wisdom and insight.

This is an excellent time for studying and broadening your understanding, either through academic methods, such as taking classes and reading books, or through conversation with others. The plans you make now will be much bolder and more innovative than usual. While your perceptions are no greater than usual, you are more willing to believe in what you see. You may feel sufficiently confident of yourself so that you can listen to others without feeling threatened by their views.

59

BREAKING UP

Summary: Breaking up rigid thinking and opinions. Disintegration. Scattering, dispersing or letting go of harmful ideas. Using religious knowledge to overcome ignorance. Causing to separate and go in various directions. Grade: C-

BREAKING UP refers to some level of ego-destruction and the dissolving of elements united in the past by the wrong principles. The present experience of letting go may be followed by a new unity. This is likely to come about when you are free from all selfish or ulterior motives about the outcome you desire. Even though some losses are certain in the shortrun, this will pave the way for union in the longrun. Generally, your success will depend on religious knowledge or guidance from the Self within.

At this time your thinking may be so influenced by your feelings that it will be difficult to think things through from an objective position. This is not usually a great problem, but it will make it difficult to share your state of mind with anyone who doesn't happen to be in the same mood. If you're upset, which is not indicated by the presence of **BREAKING UP** alone, others will find you very difficult to deal with, because you will be unable to see any position but your own. For best results you should concern yourself with the elements that bind categories together rather than those that isolate them.

BREAKING UP raises the issue of self-doubt, being deceived by others or your deceit toward others. As such, this is a bad time for making important decisions that will affect the direction of your life. Generally, you are poorly informed about what is going on.

The message of **BREAKING UP** is well described by the image of people gathered to witness an execution by guillotine. It is symbolic of letting go or giving up a cherished ideal, desire, or pattern of behavior. Getting this hexagram may be valuable for your personal growth because it brings the conditions for unhealthy goals and attitudes to dissolve. At this time you are dealing with the transformation of an old and stagnant state of mind so that things are free to move again. Generally, you can expect significant changes in your personal, interpersonal or social life.

Fierce indeed is the grip by which we hold on to our lives as our private possession.
Howard Thurman

60

LIMITATIONS

Summary: Restrictions. Achievement through discipline and self-imposed limits. Self-control. Caution. Reserve. Setting reasonable guidelines. Keeping your thoughts and emotion to yourself. Grade: C-

If you take pride in your attainment or become discouraged because of your idealistic effort, your practice will confine you by a thick wall.
Shunryu Suzuki

LIMITATIONS refers to the establishment of some boundaries beyond which your efforts do not extend. In designing these limits, you should make sure they provide you with the right guidelines for growth and opportunities for success. They must be balanced, reasonable and moderate. If they are too rigid or too mild, you will accomplish nothing. As of today, true freedom comes from understanding and accepting your personal limitations. You can only pursue your unique path of expansion within the proper limits.

Getting **LIMITATIONS** serves as a message to being self-critical and open-minded about the pros and cons of restrictions in your life. You may make great demands upon yourself, and feel you must live up to them. But they must not go beyond what is possible for you to accomplish. You will almost certainly fail to live up to any unrealistic demands, and as a result, you will disappoint your-self. The danger of making excessive demands or limitations is that they may undermine your goals.

Since ancient times the great spiritual thinkers have taught that it is good to tame the mind. But because of the flighty and undisciplined nature of your mind it may be difficult to tame at this time. Consequently, this may be a time of inner conflict that can undermine your effectiveness with others.

When **LIMITATIONS** comes up you are imprisoned by invisible ankle weights. This image brings to mind the idea that internal or hidden restraints inhibit your freedom. To be effective you should develop self-knowledge and learn to make long-term commitments. Generally, the time calls for managing the issues at hand with wise laws, reasonable controls, and moderate self-discipline.

At this time your sense of proportion is distorted so that you place too much emphasis upon matters that don't deserve such emphasis and ignore important matters. The matters that you overemphasize are those that make you afraid and fearful. However, by denying yourself rewards that you have wanted in the past, you will see that if you wait a bit, your daily life will come closer to your ideals.

61

INNER TRUTH

Summary: Following your heart, spirit or inner self. Faith, trust, inner confidence and intrinsic values. Sincerity. Reality. Faithful acceptance of the truth or inner wisdom. Understanding the feeling and views of others. Grade: C+

    INNER TRUTH refers to an opportunity to increase your sense of inner confidence. You are more in touch with your inner teacher now than at most times. You are able to handle truths about your position that you are normally reluctant to face, thereby preventing them from becoming a problem in the future. What you know about your situation is not the problem, but troubles do stem from what you are afraid of.

    INNER TRUTH calls for faith and reliance upon knowledge from the subjective Self to influence other people. It refers to having confidence and insight to gain a rapport with the people in your immediate circle. At this time your greatest strength lies in having true vision and clarity about the situation before you and the thing you desire. When your interaction with others is based upon higher truths they lead to firm and lasting bonds. By yielding to the object in question you become open and unprejudiced toward its true nature. In the end, success is the result of letting go of preconceived solutions and seeking out the voice within.

    INNER TRUTH serves as a message to seek out the truth that now evades you. It refers to an inner knowing or vision that goes beyond cultural developments, beliefs, customs, and doctrines. The situation before you can only be defined in subjective terms. Just as ignorance and suffering are the result of being out-of-touch with your inner teacher, reward, content, and inner harmony will come from being aligned with its requirements.

    This is a time for learning and gaining new experience. You should get to know yourself and what you can really accomplish. In addition, the spiritual dimension of your life may be greater now. The concrete and tangible aspects of your world are not enough. You have to know the deeper dimensions of life as well; otherwise the rest becomes meaningless.

    At this time you may learn an important spiritual lesson. Persistent thought about the thing you desire and how to attain it will pull forth the knowledge that you need to attract it. For ex-ample, persistent thought about prosperity and how prosperity comes to you will make you a magnet for prosperity. Regardless of what you desire, the thing itself will not be useful unless you know how to teach others to attain it.

If you want to know me, look inside your heart.
Lao Tzu

62

EXCESS YIN

Summary: Concentration. An emphasis on many small facts or details. Neat and exact. Seeing things as they are. Beginning in a small way. Small things can be accomplished now. Perceiving many small elements of a whole. Grade: C+

When **EXCESS YIN** comes up you are probably content to be patient and work on the outward details of your objectives. Your expectations are modest, and you are willing to do whatever is necessary to attain them. Others will find you a formidable opponent, simple because you look at all the alternatives and choose your course of action carefully and methodically. Although this is not a glamorous time in your life your actions can lead to real and lasting accomplishments.

At this time, controlled activity in any aspect of your life can do a great deal for you. You are able to direct your efforts toward building a project slowly and thoroughly, so that whatever you build at this time will probably last. Your attitude toward your objectives is reasonable and practical, which helps greatly in attaining what you want. This is not a time for big ideas, but rather for thorough accomplishments in limited areas.

The meaning of **EXCESS YIN** is well described by the image of an author proofreading the draft copy of his book. This image refers to shifting your attention from the macrocosm to the microcosm, from ideas to reality, from the general to the specific. It suggests turning away from expansion and upward movement to complete some detail. At this time the forces at work do not favor new ideas or moving beyond pre-established roles. As a whole, it is now a time to 'zero in' or focus on the small parts that make up the whole. To do this you should improve your existing position or endeavor instead of starting something new.

The presence of **EXCESS YIN** suggests that major accomplishments should not be expected. At this time self-control and attention to details will result in success. It is along this modest path that your goals can be met. Generally, manifestations of pride or flamboyance will lead you away from important insights.

There is meaning in the smallest task.
David K. Reynolds

PARTIAL COMPLETION

Summary: Attaining an important milestone. After Completion. Initial success followed by disorder. A significant point in the process of completing or bringing something to an end. Pertaining to or affecting a part of the whole. Grade: C+

PARTIAL COMPLETION refers to reaching a temporary conclusion or important stage. It is analogous to writing the first draft for a book or doing the rough carpentry work to construct a new home. It is only in regard to remaining details that the conclusion is still to be achieved. Generally, your success depends upon addressing the details that stand between your present position and the overall result. Until the present time you have been working toward an ideal; from now on your work must be more cautious and realistic.

As of today, you may attempt to cut corners because of your desire to get ahead. You must avoid becoming obsessed with any plan or course of action, and be particularly ready to re-examine your ideas of right or wrong. Stand up for what you believe is right for now, but first make sure that you are right. If you don't make the best of your present position you'll never make the best of your future goals.

PARTIAL COMPLETION serves as a message that you are adding new links to a chain that prolongs into the future. While you have reached a state of transition and things seem to be ideal, this is not the time to relax. Rather, it calls for awareness and a commitment to complete what you have started. When it comes up you have yet to complete the major details. If you fail to trouble over details the entire effort may fall apart. It is important to know that even when people get off to a good start only a few have the endurance to finish.

If you have built your position with care and persistence, and enlist the aid of others you can avoid the chaos that tend to follow **PARTIAL COMPLETION**. You should guard against being righteous. Even though your ideas may be good, you may experience problems from the style you are likely to use. It is in your best interest to stay open to other points of view and be able to compromise or adjust.

BEFORE THE END

Summary: Exhaustion of the masculine. Almost there. Approaching some conclusion. Anticipation about an upcoming and final act, fact or outcome. Completing what needs to be achieved through deliberation and caution.   Grade: C-

BEFORE THE END serves as a message that you near the final stage of an endeavor. It signals the birth of something new and holds great promise for the future. While the preceding hexagram offers an analogy to writing the first draft for a book, this one offers a related analogy: completing the final draft. Although success is certain, the situation calls for caution because the final goal has not yet been reached. By watching your step and avoiding arrogant efforts to move forward you can avoid needless disasters. You should proceed with caution because your previous experience will have little or no value in the situation at hand.

The mental picture of a woman in labor is like **BEFORE THE END**. This symbolic image signifies a beginning and an ending. It refers to hidden growth being allowed to complete its natural summit. The time before any birth brings a natural anticipation, and is present before conclusions come about. At this time you are dealing with new growth that yearns for conscious form and solidity. In summary, the current endeavor leads to the realization of a valuable development based on the conclusion of some process.

The presence of **BEFORE THE END** brings both the necessity and opportunity to completely transform some aspect of your life. Today you have reached a crisis that requires you to redefine the nature of your position or status. You may feel at though you are on the verge of bankruptcy. The long-hidden tensions within your situation cannot remain that way and must therefore be released. Strains and stresses that have existed for some time may come to the surface now.

This hexagram brings a sobering message: don't count your chickens before they hatch. This is not a particularly good time to relax in your relationship or endeavor because the energies present make it difficult to settle down into any rather comfortable routine. In most cases you may be operating under unconscious compulsions that make it impossible to create a structure that is in your interest in the long-run.

Trying to control the future is like trying to take the master carpenter's place. When you handle the master carpenter's tools, chances are that you'll cut your hand.

Tao Te Ching

Appendix A

Rules for Changing Lines

1. One changing line. Examine the meaning of this line in the first hexagram.
2. Two changing lines. Examine both lines, but the higher line (being more evolved) ought to be given first priority
3. Three changing lines. Ignore the lines and study the meaning of both hexagrams as a whole.
4. Four changing lines. Examine the two lines in the second hexagram that correspond to the two non-changing lines in the first hexagram. The higher line (being more evolved) ought to be given first priority.
5. Five changing lines. Examine the line in the second hexagram that corresponds to the non-changing line in the first hexagram.
6. Six changing lines. Ignore the first hexagram and study the meaning of the second hexagram as a whole.
7. No changing lines. Study the hexagram as a whole.

Line Meanings

Line 1: The first line represents some new idea or beginning, personal thoughts and desires or seed potential that has yet to appear in the outer world. When this line changes you are thinking about some new endeavor. A yang line here refers to an emphasis on expansion or acting upon new possibilities. A yin line here represents an emphasis on introversion, consolidation, or pursuing an established order.

Line 2: The idea of seeing the "great man" is a common theme for this line. This statement and refers to finding a third party or source of knowledge or principle that can help you in the situation at hand. Although your position is that of a subordinate there is always someone who knows more than you do. A yang or yin line here can be understood in relation to the first line. That is, the second line represents the element through which your intentions are expressed.

Line 3: Among the six lines the third one is the most unfortunate because it represents the point at which your intention or influence moves from the lower to the upper trigram. This line advises caution because you are taking your first step into the outside world. The firm third line points to an emphasis on personal achievement and the future. A yielding third line points to an emphasis on personal security.

Line 4: This line deals with the fear tied to pursuing any new activity or course in the outside world. It serves as a message to proceed with caution in taking your first steps, e.g., advising another, doing something for the first time, taking a risk. As in the first line, a yang line here refers to a new beginning or, while a yin line signifies following an established reality. Unlike line one, this line describes your experience of other people and the outside world.

Line 5: This line is the natural ruler of the hexagram and suggests the best possible outcome. It serves as a message that your position is in harmony with the wisdom imparted by the hexagram.

Line 6: The top line describes the hexagram's effect or result. According to the Ten Wings this line represents danger because you have gone beyond your plan. This may come up when you have attained your original goal but look for more without knowing what you want.

Trigram Attributes

Heaven: strength, power, firmness, awareness, creativeness, excitement, external intuition.

Lake: happiness, openness, vision, excess, inner peace, wisdom, internal intuition.

Fire: clearness, illumination, dependence, attachment, objective thinking, sociable, external analysis

Thunder: shock, excitement, movement, vitality, investigation, internal analysis.

Wind: small efforts, gentle influence, sensitivity, people-oriented, friendly, external concern.

Water: uncertainty, mystery, profound, dangerous, emotional depth, internal concern.

Mountain: standing still, resting, reliability, business-like, mediating, external control.

Earth: submissive, devoted, yielding, perfectionism, factual, internal control.

Appendix B

Trigram Titles and Symbols

The Eight Trigrams	Original Titles	Element Titles	Zodiac Signs
☰	Heaven	Extroverted Fire	Aries (& half Leo)
☱	Lake	Introverted Fire	Sagittarius (& half Leo)
☲	Fire	Extroverted Air	Libra (& half Aquarius)
☳	Thunder	Introverted Air	Gemini (& half Aquarius)
☴	Wind	Extroverted Water	Cancer (& half Scorpio)
☵	Water	Introverted Water	Pisces (& half Scorpio)
☶	Mountain	Extroverted Earth	Capricorn (& half Taurus)
☷	Earth	Introverted Earth	Virgo (& half Taurus)

Since ancient times the trigrams, when expressed in the form of elements, have been used to describe the outer physical and inner psychic nature of people and things. They form the basis of many philosophical, religious, and scientific systems and doctrines throughout the world.

Examples of the trigrams may be found in the conceptual frameworks of the four elements, Jung's psychological types, the Myers-Briggs typology, and the twelve zodiac signs of astrology. By understanding the use of trigrams, or elements, among these systems you may see aspects of your own point of view so basic as to have been ignored—your grasp on the meaning of trigrams and hexagrams may be enhanced.

The terms half Leo, half Aquarius, half Scorpio, and half Taurus refer to the first part of the zodiac sign in the case of extroversion, and the second part in the case of introversion.

Appendix C

Books and Tapes You Can Order

In addition to *Vision & Change,* you can order audio tapes and carefully selected titles from other authors. They cover intuition training, psychic development, the I Ching, spiritual growth, and personality types. Publisher addressed can be found in *Books in Print*. Books and audio tapes may also be ordered from Allen Young Books, P.O. Box 232, Berkeley, CA 94705. (415) 843-1299. Shipping is $3.00 for the first book or tape series and $1.00 for each additional one. The sales tax for orders shipped to California addresses is 8.25%. Use the order blank on the last page.

Vision & Change, Elements of Intuition and the I Ching as inner teachers by Allen David Young, Ph.D. offers a proven new approach to train your intuition. Using mental imagery to perceive the universe within and a new approach to the I Ching to divinely judge your perceptions this book teaches you to discover the new, the unknown, the untested. Through an intimate gathering of examples and exercises this book shows you how to measure personality elements and their role in affecting career, relationship and the meaning of life itself. It should be used as a constant reference for students of intuition and the I Ching.

ISBN 0-9633319-1-4   Softcover, 8.5 x 11   242 pages $19.95

Using Imagery and Intuition (three audio tapes) by Allen David Young, Ph.D. This tape series and workbook gives several structured and unstructured exercises that show you how to see, hear and read answers from deeper mind. In three hours you will learn the various levels of intuitive knowing, and conditions that both impede and nurture your intuition. The tapes show you how to see and interpret colors, auras, chakras, energy patterns and much more. Through practical information and examples learn how to (1) answer the most common questions raised about imagery, intuition, and psychic abilities, (2) speak the universal language of imagery and symbols, (3) make sense out of your hunches, (4) visualize the unseen and unprecedented, and (5) create new worlds.

ISBN 0-9633319-2-2   three-tapes and workbook $25.00

Using The I Ching (Three audio tapes) by Allen David Young, Ph.D. This three-hour tape series, with workbook, offers explicit instructions to sharpen your intuition. The tapes present new techniques of inner observation and interpretation through practice with decision making examples, and methods of divination. These tape offer (1) a concise historical summary of the I Ching's development, influence, and use since 2,500 B.C., (2) five levels of depth in consulting the I Ching, (3) several methods to interpret hexagrams, (4) guidelines for asking questions, and much more. Plus real life examples of working with the 64 hexagrams.

ISBN 0-9633319-3-0   three-tapes and workbook $25.00

You Are Psychic! by Pete A. Sanders, Jr. An MIT trained scientist shares his proven techniques for training your intuition. He answers the most common questions about psychic phenomena. This easy to read book defines the major psychic abilities and provides a multitude of simple examples on how to use them. Chock-full of creative and effective psychic techniques taught to over 25,000 people by him and his associates. Highly recommended.

ISBN 0-449-90507-1   Softcover,   5 x 8   274 pages $7.96

Joy's Way, A Map for the Transformational Journey by W. Brugh Joy, M.D. clearly describes many psychic or energy-body healing exercises and techniques. This great spiritual thinker and physician shares his insights into the awakening process, your inner and outer teachers, the I Ching, the chakra system, visualization, transformational psychology, and more. In short, this book expands your vision of your own unrealized potential. Highly recommended for understanding the spiritual healing process.

ISBN 0-87477-085-8   Softcover,   5.5 x 8   290 pages $9.95

The I Ching or Book of Changes by Richard Wilhelm and Cary F. Baynes is the *Bible* of the I Ching. Written by Wilhelm, a Christian missionary who spent much of his life in China, this is the first and only complete English translation of the Book of Changes. From original hexagram meanings to the *Ten Wings,* this book covers it all and tells you, step-by-step, how the ancient Chinese saw this holy text. If you use the I Ching and find it useful you need this book.

ISBN 0-691-09750-X   Hardcover,   5 x 8   741 pages $18.50

I Ching, The Book of Change by John Blofeld provides clear and in-depth commentary on the 384 hexagram lines. Although weak on the meaning of hexagrams, it does a superior job in translating the original Chinese interpretations of the lines. In this regard this book is better than all other versions of the I Ching. Great insights on the background of the I Ching. Essential reference.

ISBN 0-525-47212-6   Softcover,   4 x 7   228 pages $9.95

Astrology, Psychology and The Four Elements, An Energy Approach to Astrology & Its Use in the Counseling Arts by Steven Arroyo is the best exposition on the four elements that I have been able to find. Easy to read. This book is geared toward the layperson with no prior knowledge of astrology or the elements, and those engaged in any form of the counseling arts. In this book the elements are not merely symbols or concepts, but rather they refer to the vital forces that make up the entire creation. An emphasis on the philosophical, religious and mythological traditions of the elements.

ISBN-0-916360-01-6 Softcover, 5.5-x-8.5 188-pages $9.95

Telephone   Consultations

To arrange a telephone consultation with Allen David Young call (510) 843-1299. There is no charge for discussing any questions you might have. After we agree upon exactly what you want, have your Visa or MasterCard ready and we'll start your reading. When you call I can tape record the entire consultation and send you the tape. The cost is prorated at $75 per hour.

My consultations draw upon the intuitive tools explained in *Vision & Change* plus astrology or tarot if appropriate. They give reliable insights on your specific (or general) issues or questions on job/career planning, personal relationships, spiritual direction, health, decision making, etc. Topics are only limited by the questions you raise.

Notes

1. Introduction

1. Stanford, John A. *Healing and Wholeness.* New York, N.Y.: Paulist Press. 1977, p. 188.

2. Self-Study

1. Underhill, Evelyn. *Practical Mysticism.* New York, N.Y.: E.P. Dutton. 1915, p. 3.

2. Holmes, Ernest. *The Science of Mind.* New York, N.Y.: Dodd, Mead and Company. 1938, pp. 328-329.

3. Wilhelm, Richard. *The Secret of The Golden Flower: A Chinese Book of Life.* (Translated by Cary F. Baynes), New York, N.Y.: Routledge & Kegan Paul and Harcourt Brace Jovanovich. 1931, p. 63.

3. Your Elements and Relationships

1. Metzner, Ralph. *Know Your Type: Maps of Identity.* Garden City, N.Y.: Anchor Press/Doubleday. 1979, p. 72.

2. Myers, Isabel Briggs with Peter B. Myers. *Gifts Differing.* Palo Alto, CA: Consulting Psychologists Press. 1983, pp. 1-4.

3. Jung, C.G. *Psychological Types.* (originally published in 1921). Princeton, N.J.: Princeton University Press. 1976.

4. Myers, Isabel Briggs with Peter B. Myers, ibid.

5. Arroyo, Stephen, M.A. *Astrology, Psychology, and The Four Elements.* Reno, Nevada: CRCS Publications. 1975, pp. 114-121.

6. Joy, W. Brugh, M.D. *Avalanche: Heretical Reflections on the Dark and the Light.* New York, N.Y.: Ballantine Books. 1990, p. 76.

4. Imagery and Intuition

1. Bry, Adelaide. *Visualization: Directing the Movies of Your Mind.* New York, N.Y.: Harper and Row. 1976.

2. Lüscher, Max. *The Lüscher Color Test,* New York, N.Y.: Pocket Books. 1969.

3. Sams, Jamie and Carson, David. *Medicine Cards.* Santa Fe, NM: Bear and Company. 1988.

4. Jung, C.G. *Synchronicity: An Acasusal Connecting Principle.* (Translated by R.F.C. Hull), Princeton, N.J.: Princeton University Press. 1973, p. 40.

5. Campbell, Florence. *Your Days Are Numbered.* Ferndale, Penn: The Gate Way. 1931.

6. Wallace, Amy and Henkin, Bill. *The Psychic Healing Book.* Berkeley, CA: Wingbow Press. 1981, p. 20.

7. Ramacharaka, Yogi. *Yogi Philosophy and Oriental Occultism.* Chicago, Il: The Yogi Publication Society. 1931, pp. 64-66.

8. Wallace and Henkin. pp.25-31, ibid.

5. Elements of the I Ching

1. Jung, C.G. *Psychology and the East.* (originally published in 1938). Princeton, N.J.: Princeton University Press, 1978, p. 23.

2. Metzner, Ralph. *Maps of Consciousness.* N.Y.: Macmillian Publishing Company. 1971, p. 16.

3. Wilhelm, Richard and Baynes, Cary F. *The I Ching or Book of Changes.* N.Y.: Bollingen Foundation. 1950, p. 348.

4. Blofeld, John. *I Ching.* N.Y.: E.P. Dutton & Company. 1968, p. 45.

5. Wilhelm/Baynes. p. 349, ibid.

6. Counseling or Psychotherapy

1. LeShan, Lawrence. *The Medium, The Mystic, and The Physicist.* New, York, N.Y.: Balantine Books. 1975, p. 35.

2. Prioleau, L., Mardock, M., and Brody, N. (1983) "An Analysis of Psychotherapy versus Placebo Studies." *Behavioral and Brain Sciences*, Volume 6, pp. 275-285.

8. Consulting the I Ching

1. Schoenholtz, Larry. *New Directions In The I Ching.* Secaucus, N.J.: University Books. 1975 (especially chapter 4, "The nuclear Concept of Change")

2. Wilhelm, Hellmut. *Heaven, Earth and Man in the Book of Changes.* Seattle, WA: University of Washington Press. 1977, p. 15.

3. Blofeld. pp. 62-64, ibid.

Recommended reading

These books are organized according to their principal topic. Some could overlap into more than one category, and a few could be listed in all categories. Vist metaphysical bookstores regularly to check their bookshelves for the latest arrivals.

Intuition Training

A USER'S GUIDE TO PSYCHIC READINGS—Frederick G. Levine. Body, Mind and Spirit Magazine. March/April 1989.

IMAGINE THAT—David Meier. Training and Development Journal. May 1984.

INTUITION WORKOUT—Nancy Rosanoff. Aslan Publishing.

LOOKING INTO THE INVISIBLE *Intuition, Clairvoyance, Dreams*—Omraam MIkhaël Aïvanhov. Editions Prosveta.

PYSCHIC HEALING BOOK, THE—Amy Wallace. Bill Henkin. Wingbow

VISUALIZATION *Directing the Movies of Your Mind*—Adelaide Bry. Harper & Row.

WHAT COLOR IS YOUR AURA? *Personality Spectrums For Understand and Growth*—Brabara Bowers, Ph.D. Simon & Schuster Inc.

YOU ARE PSYCHIC!—Pete A. Sanders, Jr. Ballantine Books.

The I Ching

HEAVEN, EARTH AND MAN IN THE BOOK OF CHANGES—Hellmut Wilhelm. University of Washington Press.

I CHING—John Blofeld. E.P. Dutton & Company.

I CHING AND ITS ASSOCIATIONS—Diana ffarington Hook. Routledge and Kegan Paul.

I CHING *A New Interpretation For Modern Times*—Sam Reifler. Bantam Books.

I CHING ON BUSINESS & DECISION MAKING, THE—Guy Damian-Knight. Destiny Books.

I CHING *or Book of Changes,* THE—Richard Wilhelm. Cary F. Baynes. Princeton University Press.

I CHING WORKBOOK, THE—R.L. Wing. Doubleday & Company.

INNER STRUCTURE OF THE I CHING—Lama Anagarika Govinda. A Wheelright Press Book.

NEW DIRECTIONS IN THE I CHING—Larry Schoenholtz. University Books.

RESEARCHES ON THE I CHING—Iulian Shchutskii. Princeton University Press.

Element Types

ASTROLOGY, PSYCHOLOGY AND THE FOUR ELEMENTS—Stephen Arroyo, M.A. CRCS Publications

GIFTS DIFFERING—Myers, Isabel Briggs. Peter B. Myers. Consulting Psychologists Press.

HOROSCOPE SYMBOLS—Robert Hand. Para Research.

MAKING VOCATIONAL CHOICES *A Theory of Careers*—John I. Holland. Printice-Hall.

KNOW YOUR TYPE *Maps of Identity*—Ralph Metzner. Anchor Press/Doubleday.

PSYCHOLOGICAL TYPES—C.G. Jung. Princeton University Press

TYPE TALK *The 16 Personality Types That Determine How We Live, Love, and Work*—Otto Kroeger. Janet M. Thuesen. Dell Pub.

Spiritual Growth and Mysticism

AVALANCHE *Heretical Reflections on the Dark and the Light*—W. Brugh Joy, M.D. Ballantine Books.

COLLECTED ESSAYS OF THOMAS TROWARD—Thomas Troward. DeVorss & Co.

CREATIVE PROCESS IN THE INDIVIDUAL—Thomas Troward. DeVorss & Co.

INWARD JOURNEY, THE—Howard Thruman. Harper & Row.

IMPERSONAL LIFE, THE—DeVorss & Co.

JOY'S WAY *A map for the Transformational Journey*—W. Brugh Joy, M.D. J.P. Tarcher.

PERENNIAL PHILOSOPHY, THE—Aldous Huxley. Harper & Row.

PRACTICAL MYSTICISM—Evelyn Underhill. E.P. Dutton.

ROAD LESS TRAVELLED, THE *A New Psychology of Love, Traditional Values and Spiritual Growth*—M Scott Peck, M.D. Simon and Schuster.

SCIENCE OF MIND, THE—Ernest Holmes. Dodd, Mead and Company.

SECRET OF THE GOLDEN FLOWER, THE *The Classic Chinese Book of Life*—Thomas Cleary. HarperCollins.

SERMON ON THE MOUNT, THE—Emmet Fox. Harper & Row.

TAO TE CHING—Stephen Mitchell. Harper & Row.

THIS THING CALLED YOU—Ernest Holmes. Dodd, Mead and Company.

WATER BEARS NO SCARS *Japanese Lifeways for Personal Growth*—David K. Reynolds, Ph.D. William Morrow and Company.

Other Reference Books

ASTROLOGER'S GUIDE TO COUNSELING, THE—Bernard Rosenblum, M.D. CRCS Publications.

EMERSON'S ESSAYS—Ralph Waldo Emerson. Harper & Row.

ON BECOMING A PERSON *A Therapist's View of Psychotherapy*—Carl R. Rogers. Houghton Mifflin Company.

ROOTS OF CONSCIOUSNESS, THE *Psychic Liberation through History, Science and Experience*—Jeffrey Mislove. Random House.

ZEN MIND, BEGINNER'S MIND—Shunryu Szuki. John Weatherhill, Inc.

Index

A
Abundance, 215
Abyss, The, 189
According With, 158
Adversity, 159
After Completion, 159
Advertising
    brochure text, 144
    Common Ground, 144
    newspaper, 143, 145
    Open Education Exchange, 143
    workshop flier, 146
    Yellow Page Ads, 143
Approach, 158
Army, The, 167
Arousing, The, 159
Arroyo, Stephen, 53
Ascending, 206
Assembling, 159
Astrologer's Guide to Counseling, 117
astrology, 28
    See Appendix B
Astrology, Psychology, and the Four Elements, 53
Attraction, 158
aura
    aura colors, 69
    aura layers defined, 71
    Reading the aura, 68
Avalanche, 61

B
Baynes, 19
Becoming Great, 179
Before Completion, 159
Before The End, 224
Biting Through, 181
Blofeld, John, 92
Body Mind and Spirit, 85
Book of Changes, 91-93
Book of History, 93
Breaking Up, 219
Breakthrough, 203
Bry, Adelaide, 68

C
Campbell, Florence, 68
Carson, David, 68
Cauldron, The, 210
centroversion, 36
chakras defined
    fifth chakra, 73
    first chakra, 74
    fourth chakra, 73
    second chakra, 74
    seventh chakra, 73
    sixth chakra, 73
    third chakra, 73
Changing, 209
changing lines, 106
Chinese Buddhism, 93
Christian, 17, 94
Christian Science, 65
clairvoyance, 15, 65, 69, 82
    reading, 65, 66
    mental imagery, 65, 66
    movies-of-your-mind, 66
    psychic reading, 114
clairvoyant reality, 111
Clan, The, 159
Co-ordination, 158
Coming to Meet, 159
common colors defined, 69
    black, 69
    blue, 69
    brown, 69
    gold, 70
    green, 70
    grey, 70
    orange, 70
    pink, 70
    purple, 70
    red, 69
    silver, 70
    white, 70
    yellow, 70
Conduct, 170
Conflict, 166
Confucianism, 93

Confucius, 93
Contemplation, 180
consulting the I Ching, 152-157
counseling
    astrologers, 117
    counselors, 117
    guidelines, 117-119
    psychic counseling, 85, 114, 121
    psychotherapy, 114-115
    therapy, 114-115
Creation, 161
Creative, The, 158
creative process, 39

D
Danger, 189
Decoration, 182
Decrease, 201
Defeat of the Light, 196
Deliverance, 159
Desisting, 159
Diagrams for Living, 21
Difficulty at the Beginning, 158
Disintegration, 159
Dispersion, 159
divining, 97
divining and sampling, 17, 96
Duration, 192

E
Elegance, 158
element pairs, 55
    air and earth, 58
    air and water, 57
    fire and air, 55
    fire and earth, 57
    fire and water, 56
    water and earth, 59
Element Type Model (diagram), 43
element type survey, 47-48
element types, list, 44
elements, 28
    air, 31
    earth, 35
    fire, 30
    water, 33
elements and occupations, 50
elements and the creative process, 39

Enthusiasm, 158
Estranged, The, 159
Excess, 158
Excess Yang, 188
Exhaustion, 207
extroversion, 36

F
Family, The, 197
Fellowship with Men, 158
finding your element, 47
Fire, 158
Fixing, 178
Flowering, 171
Following, 177
Fox, Emmet, 21
Friends, 158
Fulfillment, 162
Fullness, 159

G
Gain, 159
Gathering Together, 159
generalist element type, 44
Gentle Penetration, 217
Glasser, William, 23
Gnawing, 158
Grace, 158
Gradual Development, 213
Gradual Progress, 159
Great Possession, 174
Great Power, 194

H
healthy personality, 60
healthy relationship, 62
hexagram elements, 98
hexagram grading from A to F, 107
hexagram interpretation
    clairvoyance and the I Ching, 109
    inside methods, 108
    outside methods, 109
hexagram lines defined
    line 1, 102
    line 2, 103
    line 3, 103
    line 4, 104
    line 5, 104

line 6, 104
hexagram stability, 106
hexagrams titles, 158
Holding Together, 168
Holland, John I., 50
house reading, 76
rudiments of house-as-self defined
    backyard, 78
    bathroom, 78
    bedroom, 77
    front yard, 77
    house, 77
    kitchen, 77
    living room, 77
    neighborhood, 77
    timing, 77
    weather conditions, 77
Hsi, Chu, 106
Huxley, Aldous, 14

I

I Ching, 9, 19, 21, 39, 91, 108
    guidelines for consulting, 150
    paths to study I Ching, 93
    the I Ching as defined by itself, 95
I Ching, 92
I Ching for Beginners, 106
I Ching or Book or Changes, 19, 91
I Ching Workbook, The, 19
Imagery, *See* mental imagery
imagery and structure, 67
imagery, open-ended, 68
Increase, 202
individuation, 41, 45, 46
Influence, 191
Initial Difficulty, 163
Injury, 158
inner teacher, 9, 20, 91, 151
Inner Truth, 221
Innocence, 185
Integrity, 158
introversion, 36
intuition, 65-66
Inward Confidence, 159
Inward Journey, 13

J

journal, 20-21

Joy, 218
Joyous, 159
Joy's Way, 73
judging, 36
Jung, C.G., 61, 45, 68
Jung's theory of psychological
    types, 46

K

Keeping Still, 212

L

LeShan, Lawrence, 111
Levine, Frederick, 85
Limitations, 220
Lines, *See* hexagram lines
Litigation, 158
Long Enduring, 159
Looking Down, 158
Loss, 159
Lüscher, Max, 67
Lüscher Color Test, 67

M

Major Accumulation, 186
Making Vocational Choices, 50
Marrying Maiden, The, 159
Medicine Cards, 68
*Medium, The Mystic, and The
    Physicist, The*, 111
Meeting of Opposites, 204
methods of consulting the I Ching
    guidelines, 154
    one-coin examples, 152, 156
    one-coin method, 152
    yarrow-stalk method, 153
    three-coin examples, 154, 157
    three-coin method, 153
methods of interpretation
    See hexagram interpretation
Metzner, Ralph, 28
Minor Accumulation, 169
Mishlove, Jeffrey, 73
Modesty, 175
Mountain, 159
multiple personalities, 60-61
Myers-Briggs, 36, 46
mysticism, 13-14

N

National Institute of Mental Health, 61
Nourishment, 187
numbers, 86

O

Obstacles, 199
Obstruction, 159
one-coin examples, 152, 156
one-coin method, 152
open-ended
    visualization, 24, 80-81
        questions 80
Opposites, 159
Opposition, 198
Oppression, 159
Outsider, An, 214

P

Partial Completion, 223
Peace, 159
Peeling Off, 158
perceiving, 36
Perennial Philosophy, 14
permission to consult the I Ching, 151
Positive Addiction, 23
Possession in Great Measure, 158
Power of the Great, 159
Practical Mysticism, 13
predicting the future, 84
Preponderance of the Great, 158
Preponderance of the Small, 159
Progress, 195
Promotion, 159
Providing Nourishment, 158
psychic, 72, 75, 85, 114, 121
psychic counseling, 85, 114-116, 121
psychotherapy, 114-116
Pushing Upward, 159

R

Radiance, 190
Ramacharaka, Yogi, 69
Receptive, 158
Reduction, 159
Relatives, 173
Release, 159

Religions
    Chinese Buddhism, 93
    Christian, 17, 94
    Christian Science, 65
    Confucianism, 93
    Religious Science, 65
    Taoism, 93
    Zen Buddhism, 94
Renewal, 184
Repose, 158
Resolutness, 159
Resolution, 159
Restraint, 60
Retreat, 193
Return, 158
Reunion, 205
Revolution, 159
Roots of Consciousness, 73
Rosenblum, Bernard, 117

S

Sacrificial Vessel, A, 159
sampling, 17, 97
Sams, Jamie, 68
Sensation, 158
sensory reality, 111
shadow, 45
Shocking, 211
Solution, 200
specialist element type, 44
spiritual growth, 14, 93
Splitting Apart, 183
Stagnation, 158
Standstill, 172
schronicity, 97
Schronicity: An Acausal Connecting Principle, 68

T

Taming Power of the Great, 159
Taming Power of the Small 158
Tao, 91
Taoism, 93
Ten Wings, The, 91, 93
three-coin examples, 154, 157
three-coin methods, 153
Thunder, 159

Thurman, Howard, 13, 19
Traveller, The, 159
Treading, 158
trigram, lower, 101
trigram, upper, 102
    trigrams defined
        earth, 100
        fire, 99
        heaven, 99
        lake, 99
        mountain, 100
        thunder, 100
        water, 100
        wind, 100
trigrams related to zodiac signs
        See Appendix B
Trouble, 159
Turning Point, 158
Tzu, Lao, 93

U
unconscious, 15, 22-23, 52, 60, 66, 95-97
unconscious, communicating with, 23, 97
unconscious elements defined
    air, 54
    earth, 54
    fire, 54
    water, 54
Underhill, Evelyn, 13
Unexpected, The, 158
Unity, 158

V
View, 158
Visualization, 22, 24, 65-66, 225

W
Waiting, 165
Wandering, 216
Water, 158
Well, The, 208
Wilhelm, Richard, 94
Willing Submission, 159
Wind, 57
Withdrawal, 159
Wooing, 158
Work on What Has Been Spoiled, 158

Y
Yielding, 159
Yogi Philosophy and Oriental Occultism, 69
Your Days Are Numbered, 68
Youthful Folly, 158
Youthful Ignorance, 164

Z
Zen Buddhism, 94

Ordering Form

Send this form or a copy of it or your written request/order with check or money order payable to: Allen Young Books.

Postal orders:
Postal address: Allen Young Books, P.O. Box 232, Berkeley, CA 94705.
Street Address: 2625 Alcatraz Avenue, Berkeley, CA 94705, **or**

Telephone orders:
Call (510) 843-1299. Have your credit card ready. For faster service, fill out order blank first. If the office is temporarily closed when you call, voice mail (recorded) messages or orders may be left at any time.

Books and Tapes:

___ *Vision & Change* $19.95

___ *Using Imagery and Intuition* (Tapes) $25.00

___ *Using The In Ching* (Tapes) $25.00

___ *You Are Psychic!* $7.96

___ *Joy's Way* $9.95

___ *The I Ching or Book of Changes* $18.50

___ *I Ching* $9.95

___ *Astrology, Psychology, and The Four Elements* $9.95

_____ Total Order Amount

Ship to:

Name_____

Address_____

City/State_____ZIP_____

Telephone number, just in case_____

Payment: VISA   MasterCard

___ Check or money order payable to: Allen Young Books

___ Credit card: Expiration date:_____/_____

Please charge my_____Visa or   _____MasterCard

Card number:_____

Name on card:_____

Signature:_____

Shipping:
$3.00 for the first book or tapes series and $1.00 for each additional one. Orders are usually shipped via the Postal Service's *Book Rate*. On request your order will be shipped UPS or overnight delivery.

Sales tax:
California residents add 8.25% sales tax.